# Letters from Bath

## 1766–1767
### by the Rev. John Penrose

D1347787

Silhouette of the Rev. John Penrose

# Letters from Bath

## 1766–1767
### by the Rev. John Penrose

With an introduction
and notes
by
Brigitte Mitchell & Hubert Penrose

ALAN SUTTON

ALAN SUTTON PUBLISHING
BRUNSWICK ROAD · GLOUCESTER

ALAN SUTTON PUBLISHING INC
WOLFEBORO FALLS · NEW HAMPSHIRE
NH 03896–0848

First published 1983
Reprinted 1990

ISBN 0 86299 112 9

Typesetting and origination by
Alan Sutton Publishing Limited
Photoset Garamond 12/12
Printed in Great Britain by
Dotesios Printers Limited

# Preface

The publication of these Letters is a joint venture between Hubert Penrose, owner of the original letters, who has for many years been researching his family history, and Brigitte Mitchell who lives near Bath and who wrote her doctoral thesis for the Sorbonne on *English Spas 1660–1760.*

The letters were written by a Cornish parson, John Penrose, in 1766 and 1767. The possibility of publication was mentioned, jokingly, at the time when they were written. But it was not until two hundred years later that they were transcribed and a publisher sought, though nothing came of it.

Then recently a transcript came into the hands of Derek Wallis, antiquarian bookseller of Bath, who was enthusiastic about their content and put Brigitte Mitchell in touch with Hubert Penrose.

The letters have been transcribed with the original spelling and punctuation. The random capital letters of contemporary writing have been preserved.

Our thanks are due to Simon Hunt, Curator, and Jill Knight, Keeper of Art, Bath Museums Services; to the staff of Avon County Library, for their kind help in providing illustrations for this book.

Brigitte Mitchell & Hubert Penrose.

# Illustrations

All the illustrations are by courtesy of the Victoria Art Gallery, Bath, with the exception of the frontispiece and that on p. 159 which come from the Penrose family collection.

# Introduction

## 1. John Penrose and his Family

These Letters were written home by my great-great-great-great-grandfather, John Penrose, Vicar of St. Gluvias (Penryn) with Budock in Cornwall, during two visits he made to Bath to take the waters in 1766 and 1767.

He came of an ancient family, once numerous in the west of Cornwall, who first appear in the records in 1195. His own branch can be traced to Truro in the days of Queen Elizabeth. Thereafter they moved to a farm on the outskirts of Bodmin, whence his father, Joseph, was called to Exeter by an aunt to learn the trade of tailor and to take over her late husband's business. In 1711 Joseph married Frances Paul of Exeter, and their first son Joseph was born in 1712, followed by their second son John in 1713.

John was educated at Exeter High School and, as a poor scholar, at Exeter College, Oxford, taking his degree in 1736. John forthwith took holy orders and, after short periods as curate at Malling, in Kent, and Shobrooke, in Devon, became Rector of Sowton, near Exeter. In 1737 John married Elizabeth Vinicombe, daughter of one of the clergy of Exeter Cathedral. In 1741 John was collated by his friend and patron, Bishop Weston of Exeter, to become Vicar of St. Gluvias (Penryn) with Budock. Here he lived and brought up his family; and it was at St. Gluvias Vicarage that he died in 1776.

His family consisted of five daughters and two sons.

*Frances* ("Fanny"). Born 1742.
>    Accompanied her father and mother to Bath in 1766 and wrote some of the early Letters for him. But, in 1767 she remained in charge of the family at Penryn. In 1768 she married Rev. William Hocker, who had succeeded her uncle, Rev. Thomas Bennett, in 1767, in the living of St. Enoder. She died in 1834.

*Elizabeth* ("Betty"). Born 1745.
>    In 1764 she married Mr. "Neddy" Coode, son of "Doctor" Edward Coode ("The Doctor") of Methleigh and Penryn. The eldest of their thirteen children, Molly, was a baby in 1766; and by 1767 her second child Edward had been born. She died in 1823.

# JOHN PENROSE AND HIS FAMILY

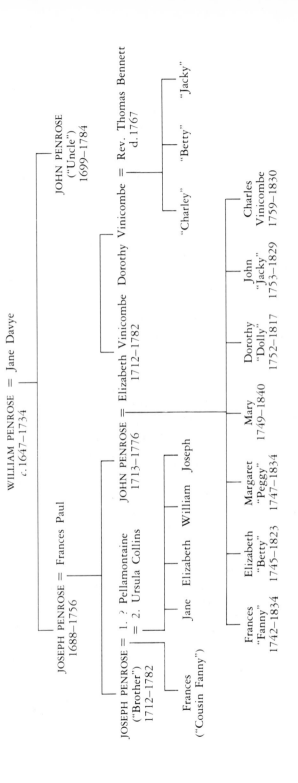

*Margaret* ("Peggy"). Born 1747.

In 1766 it was she who was left, at the age of 19, in charge of the younger children at St. Gluvias Vicarage when her father went to Bath, and to whom most of the Letters are addressed. She did not marry and remained a much loved aunt and great-aunt to the family until her death in 1834.

*Mary.* Born 1749.

In 1780 she married Rev. Thomas Donnithorne of Lansallos (near Looe), then Cuckney (near Worksop) and later of Holmepierrepont. She died in 1840.

*Dorothy* ("Dolly"). Born 1752.

In 1767 she was put to boarding-school in Bath. In 1784 she married Captain (later Admiral) Francis Pender, R.N., and lived first at Trelissick on the Fal river, and later at Hardenhuish House, near Chippenham, Wilts. She died in 1817.

*John* ("Jacky"). Born 1753.

In 1767 he started attending boarding-school in Truro. In 1778 he married Jane, younger daughter of Rev. John Trevenen of Rose-warne. He became Rector of Cardinham, near Bodmin, and later of Fledborough in Nottinghamshire. He died in 1829. It is he who was my direct ancestor. His daughter Mary married Rev. Thomas Arnold of Rugby and was the mother of Matthew Arnold, the poet.

*Charles Vinicombe* ("Charles"). Born 1759.

In 1787 he married Elizabeth, elder daughter of Rev. John Trevenen of Rosewarne, and sister of his brother's wife. He entered the Royal Navy and became Vice-Admiral Sir C.V. Penrose, KCB. For many years he lived at Ethy, near Lostwithiel. He died in 1830.

John's father Joseph and his mother Frances (née Paul) moved from Exeter to Falmouth, and both died there in 1756. Their eldest son, Joseph, joined his father as a tailor and moved with him to Falmouth. In about 1738 he is said to have married a Miss Pellamontaine, by whom he had a daughter Frances ("Cousin Fanny"), who became a formidable and well-known character and died at the age of 96. Perhaps her mother had died in childbirth, because in 1739 her father, Joseph, married again to Ursula Collins of Truro. By her he had several children who are mentioned in the Letters.

Also mentioned is "Uncle" John, Joseph senior's younger brother, who had a small holding at "Little Cripstone" in Broadoak parish, near the Lostwithiel–Liskeard road; which provided a useful stopping-place

on the journey to Bath. Another family who appear in the Letters are
Rev. Thomas Bennett of St. Enoder and his wife Dorothy. She was
sister of Elizabeth (née Vinicombe), John's wife, and had children
referred to as "Charley", "Betty" and "Jacky". He died in 1767 and,
after some negotiation, his living was granted to Rev. William
Hocker, whom Frances Penrose married in the following year.

*John Penrose, as a person*

The surviving silhouette of John Penrose gives little clue to his
appearance or character. Family tradition is that he was a handsome
man of small build. He seems to have been a man of simple, forthright
and attractive character. Although a strict father, he was much loved
by his family and highly regarded by friends in many walks of life.

He was a diligent and painstaking pastor in an age when such were
far too rare, and a forerunner of the Evangelical movement in the
Church of England. At a time when John Wesley was actively
preaching Methodism in Cornwall, John Penrose was a member of the
clerical club formed by some seven or eight Cornish incumbents, who
met frequently to discuss their problems and rekindle their enthusiasm
for the Established Church. That his ministry had a lasting effect is
illustrated by the following story, taken from a family notebook of
Victorian days.

> Mrs. Benny of Truro, who gets her living from letting out boats,
> when the new Cathedral was begun, determined to collect money
> to buy chairs for the Cathedral. She had collected enough for
> 1,000 chairs, but finding that 600 more were wanted, was going
> on with her collection. In November 1887, when Rev. John
> Penrose (great-grandson of Rev. John Penrose of St. Gluvias)
> went to view the new Cathedral, his attention was called to her,
> and he gave her a subscription. Mrs. Benny asked his name, and
> on hearing it said, "Penrose, that's an honoured name in West
> Cornwall; there was Mr. Penrose of Gluvias and Penryn".
> "Why", said John Penrose, "that was my great-grandfather".
> This happened one hundred and eleven years after the death of
> Rev. John Penrose of St. Gluvias.

Surprisingly, another admirer of John Penrose was Elizabeth
Chudleigh, a distant cousin of his wife. Her career was notorious.
After being made, in 1741, a Maid-of-Honour to the Princess Augusta
of Wales, she contracted a clandestine marriage to a young naval
officer, Augustus Hervey, by whom she had a son, who did not live
long. During her somewhat scandalous life at Court she refused to

acknowledge Hervey as her husband, though to her chagrin he eventually succeeded to the Earldom of Bristol. She later "married" the Duke of Kingston, but was tried and convicted of bigamy in the House of Lords; having to flee to the Continent. That she had a high regard for John Penrose is illustrated by the patronage she extended to his children. His daughter Mary was a sort of maid-of-honour to her for several years, and, after Mary's marriage, her husband was given livings by the Duke of Kingston. Rev. John Penrose, junior, ("Jacky" of the Letters) was also given a living by the Duke; and in her will Elizabeth tried to leave him her own small estate of "Hall" in South Devon; though he was prevented from obtaining it by the Duke's successor.

On John Penrose's death in 1776 the following appeared in the *Exeter Journal*.

> On Tuesday, the 25th instant, died, greatly and deservedly lamented the Rev. Mr. Penrose, Vicar of Penryn in Cornwall. As a faithful Pastor he was assiduously watchful over the flock committed to his care, enforcing the Doctrine of this Master by example as well as by Precept. Worn out by an intense application to his studies, and by a regular Discharge of the Duties of an extensive and laborious Cure, he yet retained, to the last, that complacence and serenity of mind, which a true sence of Religion, and consciousness of life well spent, can alone inspire. By his death the poor have lost a generous Benefactor; his flock their much loved Sheperd; the World a Friend; and his family have sustained a loss irreparable.

His epitaph, which still survives on the wall of St.Gluvias Church, was composed by the writer Hannah More. In her letter to his widow she describes him as the "worthy and amiable man you lament".

*The Journey to Bath*

The first four Letters of 1766 describe the journey from Penryn to Bath; three of them were written by Fanny, her father being too ill to write. Such a journey needed considerable advance planning. Good horses were essential and they, almost more than the travellers, needed "baiting" (halts for water and fodder), and decent quarters for the night.

The journey from Penryn to Bath – some 180 miles – would today take a few hours by car: but it took John Penrose a week. By chaise, with your own horses, you could expect to cover no more than 25–30 miles a day. By stage-coach, even with a change of horses, roads in the West Country would only allow you to do some 40–50 miles a day. If your heavy luggage was following by carrier, a plodding conveyance, it would take a long time to catch up with you.

On Wednesday, 1st April, John Penrose (Papa), Mamma and Fanny set out from Penryn in the vicarage chaise. George, the family servant, presumably rode the lead horse of the pair of chaise horses. They were accompanied by Mr. Hocker (Fanny's future husband) and Jacky (aged $13\frac{1}{2}$) on horseback. They baited at Grampound, but diverged from the turnpike on a bad side-road to visit Mr. Walker at Lanlivery. To their annoyance, in spite of advance warning, he was away from home. They eventually met him at Lostwithiel, where they stayed the night at Mrs. Arthur's Inn.

On Thursday, 2nd April, they left Lostwithiel at 7.30. After half a mile Mr. Hocker and Jacky turned back and rode home to Penryn. The chaise party baited at Red Gate and, after some very narrow and hilly roads, reached Trebartha, a mile N.W. of North Hill by 1.30, to stay the night with Mr. Rodd.

On Friday, 3rd April, they left Trebartha at 9.30 for Okehampton, baited at Bridestow, and arrived at 5.0 to stay with Mr. Hocking.

On Saturday, 4th April, they drove from Okehampton to Yendacot to stay with Mr. Pierce, baiting at Bow and arriving at 4.0. Yendacot lies about 4 miles N.N.W. of Exeter and within a mile of Shobrooke, where John Penrose had once been curate. Hence the family friendship.

On Sunday, 5th April, Papa was too ill to go to church; but in the afternoon they went the short drive to Cullompton, so as to catch the stage-coach there at a reasonable hour next morning, rather than have to catch it at Exeter at 5.0.

On Monday, 6th April, Papa, Mamma and Fanny boarded the stage-coach at Cullompton at 9.0. George had to carry Papa to the coach and then took the chaise back to Yendacot. There the chaise was laid up ready for the return journey from Bath, and George, over the next few days, took the chaise horses back to Penryn, presumably riding one and leading the other. Meanwhile the coach party had stopped for a meal at Taunton and reached Bridgwater for the night.

On Tuesday, 7th April, Papa, Mamma and Fanny again took the stage-coach from Bridgwater, stopped at Old-Down, and arrived in Bath. Col. Sewell had arranged lodgings for them, and his servants were waiting to conduct them there, Mamma and Fanny on foot, and Papa in a chair.

Hubert Penrose
Bishop's Waltham
1983

2.    Eighteenth Century Bath through the eyes of John
                                Penrose

The city which the Penrose family visited for the first time in 1766
had been a fashionable spa since the beginning of the eighteenth
century. Although the healing virtues of its hot mineral waters had
been known and used from time immemorial, it was the two
successive visits of Queen Anne and her consort, Prince George of
Denmark, in 1702 and 1703 that had given Bath the impetus to
overtake its seventeenth century rival, Tunbridge Wells.

The Royal visits set in motion a chain of events. Two years later,
Richard Nash, better known as Beau Nash, settled in the small
provincial town and started to take charge of the recreation of its
visitors. Nash's efforts, however, remarkable as they were, would not
have been enough to change profoundly the destiny of Bath. The
extraordinary progress of the spa in the eighteenth century may be
attributed to the combined action of four men, Richard Nash, Ralph
Allen, John Wood and doctor William Oliver. Each, of great talent
and ingenuity in his own field, made an important contribution to the
metamorphosis of the town.

A Welshman by birth, Beau Nash was a gambler who arrived in
1705 from London where he already moved in fashionable circles. His
influence was felt at once in Bath. The first Assembly Rooms were
built at his instigation in 1708, and the fact that he was made an
honorary freeman of the city in 1716, indicates that he had already
made himself indispensable to the Corporation by organising and
regulating the pleasures of the nobility and of the gentry who flocked
to Bath in increasing numbers.

On the other hand, although Ralph Allen and William Oliver both
settled in Bath early in the century, the former in 1712, the latter in
1728, some years were to elapse before their contribution was felt.
Ralph Allen, who had made his fortune in the re-organization of the
Post Office system, invested his huge profits in the Combe Down
quarries. He began to commercialise the Bath stone around 1725.
This was the same year the architect John Wood the Elder – the only
member of this remarkable quartet who was a native of Bath – turned
his thoughts towards the improvement of the city. William Oliver, a
Cornishman like Allen, with whom he shared literary interests, tended
the poor in the hospital as well as the fashionable invalids.

These four men are the key to the history of eighteenth century
Bath. Although their accomplishments were so diverse and their
personalities so different, yet their talents were most successfully

united in one important enterprise, the General Hospital. This charitable institution, which opened its doors in 1742, was placed under the care of doctor William Oliver. He was not only the chief physician there, but also the chairman of its executive committee until 1761. Ralph Allen donated the freestone and a sum of 500 pounds. John Wood designed the building in true Palladian style, while Richard Nash raised the necessary funds and became its first treasurer. At the time when the Penroses first visited Bath, the hospital housed seventy in-patients. John Penrose heard a sermon preached on behalf of the hospital and was impressed with the procession of the beadles and invalids as they lined the aisles of the Abbey after the service.

In 1766, the date when the vicar of Penryn came to take the waters, the four men responsible for the transformation of Bath had just died, Wood the Elder in 1754, Richard Nash – a very old man of 86 – in 1761, followed by Ralph Allen and William Oliver in 1764. John Wood the Younger was in the course of completing his father's projects. John Penrose's visit, therefore, takes place at a crucial moment in the history of Bath, when the influence of the four men could still be felt in many ways. Yet socially and architecturally changes were taking place. In his letters we therefore have a valuable record of the transformation of Bath's medical, architectural, social and religious scene.

*The Medical Scene*

John Penrose's reason for coming to Bath was to improve his health. Like many of his contemporaries he arrived in the city suffering from a severe attack of gout. He placed himself under the care of Mr. Haviland, an apothecary, who had been recommended to him, as dealing with "the best families". His case being a straightforward one, the services of a physician were not required and a well-established Bath apothecary was thought to be as good as a doctor elsewhere. John Penrose suggests that his Penryn physician, "Doctor" Coode, was not in fact a qualified physician, and would have been known as an apothecary outside Cornwall, especially in a town which included such eminent members of the medical profession.

Various forms of treatment were available. Bathing, once the only form of cure in a city rich in hot waters, was still fashionable. The Penrose family watched people bathing in the King's Bath. They also inspected, out of curiosity, the new Baths opened by the Duke of Kingston in 1755. Admission was expensive – five shillings – although the high cost of entry guaranteed privacy and exclusiveness, while the other baths, the property of the Corporation, were over-crowded. John Penrose was simply prescribed to drink the waters. At first he drank a mixture of the Cross Bath waters and King's Bath waters but afterwards waters taken solely from the King's Bath.

During the first week of his stay, the mineral water was brought to his lodgings, as his gouty foot prevented him from venturing outside. As his condition improved, his visits to the Pump Room regulated the schedule of his day. At first he seems to have been rather shy and avoided busy hours, but by the end of his stay one has the impression that he was thoroughly enjoying his visits there. The first Pump Room, built by the stonemason John Harvey in 1706 was, according to John Wood, "considering the time when built . . . one of the best Pieces of Architecture the City could boast of." Owing to Bath's unprecedented success, it was enlarged in 1751 to accommodate the growing numbers of people resorting to the spa. It nevertheless retained some of its original features, duly recorded by John Penrose in one of his letters, especially the time-piece presented by the famous clockmaker Thomas Tompion in 1709, still to be seen there today. In 1753 a statue representing Beau Nash with a plan of the hospital, given by the citizens of Bath in recognition of his services, had been placed in a niche in the right-hand corner of the east wall, opposite the musicians' gallery. This room, the very focus of Bath life, was evidently becoming too crowded by the end of the seventeen-sixties, and it remained increasingly cramped until 1780 when the architect Thomas Baldwin entirely rebuilt it on a much more extensive scale, on the same site.

While John Penrose's first letters include long accounts of his miseries and discomfort, he soon found relief and was of course delighted with the improvement in his health. He admits that although he was quite sceptical of the healing powers of the waters when he first came, he left the city a complete convert. A second visit was therefore undertaken a year later in 1767.

*The Architectural Scene*

Whereas one of John Penrose's first outings was to visit the Pump Room, he was soon well enough to explore methodically the town whose fame was well-established by the time George III ascended the throne.

Starting from his lodgings in Abbey Green, he gradually discovered the beauties of the place, with the help of a "sixpenny Guidebook", which can be identified as Cornelius Pope's *New Bath Guide or Useful Pocket Companion,* published in 1762. John Penrose relied on its information to tell his correspondent such precise details as the dimensions of the Assembly Rooms and the inscription on the

Granville Monument on Lansdown. He probably needed the help of
the guidebook when he tried to describe the ornamental details on the
façades in the Circus. For although a scholar, he was no aesthete and
was often at a loss when he came to describe religious paintings.

The Bath of 1766 was still very much centered on the lower part of
the town. A patient's daily routine included an early visit to the Pump
Room, followed by breakfast either at home, or at one of the
coffee-houses; or on special occasions, he would attend a public
breakfast, such as the one the Penrose family were treated to at Spring
Gardens. This was followed by a daily church service – for many this
would be at the Abbey – before strolling along one of the Parades.
These wide, flag-stoned promenades lined with stately houses, designed by John Wood between 1740 and 1743, were not the least
object of John Penrose's admiration. He found them convenient and
elegant and enjoyed the views they afforded of the surrounding hills,
especially that of Ralph Allen's Prior Park on the southern slope.

The two Assembly Rooms were both situated on the Grand Parade,
almost opposite each other. *Harrison's,* the first to be built, was by
1766 called *Simpson's.* It was free standing and looked over a formal
garden along the river Avon. A ballroom had been added in 1750,
during Simpson's tenancy. *Wiltshire's,* formerly *Lindsey's,* was built by
John Wood in 1728 and was incorporated in a row of houses. Its Great
Room, with a coved ceiling, was justly famous. John Penrose could
not resist peeping in, on one of his morning jaunts, but it was Fanny
Penrose alone of the family who frequented the subscription balls, held
twice weekly, on Tuesdays at *Simpson's* and on Thursdays at *Wiltshire's.*
Both Rooms were soon to be known as the Lower Rooms in order to
distinguish them from the Upper Rooms, designed by John Wood the
Younger and opened in 1771. But at the time of the Penroses' visit,
social life was still entirely concentrated in the lower town, especially
as the Playhouse was only a stone's throw away, in Orchard Street. It
was comparatively new, having been opened in 1750 and all performances took place there, as the theatre once existing in the basement of
Simpson's Rooms had been closed down in 1755.

The town, however, had started expanding to the north, outside the
medieval walls. John Wood's ambitious plans for extending the city
were materialising. A whole new district was being developed,
including Queen Square, started in 1728 and completed in 1734. Its
residents enjoyed the privilege of having their own church, St. Mary's
Chapel, situated on the south-west corner of the square. There was a
formal garden in the middle, with, as its central ornament, an obelisk
erected at Nash's expense to commemorate the visit of Frederick,

Prince of Wales, in 1738.

To the north, Gay Street had been recently completed, and a noble sight it was, according to John Penrose. Gay Street led up to the Circus, designed by John Wood the Elder, but built by his son between 1754 and 1766 when John Penrose recorded its completion except for one house. Like so many of his contemporaries, the vicar of Penryn was extremely impressed by the novelty and the boldness of its conception. He had one reservation to make, that the parapet failed to conceal the roof.

Milsom Street was being gradually developed by Daniel Milsom, a wine cooper, who had started on his scheme in 1761. While the Penroses were at Bath, the foundation stone was laid for the Octagon Chapel. Most churches, the Abbey excepted, were becoming too small to cope with the influx of visitors, and many of them had either been rebuilt, like St Michael's outside the North Gate, or were about to be, like St James' near the South Gate. A year before, Lady Huntingdon's Chapel had been opened in a place called Vineyards. Strawberry Hill Gothic was the style chosen for the sober Bath Methodists by the eccentric countess.

By contrast, the old Guildhall, situated on an island site in the middle of the High Street, must have looked strangely old-fashioned. The inside had been beautified, thanks to the generosity of Ralph Allen. There were hung the portraits of all the members of the Corporation painted by Adrian Van Diest. Other portraits displayed there included Frederick, Prince of Wales, and his wife, Princess Augusta, Lord Camden, the Town Recorder and General Wade, formerly MP for Bath.

Allen's seat, Prior Park, begun by John Wood, but finished by Richard Jones, Allen's clerk of works, dominated the city to the south. The gardens, carefully planted on the hillside with Alexander Pope's advice, were now mature. They appear to have been a favourite excursion for the Bath visitors. It was one of the first outings offered to Mrs. Penrose and Fanny when they arrived. As John Penrose did not visit the place himself, regrettably we get no account of the Palladian villa, which had been inherited by Allen's niece, Gertrude Warburton, two years earlier.

No visit to Bath in the eighteenth century seems to have been complete without an excursion to neighbouring Bristol, by the seventeen-sixties the second city in the kingdom. The Penroses were no exception. Leaving Bath early one morning in a post-chaise from the Bear Inn in the High Street, they spent a whole day in the busy port, meeting friends and seeing the principal sights; St Mary

Redcliffe "the fairest, goodliest and most famous parish church in England" as Queen Elizabeth had once called it; St Nicholas' Church, College Green, and also the Hotwells at Clifton, which were beginning to compete seriously with Bath and offered an alternative to those visitors who found the latter too crowded.

## The Social Scene

It would have been difficult for John Penrose coming from distant Cornwall on his first visit to a spa, to perceive that the social scene in Bath was changing, for its transformation was more subtle than that of the townscape. Moreover, by reason of his age and of his profession, John Penrose had very little interest in public assemblies. On one occasion he was offered a ticket for a ball and his reaction was "I would as soon sit in the Stocks"! He never went to see a play, leaving this entertainment to Fanny, his daughter. Card games horrified him, and although apparently quite tolerant, he obviously disapproved of his wife or daughter indulging in such "rakish" pastimes. Rake was one of his favourite words.

Every work written on eighteenth century Bath emphasizes Beau Nash's achievement in organising and disciplining the society that frequented the spa. John Penrose was very much impressed by the regular hours kept for balls and assemblies. The elegance of women struck him from the very moment of his arrival in the city. There was no such thing as old age in Bath, everyone, even older ladies, dressed to look young and gay. Milliners, silk-mercers, and mantua-makers came down from London for the season, bringing with them the latest fashion and plied their trade most successfully. The vicar of Penryn was not a little surprised to discover that elegant clothes were not just reserved for the nobility and gentry – "the Sexton's daughter wears a wire Cap and dresses like a Woman of Fashion". Writing to his daughter, a girl of nineteen, John Penrose was careful to keep her *au fait* with such sartorial novelties as the so-called "Minute Dress" which took one minute to put on. He was also amused by the new fashion of wearing spectacles and the vogue for being near-sighted. The whole family, sober and provincial, was caught up in the pervading atmosphere of frivolity. John Penrose had a new suit made, bought a new hat and new stockings. Mrs. Penrose acquired a new gauze apron and "Temple Spectacles". Fanny was the one who spent most money on clothes. The milliner's bill would have been difficult to pay had it not been for their friend Colonel Sewell, who obtained a discount for them.

Although delighted at first by the general air of elegance prevailing over the city, John Penrose found it rather exhausting to appear in every circumstance dressed up in his best clothes. He confessed to his daughter that he sometimes longed for the comfort of his old dressing-gown, a comfort he was seldom allowed to enjoy as a constant stream of visitors called at their lodgings, many of them previous acquaintances from Cornwall but among the newcomers were some of the clergy. It seems that there was a West Country circle from Exeter and Cornwall who enjoyed each other's company in Bath and perhaps Beau Nash had not entirely succeeded in breaking down the provincialism of Georgian England.

Bath appeared not only as the centre of fashion, but also as the land of plenty. Mrs. Penrose was amazed at the sight of the market, where meat, fish or vegetables seemed bigger and fresher than anywhere else. The cost of living was expensive but then the quality of the merchandise offered was outstanding. Luxury trade was equally prosperous due to the growing influx of well-to-do visitors from London. In the so-called toy-shops were to be found the most exquisite "trifles" to be taken home as presents – artificial flowers, miniature objects, boxes of every shape and description. But it is also interesting to note that a cheaper, more dubious market had developed. On their first visit, the Penroses carefully avoided passing through Avon Street, "a Street of ill-Fame", but in the following year, they discovered that it not only housed noisy taverns but was also the street where bargains could be found. Perhaps some of the objects offered at reduced prices were traded in by unlucky gamblers. Mrs. Penrose, who enjoyed a modest income, certainly took advantage of the shady Avon Street market. Except for an incident at the West Gate where he had a brief scuffle with a drunken man, the vicar of Penryn was also struck by the refinement of manners in general, another achievement of Beau Nash. People were extremely civil to one another. Even the local people spoke in a very fine manner, without a trace of a country accent. John Penrose admitted he found himself addressing people with more politeness than usual, a habit he will lose, he said, "by the time I cross the Tamar".

Bath was a world of its own with its own customs, its own code of behaviour, which the newcomer only discovered by experience. There were a few ritual ceremonies of initiation. The City Waits came and played to welcome visitors at their lodgings. The Abbey bells pealed to announce the arrival of an important visitor. John Penrose was slightly hurt that they did not ring for him, but his mind was put at ease when he was informed that they rang for nothing less than a lord. On the other hand, he had the satisfaction of reading his and his wife's name among those of the latest arrivals in the *Bath Journal*, although, sadly, Fanny's had been left out.

All these gratifying attentions, first introduced by Beau Nash, were still flourishing after his death. The most significant change was that while the former Master of Ceremonies had insisted that all pleasures had to be taken communally at the Assembly Rooms, private parties were now the general rule. "Tea-visits" took place every day. People called on each other so frequently that on some occasions John Penrose, to his deepest regret, missed going to church for evening prayers.

## The Religious Scene

We are never allowed to forget, as we read his letters, that John Penrose was first and foremost, a clergyman. While the letters convey valuable and original information about the medical and social customs of Bath, about famous visitors and about the city's architectural novelties, his favourite topic was undoubtedly the religious scene.

Far from restricting his religious duties to the neighbouring Abbey, described outside and inside in minute detail, he also explored methodically all the other Bath churches, except the dissenting chapels. He attended divine service in two other parishes, St James' and St Michael's, in the newly-built chapel in Queen Square and in the rather neglected chapel of St John the Baptist, near the Cross Bath, where he pointed out to the incumbent the presence of cobwebs. Venturing further afield, he also went to Walcot Church, and to the little country parishes, such as Widcombe and Bathwick, reached by means of a ferry across the river Avon. No effort was too great when duty called him. But his preference was for the great Abbey Church, where the congregation impressed him both by their number, especially that of men, and by their exemplary behaviour during the service. None of them seemed to refuse to repeat the Athanasian Creed, a point on which he seemed to have experienced some difficulty with his Cornish parishioners.

In the Abbey he witnessed splendid processions on various festive occasions and heard famous preachers. The latter he found a stimulus to his own faith. He himself preached there many times as the local clergy, perhaps overworked during the season of the Bath waters, seem to have enrolled visiting members of the Church to assist them in their religious duties. John Penrose willingly accepted their invitation and wrote: "Once I am found out, I expect full Employ". He was never entirely on holiday and found, to his surprise, he was one of the few to wear his cassock and bands in Bath.

Lodging with Dr. Grant, himself a clergyman, he was soon in touch with other members of the Church of England and enjoyed meeting and discussing religious topics with them. Some members of the Bath clergy become quite familiar figures in the letters. We often hear about Mr. Taylor, the Abbey Reader. The themes chosen for the sermons were also carefully noted and commented upon; perhaps for his own sermons later, a common eighteenth century practice.

There is one particular subject which excited John Penrose's curiosity and interest, the Methodists. Bath had been a stronghold of Methodism for nearly thirty years. The famous altercation between John Wesley and Richard Nash had taken place in 1739, and the Master of Ceremonies, for all his influence, had failed to prevent the two brothers John and Charles Wesley, or George Whitefield, from making more and more converts over the years. Nash's opposition was complicated by the fact that Methodism's most aristocratic convert, Lady Huntingdon, was determined to make Bath a place where she could spread the new religion to the upper classes. In 1765 she had opened a chapel there. It was a showpiece from the outset. Attendance, curiously, seems to have been by invitation only. Mrs. Penrose was given one of these cards and the vicar of Penryn lost no time in attending a service in the brand-new gothic chapel. John Penrose's long account of his visit to Lady Huntingdon's Chapel may be compared with a letter of Horace Walpole, who also attended a service there in October of the same year. Both men emphasised the theatrical side of the service, which Walpole called "Mr. Wesley's opera". Walpole, of course, was only amused. John Penrose was horrified. He was a loyal supporter of the Church of England and could not tolerate the sentimental, emotional approach of the Methodists. This kindly man clearly enjoyed reporting rumours about Lady Huntingdon's sanity, and one has the impression that he was only too happy to notice the links between the Bath Methodists and the Bath playhouse. A traveller whom the Penroses met on their journey from Cornwall and whom they had liked very much became less sympathetic the moment they found out he was a regular attendant at Lady Huntingdon's Chapel.

It is surprising that John Penrose was not more amused by Christopher Anstey's *New Bath Guide,* which was published while the Penroses were in Bath and which the vicar of Penryn read during his stay. The Bath poet poked fun at the Methodists and accused them of using all sorts of tricks to convert women to their creed. It is possible that John Penrose found the satire in bad taste. In any case, it was not the sort of topic to write about to his daughter Peggy, a tender girl of nineteen.

A few years later, in 1771, Richard Graves, the rector of Claverton, a parish near Bath, in his turn satirised the Methodists in his novel, *The Spiritual Quixote*. Feelings against the disciples of Wesley and Whitefield by then reached a climax. John Penrose's reaction illustrates the attitude of the Church of England towards Methodism a few years earlier.

Letters describing life in Bath in the mid-eighteenth century often mention the magnificence of the balls, or the jostle in Pump Room. There is less information about religious life and this last aspect is the most original and the most valuable contribution which the Penrose letters make to our knowledge of Georgian Bath.

*John Penrose as a writer.*

The Letters are a day-to-day account of the Penrose family life at Bath. The fact that they were all destined for the same correspondent gives them the unified quality of a journal. They must have received an enthusiastic welcome at the vicarage of Penryn as their author was pressed for more details. The letters were meant to be kept as a record of what was certainly a great adventure in the life of this Cornish parson and his family.

There are only twenty letters written during the second visit made, at the same time of year, in 1767. Several explanations come to mind. Firstly, John Penrose became seriously ill with jaundice and probably found writing a cause of fatigue. Secondly, the novelty of Bath had worn off and there was no need to describe the places of interest so extensively. Thirdly, Fanny to whom several of the letters are addressed knew Bath already. Nevertheless the letters of 1767 are a welcome and useful complement.

John Penrose clearly enjoyed writing and he was a lively correspondent. Sometimes dialogues are quoted *verbatim*. He has an excellent eye for detail, as in his description of lodgings, food and houses; for example Mr. Loscombe's house at Bristol and the dinner at Mr. Brinsden's. In this he is sometimes as good as Parson Woodforde in his accounts of meals and domestic arrangements. The letters also show how preoccupied a clergyman was with prices and expenses – the secondhand silk, the indifferent food eaten in their lodgings, the shabby gentility. This is "economy" Bath in sharp contrast with other accounts from the nobility who were less concerned with the cost of living.

Contemporary accounts of eighteenth century Bath are often biased. The medical tracts extol the therapeutic virtues of the waters and the superiority of the city over other spas. Even John Wood was rather partisan in his *Essay towards a Description of Bath* and claims full credit for the improvement of the town. Other writers were inspired by resentment or spite. The novelist Tobias Smollett, dissatisfied for not being accepted as a doctor by his Bath colleagues, lost no opportunity to attack Bath. The Spa was always a favourite target for satirists, from 1700 with Ned Ward's *A Step to the Bath* to Christopher Anstey's *New Bath Guide* published in 1766. John Penrose, on the other hand, had no axe to grind. He was a dispassionate, gentle observer of Bath's social life and customs and of the visiting celebrities. For this reason his objective testimony is of more historical value.

Brigitte Mitchell
Dyrham Park
1983

A Southwest Prospect of the City of Bath in 1757, engraved by H. Roberts after a painting by Thomas Robins.

# VISIT OF 1766

Trebartha, Apr: 3rd. 1766.

My dear dear Peggy,

You see, by the Date above, where I now am; Your Mamma, Fanny, George,[1] and I all very well: so are our Cattle. Mr. Hocker and Jacky doubtless let you know all that passed till we parted.[2] However you shall have an account from me in Brief, to refresh your memory, and because we think it will give you Pleasure; and whatever will give you Pleasure, I shall always readily comply with. Mr. Bolitho and Mr. Williams were so kind as to accompany us from home, the latter so far as Perran Poor-house, the former to the third mile stone from Truro. Our obligations are to both of them, for their Kindness. We designed to bait at Truro; but Mrs Walker being ill, we proceeded to Grampound without baiting. By the way we called at Keggon Bridge upon Mrs. Cozion, who has been ill, but is now better: let Mrs. Virginia and Mr. Islington Bolitho know it. At Grampound we refreshed ourselves and Horses: price three shillings. At St. Austell we called upon Mrs. Vivian, saw her and the child, but did not alight. At St. Blazey, Mr. Grant and his Lady would fain have made us drink Tea with them, but as we had acquainted Mr. Walker that we would drink Tea at Lanlivery, and Mr. Walker had acquainted us that he should be at home the Wednesday, tho' engaged the following Days, we (tho' with much ado) declined the kind Invitation. The only Difficulty we met with in the Road, was in going from the Turnpike Road to Mr. Walker's. No danger, only Mamma a little frightened, and Fanny somewhat more. But what Difficulty would deter us from going to see an old friend? However our old friend happened not to be at home. Business called him to Lostwithiel, and Mrs. went to take care of him. Orders were left to make Tea for us, and a Bed in the Evening, when Mr. & Mrs. Walker were both to return: but we went on to Lostwithiel; and at Mrs. Arthur's Inn, we met them whom we expected to have found at Lanlivery. Many apologies made, and all very good friends: But I think we should not have been out of the way,

1 George was the family servant.
2 Mr. Hocker and Jacky returned to Penryn from Lostwithiel.

if they had been coming to Vicarage, or any other friends. Supper at
Lostwithiel, Veal cutlets and Tarts, poor Cyder, stale Ale, good
Punch. Drank [to] all at Vicarage and Penryn. Expence, Landlord's
Bill 18s.7d. – Gave the servants 2s.5d. – Total One Guinea. – What
was laid out in Turnpikes, not yet paid George. Jacky and Mr. Hocker
went with us this morning half a mile's ride: then we parted. We
hope, they had a pleasant Journey to Penryn: we went on very well,
thank God, tho' a little down in the mouth at Parting: even Fanny
herself Full heavy-hearted at the leaving such Friends as those: e'en yet
'tis grieving. We passed along in Sight of Uncle's, but having sixteen
or eighteen miles to travel, and no Turnpike Road, we could not stay
to see them, which we should gladly have done, had opportunity
served. At Red-gate we baited, spent 9d. and gave 6d. to a girl of
Budock, who lives there a Servant. Her name is Gordon, a Daughter
in Law to one Eustace, who lives just by the River you go over to go to
Falmouth. Tho' we set out from Lostwithiel half hour after seven, we
did not reach Trebartha till half hour after one: the Ways being mostly
very narrow, and very hilly; in other Respects not to be complained of,
for common Roads. Fears of being out of our Way, sometimes
disconcerted us a little; but we did not really lose our Way at all, nor
have we met with any the least accident, since our first setting out.
God send us as pleasant, at least as prosperous Journey, from this
time, as we have had hitherto! Mrs. Rodd and the Child very well: Mr.
Rodd is gone to a Meeting of Justices at Callington, but will return
this Even. Mrs. Rodd very glad to see us. I can say nothing of the
Place in this Letter, because I have not walked out to look about me.
Our Dinner boil'd Beef, Shoulder of Mutton roasted, Hogs Pudding,
Oysters fried in Batter, Black-curran Tart, Garden-Stuff, etc. Writing
about Dinner, again minds me of my Breakfast at Lostwithiel;
excellent hot Rolls with our Tea. Dr. Stackhouse lay at the same Inn,
where we lay; but went away in the morning, too soon for me, a
lie-a-Bed, to speak to him. Mr. Baron and Mr. Jones came to the Inn
to see me, very kind of both of them. Miss Baron came to see Sister,
and Miss Bennet supped with us. – Ask Mr. Coode for a copy of the
Advertisement about the strayed Flanders Mare and Filly, and send it
us. Remember our Love to the Doctor, and to Mr. and Mrs. Coode,
not forgetting precious Molly, who bears the Bell yet from any little
Miss I have seen in my Travels so far. 'Tis our Desire, my dear Peggy,
that you want for nothing, nor any one with you. Give our Blessing to
your Brothers and Sisters. May God for ever bless you yourself! And
you cannot conceive, what a Pleasure it will give us all, to hear that
there is perfect Harmony among you. Remember us to the two

Betties.[3] I forgot to tell you, that a little this side Red-gate the Snow still lies on the Ground. Indeed the country thereabouts is so very cold, that I should not wonder to see Snow there at Midsummer. You will let Mrs. Hearle know, the family at Trebartha are all well; but don't shew my Letter to any but very intimate friends. Mr. Hocker, I suppose, will be gone West, before you receive this; otherwise he will be glad to hear we are all well, and in his Interest. Tho' I say, we are all well, I must own, I have a little stitch in the left side of my neck, but I hope it will wear away by to-morrow morning. I am, my dear Peggy, praying God to protect you all.

Your ever loving Father

JOHN PENROSE.

P.S. A line hereafter from Mary, Dolly, and Jacky, and a mark from Charles Vinicombe, will be very welcome. Let the Clark speak to Wordell about the money for the Trees; and get what he can of that money, or any other, for your Supply. If you can let my Brother at Falmouth know whenever you hear from us, pray do. I hope, you have sent the Letter to Mr. Padgett. We are very glad, we did not take a Post-Chaise.

Oakhampton. April 4th, 1766.

My dear Sister,

Papa wrote you a letter yesterday at Mr. Rodds, intending to put it in the Post-Office as we went through Lanceston, but when we came there we found the western post had been gone out some time; this very much disapointed us, as we thought you wou'd all be uneasy at not hearing from us, according to promise, but very fortunately, we met Mr. Enys's servants soon after, who promised to let you have it to morrow as soon as possible. We set out from Mr. Rodds this morning about a half an hour after nine, we stopt at Bridestow to feed our Horses, and we eat some Bread & Cheese, then we set out for this place, & got here about five o'clock. Papa's neck is very stiff, Mama & I are very well only my bones ake a good deal, which is no wonder, considering the bad roads. We came here at Mr. Hocking's intending to drink tea, & then go to the Inn, but he desired us to lodge here, which we accepted. Mrs. Hockin is not home, but Miss is, & Mr. Kingdom is here. We intend setting out for Yendicott to morrow

---

3   Betty Coode (née Penrose) and her cousin Betty Bennett.

morning as soon as we have Breakfasted. Papa had the misfortune to loose his Cane out of the Chaise to-day between Lifton & Bridestow. We were entertain'd at Trebatha with the Utmost civility. I think it a very pretty place. I hope you'll excuse my not being more particular at present as tis almost dark. Papa & Mama join with me in remembering to you & dear Brothers, Sisters, Mr. Coodes, little charming Molly, etc. Believe me to be dear Sister Peggy yours affectionately

### FRANCES PENROSE.

Remember us to both Betty's. Pray excuse haste. I believe you will not be able hear from us again till you see George which I hope will be next Wednesday even.

To:   Miss Margaret Penrose,
at Gluvias Vicarage,
near Penryn,
Cornwall.

Yendicott, Sunday morn.
April 5th. 1766.

Dear Sister,

We got safe here yesterday afternoon about four o'clock, our being so late was owing to the badness of the roads. I am sorry to tell you that Papa has been very bad ever since he wrote you from Mr. Rodds, in his Neck and Sholders. Mama and I thought yesterday morning at Mr. Hockins that we shou'd not be able go any farther, but Papa was willing to try, and had his Clothes put on with great dificulty, but he was as well, (or better) on the road then we could expect, this morning his chief complaint is in his knee. We were received here with the utmost civility, by Mr. Mrs. Pearse, Mrs. Taylor, Miss Savory & Master Pearsy, who is a very fine Boy. Our Mr. & Mrs. Pearse are expected here to day. As Papa would find it very troublesome to get up so early to morrow at Exeter to go in the Coach, we intend going to Cullumpton this evening instead of Exeter, so the Coach will take us up there to morrow morning about nine o'clock. George is now gone to Exeter to let Mr. Paul[4] know it, and to desire him to come here to us. Papa is not able to go to Church, and Mama is going to tarry with him. I dare say you will all pitty us, as you must needs think it very

---

4   Robert Paul, a cork-cutter of Exeter, was evidently a cousin, through John Penrose's mother née Frances Paul.

dismall for us. I shall be very thankfull, if it Please God, we can get to Bath at the time we proposed. One very great happiness is, that we have had such fine Weather. I am now come from Church, and have the pleasure of finding Mr. & Mrs. Pearse here, who desire their love to you, Mrs. Coode etc. Papa Mama join this family in love and Compliments as due. Be assured that I am my dear Sister Peggy

Yours affectionately
FRANCES PENROSE.

Exon. April 7th 1766.
Cos. Peggy

I was desired to open this to let you know, that George went yesterday to Collumpton, with your Papa that you should not be uneasy, if he should not get home the day that you expect him. I wish Cos. Penrose was got safe to Bath and hope he will find great Benefit. Please to remember me to your Brother and Sisters,

from your
Affectionate Cos:
ROBT. PAUL.

They expected a letter from you, to be left with me last Saturday.

To: Miss Margaret Penrose,
at Gluvias Vicarage,
near Penryn,
Cornwall.

Bath. April 9th. 1766.

My dear Sister,

Thanks be to God we got safe here last evening, about a half an Hour after Six, and this morning had the very great pleasure of receiving your letters. As I know it will give you satisfaction, I will first give you an account of our Journey. I wrote you a letter last Friday from Mr. Hockin's which gave you an account of the days journey, and of Papa's being much out of order, but on Saturday morning, he was so bad when he came to get up, that we thought he would not be able go on, in his journey, but he with dificulty got into the Chaise, but his Neck was so bad that he cou'd not put his hand to his Mouth; we rid through a good deal of very bad roads, and stop't at a place call'd Bow, to bait our Horses, and we eat some Biskits and drank some Wine, and then went on to Yendicott, but so late that they had dined, tho' not eat up all the meat, for we had brought to Table for us, part of a fine boiled Turkey a breast of Veal, Pork and Pease and Tarts, and a very elegant Supper in the evening. Sunday, I wrote you an account of, in the Letter I designed to have sent you by George, but as he went on to Collomton with us I gave it to Mr. Paul to put in the Post-Office, as I wrote it before dinner I cou'd not give you an account of that genteel entertainment. The first course was a fine dish of Fish, a rump of Beef roasted, Ham and Fowls, a fine Sallad, two small plates of Garden-stuff, answering each other and two Bread Pudins. I think our Mr. and Mrs. Pierce are looking old, one of the first things she said was, how did I come to let my younger Sister be married before me. I told her it was the fashion in our Town. She was dressed in a brown Satin Night Gown and a purple Sattin Hat and Cloke. She says she longs to kiss Betsy's Child.[5] I suppose George told you the dismal condition Papa was in upon the road he was obliged to be carried in and out to the Coach all the way. It was as easy a Carriage as ever I road in, in my life, only one person in it besides ourselves, and that a young Gentleman one Mr. Cook, who is going to set up his business (which is that of an Apothecary) here at Bath, his Mother is the person Mrs. Walker taulk's so much of. It was very happy for us that we met with so agreeable a companion for he was very usefull to Papa on the road. We dined on Monday at Taunton, a very large Town; as we went out of Town there was a Woman an outside passenger taken up, who road by the Coachman's side on the Box, so you may tell Mary we had no one on top of the Coach, no legs hanging down in the way. We lodged that night at Bridge-water, and had a Clergeman who lives there, one Mr. Borows [Burroughs] to sup with us. Yesterday we had in our view most part of the way, the finest prospects I ever saw, we went through Wells, but did not stop till we came to a place call'd Old-down, where we dined, and then set out for this place. We saw Coll. Sewell's man as soon as we came, he had been waiting for us two hours, the Col. came to the Inn and went with Mama and I to our Lodgins, Papa was carried in a Chair. Our Lodgins are excessive handsome, we have a Parlor and two lodging rooms all down stairs, which is very convenient, as Papa is not able walk. This place is call'd Abby Green at the house of one Mr. Grant a Clergeman. Mrs. Grant is a very fine Lady. We were all not a little disconcerted when first we came here, for Mrs. Grant was surprised to find we had not brought a servant with us and said we

5   The baby, Molly Coode.

must take one for it was a thing impossible to do without one, so we have taken a Girl of about 15 year old, and we are to give her her meat and 2s. per week. There are two Ladies that lodge in the House with us, that are very kind, and have offer'd us that their maid shall do any thing for us, one of 'em is a Sister [in] Law to Sir Edward Turner our Member. They told me I shou'd have a Ticket of 'em any time to go to the Ball. It is impossible for me to describe how kind the Col. & Mrs. Sewell are, Mrs. Sewell is not well, so I have not seen her, Mama call'd upon her this afternoon. Mr. & Mrs. Robinson were here this morning. We were greatly disappointed at not hearing from you by Saturdays post, I dare say Mr. Hocker was sorry that he forgot, and think he was much more to blame in his proposal, than in forgetting the letter. We are glad every one is so kind to you. You have all gave us great pleasure, in sending us such pritty Letters. My dear Mary must excuse my not writing her this post, tell her I will soon, and that I was obliged to cut my ruffle sleeves this morning, and have wore 'em all day without hemming. I hope our clothes will come to night, or I know not what I shall do. We expect Papa to be confined to his bed every hour. As I must write Mr. H – to night I can't stay to enlarge at present, tho I have wrote so much I have a Thousand things more to say if I had time. Papa and Mama join with me in remembering you all, and Compts. to all friends. Tell Mrs. White Mrs. Aurelia[6] is well, and will write her next time I send you a letter, and tell her she may send a letter whenever you write under your cover. I remain

my Dear Peggy your affectionate Sister
### FRANCES PENROSE.

P.S. I omitted the second course at Yendicott, which was Roasted Sweet breads, Lobsters, Trifle, 2 Plates of Almonds and Raisins, Baked Pares and Potted Meat, etc. We are sorry Dr. Coode is so much out of order.

Bath. April 10th, 1766.

My dear Peggy,

And all the rest of my dear Children, I pray God bless you all. You have heard so much of my Disorders, (and indeed I have been disordered greatly) that I thought you would all be glad to have a Line

6 Mistress Aurelia was servant to Col. and Mrs. Sewell in Bath. Her mother Mrs. White evidently lived in Penryn and may have been employed by the Penrose family there.

again under my own hand, tho' but a line. Last Night is the first Night I have been able change Posture in the Bed, for 5 or 6 Nights: and till to-day noon, I have not been able put my hand to my mouth, but have been fed like a child, since I left Oakhampton. Judge you, what an uncomfortable Journey I have had, and your Mamma's and Sister's Discomfort not less than mine. I cannot now stand on my feet, not even supported by two; but I hope, I am in all Points bettering. The only Gout I have remaining, worth mention, is in the great Toe of my left Foot: which alone, had I otherwise been disposed, would have prevented my Dancing this morning, when the City Music came to the Door of our Lodgings with a Welcome to Mr., Mrs. and Miss Penrose to Bath. Whether or no the Music was enchanting as that of Orpheus, in Poetic Story, I am not Judge enough, having Midas's Ears, to take it upon me to determine: but, if he made Stones and Trees dance after his Lyre, the Bath Musicians made Silver dance out of Mamma's Pocket, at the distance of a large Room between, and, we are credibly informed, their attempts are succeeded by a like effect on almost every Stranger that comes here. If this be too learned a Sentence, your Brother will unriddle it to you. The Bells have not rung since our Arrival: Perhaps the Ringers have heard, I can't tell how, that at Lyfton and Wells the Bells rung sweetly, as We passed through, without our making the Ringers so much as drink. We came hither Tuesday Evening. Occurrences between my writing you at Trebartha and our coming hither have been so fully and elegantly set forth to you by your Sister Fanny, that I dare not say any thing which happened in that Interval; for I would willingly avoid the Imputation of Impertinence, my Fingers must be spared a little, and likely Mr. Hocker would resent it as a Reflection on himself, for somebody and he are all one.[7] Bath afforded an exceeding fine Prospect from the Hill, descending to it: and I can say no more of Bath, not having been out of Door since my arrival. One can hardly look upon the buildings too, for the multitude of fine Ladies continually passing and repassing before your Eyes, but of these and the Fashions your Sister will write Mary. Let me only make mention of one, the Mistress of these Lodgings. From the Inn, where the Coach stopt, your Mamma and Sister were escorted by the Colonel, and I conveyed in a Sedan to this Place. The first Thing, which struck us was a Lady as fine as possible who welcomed us to Bath. Scarce a minute had passed, before we are asked, if we were without a Servant. We answered "Yes". – "But it is

7   The implication here is that Fanny and Mr. Hocker "are all one" i.e. courting. They married two years later.

impossible you can –

### Apr. 11th.

When I began writing, I did not think I could have held it out five lines, but I held it out better than Expectation, till I came as far as you see in the preceding Page. Then I was interrupted, and could not resume the Pen any more that Day. We all thought, that we should not know here what to do with ourselves, Time would hang so heavy on our hands in a strange Place: but, on the contrary, Dinner Time excepted, or between three and five, we have no Respite. All is Hurry Hurry. We have had repeated Visits, not only from the Colonel, whose Kindness is beyond compare, but from Dr. Grant, a Clergymen, who is Master of these Lodgings, and Mrs. Grant many Times, the fine Lady mentioned a little before; Two ladies, who lodge in the first Floor over our Heads, daughters of Dr. Leigh master of Balliol College in Oxford, the elder one married to a Clergyman of great Fortune, of the same name; Mr. and Mrs. Robinson, and Mr. Grylls; and an old School-acquaintance of mine, who generally resides at Bristol, occasionally at Bath, Major Tucker. Now again all is quiet, and I am glad to go on with the rest of my Story. But first I must tell you, we this Day heard from Cousin Fanny, who is pleased with her Journey, and pleased with London: and that this morning, by advice of Mr. Haviland, an experienced Apothecary, who has lived in Bath upwards of thirty years, and been employed in the best Families, I began to drink the Waters, a quarter of Pint at seven, ditto at twelve in the morning, which I like very well, I beg you and all my Friends to pray for a Blessing on them. Should I need a Physician (which I hope I shall not, as I do not find mine to be a case uncommon) by the kind Recommendation of the Colonel, Dr. Schomberg one of the Top Physicians, Has promised his advice and assistance without Fees.

[April 10th continued] – do without one." "Why, Ma'am, we thought the servants of the House, did every thing for us, which we wanted". – "Oh, no, Mem, the Servants of the House clean the Rooms, make the Beds, light the Fires, dress the Victuals: But, who, Mem, shall go off Errands, lay the cloth, wait on you at Table, at Tea, and do the many other little Things which necessarily occur?" – "We were informed, Ma'am, that all these things would be done by your Servants, by Persons who have been at Bath, some in like circumstances." – "Indeed, Mem, I know no such Thing: perhaps, it may be so at a Boarding House, but surely, Mem, not at Lodgings." – "What then, Ma'am, would you advise us to do if we are utter Strangers here." – "Really, Mem, I can't tell: but I am certain you cannot do without a

Servant." – You begin to think, honest Peg, that we were in a deplorable Situation, and that we went to bed supperless. I do not know, but we should, if it had not been for the Colonel, who employed Aurelia and John[8] to look out for us a temporary Servant, which they soon got, a girl of twelve,[9] who had never been out before; and John got us some Bread and Cheese, some Ale and Wines and afterwards the Landlady offered us Civilities, and has not been wanting in Kindness ever since. And the Two, Mistress and Miss Leighs, are exceedingly kind indeed, have offered to help us in all our Needs, and the Assistance of their Servants. However, I hope, by God's Help, who brought us hither well, we shall do well while here. And, indeed, like Robinson Crusoe, we begin to see our affairs a little flourishing. We have not only an inexperienced Servant, but Household-goods, viz. a Tea-kettle and Saucepan, 2 Tea-pots, milk-pot, Butter-dish, Pint and half-pint Mugs, Bason to keep Salt in, (a Three shilling Barrell of Small-Beer, a doz, of Wine) a thumb-bottle for Ink, a Pint Bottle for Bath Water, and a small Phial for Vinegar. All these our own Property. Of the Colonel's, half dozen plates, a slop-Bason, two Tea-Waiters. The Mistress of the House has lent us, a Pair of Salts, 4 wine glasses, a Tumbler, 2 silver spoons, and Tea-Things till the carrier comes with our Box, who is expected to-night. Our apartments consist of three Rooms, a Parlour and Two Bed-chambers, the Parlour and our Bed-chamber handsomely cieled, and Fanny's papered. – The Parlour hath in it a Beaufet, 6 Mahogany Chairs with Hair-Bottoms, an Easy-Chair, a Dining Table, and Pillar and Claw Table both of Mahogany, Chimney Looking Glass, and Looking-glass against a broad Mullion between the Window Frames. Handsome Chimney-Furniture with Marble Hearth. All the Houses here are sashed.[10]

## April 12th.

Left off writing yesterday, because I was much out of Order: and so I am still. My left Foot is swell'd prodigiously. Tom Pearce's Shoes not worth a half-penny. Almost every thing I eat or drink, comes up again. Your Mamma hath been to-day at the Market, which she thinks a very fine one: bought a Neck of Veal; 12d. of Tripe, worth 3d. at home, and not a farthing here after it was cooked; Potatoes, Onions,

8   John was Col. Sewell's other servant.
9   But Fanny, in a previous letter, said that she was about 15 – which seems more likely.
10  At this period it was fashionable to replace mullioned windows with sashed frames. John Penrose had done this in St. Gluvias church – which is nowadays considered almost an act of vandalism.

etc. Your Mamma and Fanny have both been at the Abby-Church, at different times: There they might go in any Dress; but no fashionable Place can be approached, without much Form; and we had not our Box from the Carrier till this morning. Every thing was safe, except one large Saucer a little broke at the Brim. After I wrote yesterday Dr. Stackhouse called in. Fanny is just now gone out, to buy fine Things against the Ball: and she is offered as many Tickets as even she will have.

Our Lodging Room has a blew and white flowered Linen Bed, Window Curtains the same, Walnut Chairs with blew Bottoms, Chest of Drawers, Dressing Table, Looking-Glass: Inside, a closet with hanging Press and Shelves. Fanny's Bed white, with all conveniences, and a closet. The House we live in, is on the west side of Abby Green, fronting East and West: but Fanny's Room has a window, which looks up a long Lane towards the Church-yard. – My Library consists of the *Bath Guide,* a sixpenny Pamphlet:[11] and a *Map of Bath,*[12] in which I can shew you exactly where we are situated. It is inconceivable, what a number of fine Ladies and Gentlemen (the Gentlemen far inferior in Numbers to the Ladies) pass before our Parlour Window, going to the Grand and South Parades, which are the most public Walks: Your Mamma and Sister have not seen them yet: tho' by what I can learn, they are little farther from us, than Mr. Bolitho's from you.

## Apr. 13th.

Left off writing yesterday, because Mrs. Leigh and her Sister came a visiting, the only Tea Visitors we yet have had. Mr. Arch-deacon Sleech was here this morning, after preaching at the Abby; and Mrs. Snow, wife to Mr. Snow, Chantor of Exeter Cathedral. Your Sister was at Church this morning, and your Mamma is just now gone. Thank God, tho' I had an indifferent Night, I am much better to-day than I have been for many days. Poor Mrs. Sewell is exceeding ill; some fears there are that she may not recover, John has been this morning to take Lodgings for the Col., etc. about half a mile out of Town, on the western side of Holloway Road. You will wonder, my dear, when I tell you, your Mamma is the only old woman in Town: Ladies without Teeth, without Eyes, with a foot and half in the grave, ape youth, and dress themselves forth with the fantastick Pride of eighteen or twenty. Even the Sexton's Daughter wears a wire cap, and dresses like a woman of Fashion. But, by the by, I am told the Sexton's Place far exceeds

11  *The New Bath Guide or Useful Pocket Companion,* printed by Cornelius Pope and first published in 1762.
12  Map of 1750 – See illustration facing p. 74.

Abbey Green, Church Street and part of the Abbey. Pen and watercolour wash by Benjamin Morris about 1785, showing on the middle left the house where the Penrose family took lodgings in 1766.

Aunt Margaret's,[13] and is worth as much as the Vicarage of Gluvias. This comes in, by the Way, for I leave all Account of Dress and Fashion to Fanny. Fanny hath bought Lace for a Tippet and Tucker, to wear next Tuesday at the Ball: she hath bought, and trimmed, a white hat bound with blue and white Ribbon. She hath been this morning upon the Parade, and likes it very well. I can go no where: my left foot wrapt up in flannel, too big for a Shoe. It is impossible to express how obliging Mrs. Grant, our Landlady is, many times a day enquiring after my health, and offering the assistance of her Servants, and the use of any Utensil in her house to do me kindness and assist your Mamma in her care for me; and the two sisters, Leigh, are as civil to Fanny as possible, with such civility as proceeds merely from goodness of Heart, and not from the constraints of Politeness and Good-breeding, tho' no Ladies possess these latter in higher degree. The Colonel is always coming or sending to know how we do, and whether we want any thing. But in a day or two he will be gone with Mrs. Sewell: I pray God heartily it may be to the Recovery of her Health. She is a good woman, and such as will be found wanting: the Col. is much affected. I have not yet increased my Draught of Waters. I presume, from the Gout's being as yet upon me. I have great Encouragement, from what I hear hourly of the Benefit persons in my case have received, to pray for God's Blessing on these means. Should I succeed, I shall not repent my Journey. But, I think, nothing less precious than Health is worth seeking in this Place of extremist Vanity: there may be more Wickedness in Vanity-Fair, but not more Vanity, tho' it gives it its Name. – Your Mamma hath bought some charming gouty socks for me, and large gouty stockings, and is pleased with finding she may have at the shops here whatever she wants. I mention these things just as they arise in my mind: for I have such frequent Interruptions, that I am all confusion. I hope my dear Peggy, you and the dear children, and the rest of the family, remember the Sabbath-day to keep it holy: your Sister and Mamma in some measure sanctifie it, but Sunday scarce shines a Sabbath-day to me. I hope your Brothers are good at Church; and I would have Jacky send me the Texts in Latin. Tell them both from me, that I beg them to remember their Creator in the Days of their youth, then God will remember them in the Day when he makes up his Jewels. What I say to them, I say to you all: be diligent as you can in serving God, then God will love you and make his Abode

---

13 We know of no Aunt Margaret in the family. It is probable that "Aunt" is used here as a Cornish colloquialism for an old woman, well known to the family, who was sexton at St. Gluvias.

with you; and those, whom God Loves, and takes up his residence with, need fear no Evil, either spiritual or temporal, either in this World or the next, for the Love of God is comprehension of every Blessing, and even the Happiness of the Saints in Heaven consists principally in their being in the Presence of God. I would have you read together *Doddridge's Sermons to young Persons*, and may the divine Blessing render them useful to your Souls! – Dear Peggy, always remember us all to Dr. Coode, whom we sincerely love, and to our dear Son and Daughter Coode, and precious Molly. I have been longing to see children carried in arms, that I might compare her with them; but have seen but one or two since I have been here. Remember us always to George, and the Maids; Mr. Bath, Mrs. Nevill, Friends at Falmouth and all inquiring friends; to my kind Assistants Mess. Evans and Osborn, and if Opportunity offers to Mess. Walmsley and Harris. Let Mr. Evans and Mr. Osborn know, what Mr. Buckingham wrote; and that, if Mr. Robinson returns before me, and Help is wanted, he will be ready to give it. Text this Day, both parts of the Day, at the Abby, Phil. IV.8. Arch. Sleech preacher. It was literally a very fine Congregation, a Congregation of fine Ladies. Your Sister saw there at one view more Ladies, than she had ever seen before in her Life-time put all together. The Chancel, which is very large, reaching to the Body of the Church from the Communion Table, was full of Ladies, all sitting on Forms matted; the Body of the Church is pewed. Sister made one among the Ladies on the Mattin.


### Apr. 14th. Monday.

This morning before I was up, I received the most comfortable of Cordials, six Letters from six dear Children. I cannot answer them, as they do the King's Speech, Paragraph by Paragraph, but in general I thank you all, and you may be assured, that I shall read them so often, that not a Jot or Tittle in them will pass unnoticed. I must indeed particularly express my Satisfaction, at the good Report of Dolly and Charles, and don't at all doubt but they will continue to behave well. That dear little nonpareile Molly has a slight cold, may probably be owing to Teeth coming: That the Doctor is well enough to go again to Methleigh, is matter of Joy. You may shew the Doctor and Mr. Coode's family all our Letters: for I dare say they are all interested in our welfare, as much as you are, and I desire them Happiness as my own. Tell my dear Jacky, that I am not against his going a Ship board, if again invited, or any where that you approve of: you are as prudent as you are honest, and you are honest to a Proverb so that I leave such things with great Pleasure intirely to you. If Mr. Evans[14] had gone on with him in my way, it had pleased me better: however Jacky must go on in *his* way, and I am throughly satisfied, that he will by his Diligence do credit and Justice both to himself and me. Mr. Evans view is evidently enough to save himself trouble. Jacky's Letter was just such as I meant for him to write me. Mary writes like an Hero; she shall challenge all her compeers (look in *Johnson*): I cannot commend you, because 'tis to your face. But in Obedience to Mamma I acquaint you, that she vastly likes your Huswifry and good Management: and I hope, every one will consider, what a Burden it is on such tender years to provide for a family, and lighten it to you as much as they can. Poor George, it seems could not tell my Distress without Tears. He was much affected, and shewed great concern for me, and I found him wanting after he went away, no one being so handy about me except Mamma. Next Monday, Apr. 21st is Fanny's Birthday: You will excuse my giving you this Rememberancer, tho' I can't think you would have forgot the day, had I said nothing about it. Dr. Williams, Mrs. Archer, Mrs. Behenna, who have been so kind as to remember to us, have our Thanks, and compliments in Return. Give my Love to the Clark; and I am heartily glad, he is able be at Church again: I have great confidence in his care. As you have begun Walker's Xtion, keep on in it: don't leave it for Doddridge, before recommended, but possibly, you may be able to read this, now and then, by little and little, by the by. – This morning hath added an half pint tin cup to our little houshold-goods. I am a great deal Better, can put on my Shoe, and by the Help of Mamma can walk the Length of the Room. My Dose of Water, as usual. – Mrs. Sewell is better this morning. – Tell Mrs. Tabris, we remember to her. – Mamma designs writing a Line to Mrs Coode: you must excuse her not writing to you now; my Scribble must serve for us both. – Whether we are now in the Place, whence the Proverb took it's Rise of God's sending meat, and the Devil cooks: or whether our late Dining, at 3 o'clock (and Company will not let us eat a Bit of Meat sooner, tho' we were starving) takes away our Stomachs: neither of us have made the fifth Part of a Meal since our being at Bath, and your Mamma hath lost Flesh since she came from home. But truly she has gone thro' prodigious Fatigue and Anxiety of Mind (we will not lay all the fault on Bath;) all along on the Road, I was forced to be helped in and out the Coach, and carried up and down stairs, by two ruffian-like fellows; very little compassion had of my poor aching Bones: in the Coach, which was an easy one, every

14    Mr. Evans, schoolmaster of Penryn and Vicar of Tintagel, took over Jacky's schooling, whilst his father, who normally taught him, was away.

jolt, as I was pinioned, and could not move my Arms, or hold by any thing, or poize my self in the least, excited a Oh! and sometimes went to the Heart of me, always to that your tender Mamma, who always felt for me as much, sometimes more than, I did. Then the fatigue, at Nights and Mornings, especially at Bridgwater where the Stage Hour was six o'clock, was amazing. Nothing but God's Goodness, and her Love to me and the Family, could have possibly supported her. My dear Children, neither you nor I can ever be enough thankful to that providence, which was her Support, and which brought me hither, without stopping on the Road, through such very extraordinary Difficulties. −

My dear Peggy, my Letter to you was written by Fits and Starts, as Opportunity offered. The Matters in it no way digested, but set down just as they occurred. This Method, or rather this Want of Method, I have been obliged to put up with, if I would write to you at all. My Letter, my dear, may fitly enough be compared to Beef fried with potatoes, carrots, cabbage, altogether: an hodge-podge of various eatables, very different in Taste, yet eatables however. On such a miscellaneous Dish I have before now made a very sufficient and comfortable meal. If you sit down to this medley of mine with a good Appetite, (and I am no conjurer, any more than you, if this will not be the case,) I not at all doubt but you will be pleased. Don't be greedy, Peg, but invite all the family to the Entertainment: you are heartily welcome to it, such as it is; and much good may it do you!

Mr. Gregor called here this morning: he speaks greatly in Com-mendation of Bath. − Your Mamma's and my repeated Blessing on, and dear Fanny's Love to you, and all your Brothers and Sisters, conclude this rambling Epistle from,

My dear dear Peg,
Your ever affectionate Father
JOHN PENROSE.

P.S. Our Compliments wait on the two worthy families, Hearle and Heame. − Put Dr. Peter's Letter into Post-Office. − Mamma saw Mrs. Sewell to-day, who at 3 in the afternoon was to be conveyed, not to the Place I mentioned, but to Lincum Spa,[15] not far from Prior Park. The Water prescribed me is from the Cross Bath.

15   According to John Wood, Lyncombe Spa was first discovered by Charles Milsom in 1737 while preparing a fishpond. The spring disappeared but was later revived and in 1766. Christopher Anstey referred to the "charming parties made" to visit "Lincomb's shady groves."

Bath. Apr. 15. 1766.

My dear Peggy,

And all the rest of my dear children, may the watchful Providence of Almighty God keep you ever under his Protection! You see, my dears, I am still able write you: and I do not know, that I can so well, surely not so agreeably, use that ability. God is very good to me, and my Gout seems walking off. I am able to rise from the Chair, and walk the Room a few Turns by the Help of a Stick, which your Mamma this morning bought at a Toy Shop, and made me a Present of. The Doctor has altered my Regimen: I am now to take Water from the Cross Bath at 7 and 8 o'clock mornings, and from the King's Bath at 12, quarter a Pint each time. Every one, who comes in, tells me this exactness as to Time and Quantity is a mere Farce, notwithstanding the Doctors so gravely prescribe: and it may be so for ought I know; but as it may not be so, I'll try stricktly adhere to Rule. Some say, the Waters heat them; some, that they make them giddy; others talk of other Effects from them: I can only say, that I have no Effect, which I know of, from drinking the Water, but that it quenches my Thirst, which at present is an excellent Quality in it, for I have been thirsty, more or less, almost from the Beginning of my Journey. As my Gout goes off, my Thirst will abate, and I think it is not near so great as it was a day or two ago. Mamma hath sent for a Taylor to take measure of me for an outer Coat, Camblet at 3s. per yard, which will be made by Thursday Even: and the Taylor is going to let out my blue coat, which is too little, but can easily be made bigger. Don't you think, Mamma is very good to me? She hath also bought for herself a Pair of Temple Spectacles: which I am very glad of, because her common ones used to leave red marks on her Nose. Fanny is just now (almost 6 o'clock) gone in a Sedan to a Ball; Miss Leigh is with her. She had her Ticket of the Colonel. Dr. Stackhouse was so kind as to send her Tickets this morning; one for herself, and one for any friend she chose to bear her company: This was very obliging in the Doctor and I shall acknowledge the Obligation; but Fanny was supplied before, thro' Favour (as I said) of the Colonel. – Here I was interrupted till 8 O'clock; at which time Fanny came home, in a Chair; the Lady with her not chusing to stay longer. But of this, and all that relates to the Ball, I suppose Fanny herself will write a particular Account to Mary. Let me now return again to myself, and give you a Symptom that I am growing better; which is, that I made a good Dinner today, the only good meal I have made since here. We had for Dinner a Mutton-Pye, made at the Pastry Cooks, price 1s. just enough for us three, a Taste for our little

Servant, and a Bit to eat cold. Our little Servant we all wish you could see: a very likely Girl, sharp, pert; able to do little, but willing to do what she is able; wants to go into Cornwall with us, and uses many little insinuating arts to gain her ends. We could compare her with her Betters not many Miles from Home, but Comparisons are odious. The People here in general speak so fine, that our finest Ladies don't equal them: and your Mamma's Account of the Market-folks, is, that they all, even the very Butchers, mince their Words: By her Description they speak like Mrs. Behenna, when sometimes she gives herself affected Airs. So polite the ordinary People in their Dress, that a Woman went by this morning with a Horse loaden with Muffins (a sort of hot Bread) in a white shag Hat and an Habit. – If you do not see our Names among those of the Gentry arrived at Bath, in the Sherborne Paper, we have seen them in the *Bath Journal*: Mr. and Mrs. Penrose at least; but surely it was an unlucky Slip to omit Miss, the youngest of the three, and, if you had seen her just now equipped for the Ball, you would think her as well worthy Notice (for she made a smart appearance) as most at Bath. I have this Day had another fresh Visiter, Mr. Snow, Chantor of Exeter Cathedral, whose Lady I wrote in my last had before paid her Respects to Mamma. The Chimes are now going *nine*. So I wish you all a good Night.

### Wednesday, Apr. 16.

Dear Peg, Good morrow to you. Before I proceed to new matter, let me correct an erratum in what goes before. The Bath Butchers do not mince their Words, only they speak fine, as the Manner here is: so my Illustration of the matter must go for nothing. – This morning we received Mrs. Grant's Bill, which is delivered in once a week. If I should not always send it you, yet this will serve for a Specimen, and give you some Amusement, perhaps some Disgust.

Apr. 9. Boyling fish, 4d. – Frying Fish, 3d. Mem: Both boiled and fried fish absolutely spoiled. Lard for the Fry, found by us, price 2d. – No more hott suppers.

Apr. 10. Boiling mutton, 4d. – Boiling Mutton Broth, 3d. Mem: Not two different Boilings, but a little Oatmeal of ours delivered to the Cook, and two china Basons of Broth made, which we eat before Dinner.

Apr. 11. Roasting Mutton, 4d. – Mem: The only thing tolerably cooked, of all we have had. We always find Butter for Basting the meat.

Apr. 12. Boiling Tripe, 3d. – Mem: we ordered it to be fried: wretched stuff.

Apr. 13. Boiling Veal, 4d. – Boiling Bacon and Greens, 4d. Mem: A pen'noth of Spinach, and a little Bit of Bacon to eat with, or relish, the Veal.

Apr. 14. Roasting Veal, 4d. – Mem: Under-roasted, and I could not eat any of it. We have bought and boiled a few Potatoes in our own Sauce-pan; and must do more, in the cookery way, ourselves: or between the Dearness of the Meat and Dressing it we shall be ruined. This cookery Bill, is the grossest Imposition, we have yet meet with. Sunday Mamma poached two Eggs herself.

Apr. 16. One week's Lodgings, £1. 5. 0.

This and Saturday are Market-Days here. Our Marketing to-day, a Loin of Mutton, 21d. – a Fowl, 20d. Butter is 6d$\frac{1}{2}$ per lb.

We have no expectation of seeing the Colonel to-day. But Mrs. Sewell is better. So, thank God, am I. I can walk the Room without Help; and have this morning made a Visit to the Ladies up-stairs: the first Time I have been out of our own Lodgings, since I entered them. Fresh Visiters this morning, to your Mamma Major Tucker's Lady, to me Revd. Mr. Vivian of Cornwood who is now in his Tour of England with Commissioner Roger's Son, and intends staying at Bath a Fortnight. The Duke and Duchess of Beaufort[16] came to Bath Monday Evening, and went away again Tuesday morning: the Monday Evening they were at the Play, and thereby hangs a Tale. But, as Mr. Hocker's Saying is, more of this when we meet. Fanny was this morning to see Miss Stackhouse: the Doctor disordered in a cold. I have wrote Mr. Feroulhet about the *London Chronicle*, ordering it to be sent me here: so you will not be surprized at it's not coming to Penryn. The Town Papers will well enough serve Mary and Charles. – Fresh Visitor this evening Counsellor Short of Exon, an old School-acquaintance who enquired kindly after Mr. Davis. My Apothecary this Evening has ordered me, to drink now three times a Day from the King's Bath, at the usual Hours, and not to have any more from the Cross Bath; and hath increased the Quantity to a third, instead of a Quarter of a Pint, each Draught; so now I am ordered to drink what they call the Middle Glass. Oh my dear Butler, what would we give for a Night-cap of Vicarage ale!

### Thursday, Apr. 17.

Weather is wet, so that I cannot venture to go out, even in a Chair, (as I have not yet been out at all) to drink the Water at the Pump,

---

16   Henry, 5th Duke (1744–1803) who had married as his Duchess the same year, Elizabeth Boscawen from Cornwall.

where I am told it hath most Virtue. Colds here must be guarded against with all imaginable care: for if I catch cold, I must cease drinking the Water, and then I lose the Benefit of my Journey. Mamma and Sister go out, to Church twice a day, a quarter after eleven, and a quarter after four: and they are all who go to Church from this House, except Dr. Grant, the Owner, when he reads Prayers, as sometimes he does. This Dr. Grant is the Clergyman, that from the Time of the Marriage-Acts till his Leaving Scotland and coming to Bath, had his Residence on the other side Tweed, and married the People, who could not be married in England, by Reason of their Non-Age, and Want of Friends consent. It was not, in my mind, a reputable Employment but it was legal, and profitable, and the Gentleman bears a fair Character. He has offered me the use of any Book in his Study, so has Col. Sewell the Use of any Book in his, and the Ladies upstairs have lent me *Johnson's Shakespeare,* so I have not yet subscribed (and I don't know that I shall subscribe) to the Bookseller's Library. Mr. Vivian too, who is a Subscriber, has offered me any Book in the Catalogue, during the Fortnight he is to reside here. Mr. Vivian, and the Gentleman he travels with, are at a Boarding-House. They pay 20s. for 2 Lodging Rooms, 10s. for a Parlour, and 12s. a head for Eating, etc. per week: everything found them, except Tea, Sugar, and Wine. And happy for Mr. Vivian, so at least he thinks it, the Mistress of the Boarding-House is a Methodist, and has a great Reverence for Lady Huntingdon's Chapel.

No new Visiter this Day: but this afternoon we all paid a Visit to Mrs. and Miss Leigh, the first Tea-Visit we have made. Before Tea, and while Mamma and Sister were at Church, I spent an Hour with Mr. and Mrs. Grant. Our Visit to the Leighs was not protracted to any considerable Length: for one Mr. Hutchinson, Capt. of an India-man, and his Lady, drank Tea with us, and immediately after, sat down to Quadrille. You must suppose, it suited our Inclinations to get away as soon as decently could be. I shall rejoice, when to-morrow comes, because we expect to hear again to-morrow morning from you and your dear Brothers and Sisters. The Post comes in this Night, but the Letters are not delivered out till eight or nine next morning. I pray God, your Letters may bring Word, that you and all our Friends enjoy the invaluable Blessing of Health, and all other Blessings.

### Friday, April 18th.

You cannot conceive, my dear Peg, how much Fanny is admired: she is counted a very fine Woman. But indeed she need not be proud upon it: for I never saw such a Parcel of Ugly Faces, as I have seen since

I came to Bath. I believe, they look so much worse, for taking such Pains to adorn themselves. If they were in a State of Inaction, they would look like so many rotten Posts gilded. Miss Kitty Stackhouse is the only one, that has any real Pretense to Beauty. Fanny's Likeness to Lady St. Aubyn has been discovered at Bath. She expects every minute to be called upon by Mr. Vivian, Mr. Rogers, and Mr. Glynn of Helston (who is also on his Travels under Mr. Vivian's Care) to go see some Paintings, and in the afternoon (I believe) she will go with them to see Prior Park. It is very obliging in the Gentlemen, and a good Opportunity for Fanny. All our Acquaintance call in almost every day to ask how we do; and the Gentleman, who came up in the Coach with us (tell Mary) is a pretty constant visitant.

Between eight and nine this morning we received your very honest, and Mary's very comical, Letters: at the Foot of the latter were a few Lines, which by the contents come from your Brother, but by its Brevity seemed to be an Epistle from Bob Short. I would not have him neglect his Business, nor too much balk himself in his Play, but I shall be glad to see a little more of his hand-writing, carefully written. Let us know in your next, whether Jacky's Breeches are made. As Mary has a fancy to Miss Kitty's Copper-plate, your Mamma is willing to indulge it: and we do not doubt, but she will be very careful of it, and be so good a Girl as to deserve it. You are very good, my Peg, in reading with and to the Family. I hope, God Almighty will prosper your Proceedings, and make them a Blessing both to you and them. I have inclosed a Letter of Thanks to Mr. Philipps, which you may read, seal, and send. I design also this Post to order 6 Licenses to you from Mr. Geare by the Caravan. I am glad you have such a Run of Trades and wish it may continue. Your Mamma thinks the Pig turned out very well. Sister is in no small Trouble, that her Letter was shewed to Mrs. Hearle. I don't know, how you could help it: but it will be a great Bar to Freedom in writing, if our idle chit-chat, which is well enough among ourselves, be read publickly to others, who perhaps may expect fine Writing, Aphorisms, and Oracles. We may very justly expect this, that no one see our Letters, but Mr. Coode's Family; and that if you or they would communicate any Part of the contents to others, you would read such Part yourselves, and judiciously leave out such trifling Occurrences as none but you and we are interested in. We are obliged to you for your Intelligence about the Comet: Mr. Vivian saw it in his Journey: I have mentioned it to some Persons here this morning, to whom, as well as to us, it was a Piece of News. Bath is a Place, where Things below engross so much Time and Thought, that Things above may pass unnoticed, without wonder. Remember us, as

due, to Dr. Coode, Mr. Mrs. and Molly Coode, and all other friends,
as in my last: also to Mrs. Mead, Mrs. Trevethick, Mrs. Turner, Mr.
Bolitho, Ury and Jenny, and to all who inquire after us, or shew you
civility. Tell Betty Trelease, we pity her in the Tooth-ach, and would
advise her, by all means, if it be owing to a rotten Tooth, to have the
Tooth drawn. Communicate to Mr. Hocker any thing you think worth
while, with our best Love and Compliments; and when you see him,
he may see our Letters. If Mrs. Tabois's want of Coals be owing to her
not receiving money due to her, we suppose her Want to be of no long
continuance: but if it be owing to Poverty, you are commissioned by
your compassionate Mamma to desire her Acceptance of Half a crown.
We observe all the Particulars in your Letters, tho' I do not answer
them all particularly. I have answered all such, as I imagine required
an answer, I hope to your Satisfaction.

Lord Edgcumbe[17] is come to Town. The Bells rung last Evening; I
was told, for him, but he came not till this Evening. So, as soon as I
can go out, there will be a grand Visit for me to pay. The Bells ring
here, for nothing less than a Lord; so my Resentment is over, that they
rung not for us. Your Mamma and Fanny have both been to see the
Pictures, and are much pleased with them. Among the rest is a fine
Portrait of a father, mother and child: the finest Portrait, she ever saw,
and she liked it the better for the child's being very like little Molly.
Fanny's Walk to Prior Park is post-poned on account of the weather,
which is come in rainy. The Taylor hath brought home my outer coat.
'Tis made of mixt Camblet, next kin to Black. It fits me, and I like it
very well. My blue coat is also let out and made bigger, so that it will
better button over my Cassock. But I wish I may not repent of this
alteration: for I have no Reason to think of growing bigger, till I come
back to the Flesh-pots of Penryn. By the Help, however, of some
pickled Salmon, 15d. per lb., monstrous dear! I have made a good
meal to-day.

The weather clearing up a little in the afternoon, Fanny walked
with Mrs. Leigh to King's Mead, and The Square, and saw somewhat
of the new and finer Part of the City; and is now returned very well,
and delighted with her Walk. As she is frequently engaged, and I
write you pretty fully, your candour will excuse it, tho' she should not
write you so long a Letter, as you and she both desire. Her Inclinations
are to give you all the Pleasure she can: but you would not have her,
while abroad, neglect any Opportunity of seeing what is to be seen,

17    George, 3rd. Baron Edgcumbe, later Earl of Mount Edgcumbe and Admiral of
      the Blue.

especially while I am so ready to gratifie you with an Account of the minutest Circumstance relating to us. When I am able go abroad, as I hope I shall in a Day or two, unless we have bad weather, I shall have more Things to communicate to you, but less Time to communicate then: however, I hope, I shall not suffer any Company or Engagements to engross so much of my Time as not to leave myself enough of it to correspond fully and punctually with my trusty Housekeeper, and in her with all her Brothers and Sisters. To you and them your Mamma and I daily beg to God to give every good and perfect Gift. We have you constantly in our Hearts and Minds: and it is with sincerest Thanks to Heaven, that I am enabled to subscribe myself

Dear Peggy,<br>
Your, and your Brothers and Sisters,<br>
Ever affectionate and tender Father,<br>
JOHN PENROSE.

P.S. The Apothecary has this evening ordered me a fourth Glass daily 2 hours after Dinner. I desire your Sister Coode to buy for Col. Sewell a dozen of Muslin Cravats. The Colonel says, they are frequently brought to Falmouth in the Lisbon Pacquets. They must be sent to Exeter to Mr. Paul, to be forwarded by the Bath Coach to me at Mrs. Grant's in Abby Green, Bath. Mrs. Sewell is so much better, since she has been at Lincomb Spaw, a sweet Place, that she eats Two Breakfasts every morning, and can pick a Piece of roast Veal at three o'clock.

The Picture mentioned in the preceding Page cost 120£ drawing the Gentleman and Lady only. What the child's Picture cost, I can't tell. But the Limner's Price is, for a Quarter Piece 20 £; for an Half Piece, 40 £; for a whole Length, 60 £.

Bath, Abby Green, Saturday,<br>
Apr. 19. 1766.

Dear Peggy

And all the rest of my dear Children. It will be great Pleasure to you to hear, as great as it is to me to write, that I am so much bettered in my Health, as to be able walk out a little to-day. After Dinner your Mamma, Sister, and I went upstairs a visiting to Mr. Chantor Snow and his Lady till Church-Time: then your Mamma went to the Abby, and Fanny after conducting me to Mr. Robinson's Lodgings, which are next Door to Wiltshire Great Room, where the Ball is once a week. The Sash happening to be up, I had the curiosity to look in, and saw the finest Room I ever saw. It is 86 feet in length, 30 in Breadth, and 30 in Height, with a cove Ceiling. I am told, it is ornamented with a Painting and Bust of Mr. Nash, late Master of the Ceremonies, but I did not observe them. When it was done at the Abby, your Mamma and Fanny called at Mr. Robinson's, and we walked together over the Grand Parade, reckoned one of the noblest Walks in Europe, being about 190 yards long, and 20 broad, and raised on Arches above the common Level 18 feet, which commands a beautiful Prospect of the adjacent Country. Near the farther end of this Grand Parade is Duke-Street, where Mr. Vivian, and Mess. Glynn and Rogers board. We called on them, stayed a few minutes, and then with Mr. Vivian walked through the South Parade, a very grand Walk, tho' neither so long, nor so wide, as that before-mentioned: from this there is a beautiful Prospect of late Mr. Allen's House of Prior Park, and a Ferry leading into the Fields. We then came home through Pierpoint-Street, which brought us again into the Grand Parade, one end whereof is very near our Lodgings. Both Parades and the two forementioned Streets, Duke and Pierpoint, are all paved with large broad flat stones; so that it is as easy walking there, as in a floored Room. The Buildings are truly magnificent: so that I could not help thinking of the Disciples admiring Question to Christ concerning the Temple, "What Stones and Buildings are here?" My Feet are a little wearied with my circuit, and but a little. If It please God I continue to mend, as I have of late, one Week more will shew me all Bath. Mr. Vivian came home, and drank Tea with us, and permitted to my Perusal a very good Sermon, which he is to preach at the Abby To-morrow. From my own Exploits, let me return to what relates more especially to Mamma, and Huswifery Affairs: Market-day, Butter 8d. per lb: Beef and Bones 4d. Whatever relates to Victualing, a disagreeable subject. New Visiters to Mamma Mrs. and Miss Sleech, wife and daughter to the Archdeacon of Cornwall. This morning the Duke and Duchess of Beaufort revisited Bath, in a Phaeton with six Horses: I hear, they were to go again to Badington,[18] their Seat, this Evening. – I have sent Ld. Edcumbe a Ticket of Compliment; but His Lordship was abroad. – I believe I forgot to tell you, that when you receive the Licenses from Exon, Jacky or some one else, before they are granted, must write my Name under the Seal, John Penrose surr. [surrogate] – Mr. Robinson and his Family, and Mrs. and Miss Leighs, all intend to leave Bath

18   Badminton House, Gloucestershire, second half of the seventeenth century, altered by William Kent circa 1740.

next Wednesday sen'night. We shall be very sorry, to lose so good friends and neighbours.

### Sunday, Apr. 20.

Dear Peggy, This is a Day of serious Reflection: and it comes into my mind, that we are here as Strangers and Pilgrims, and so are all of us in this World. We here are provided of commodious Lodgings, and want no Necessaries: surely then we may very well put up with want of Delicacies. Were every thing here such as Heart could wish, we neither could, nor (if we could) should we chuse to stay here. Tho' our Lodgings were adorned with the richest Furniture, and our Table spread with the greatest Variety, yet this is not our Home: we must and would leave it. So, if Christians would consider, how little, and for how little a while, they are concerned in any Thing in this World, they would go thro' any State, and any changes of State, either to the better or the worse, with composed equal minds, always moderate in their necessary cares, and never taking any care at all for the Flesh, to fulfil the Lusts of it. They, who have no better Home to lay claim to, than this World, may live here as at Home, and serve their Pleasures: they, who have all their Portion in this Life, may enjoy the poor Vanities that are here. But such, as know that their Estate is in Heaven, and Riches and Pleasures are reserved there for them, will let their Hearts be there, their conversation there. This is not the Place of a Christian's Rest or Delight, unless he would be willing to change, and have his good Things here; as there are some foolish Travellers, who spend the Fortune they should live on at Home, in silly Pomp a little while abroad among Strangers; selling Eternity for a Moment, and such Pleasures for Trifles, as a Moment of the former is more worth than an Eternity of the latter. The Day and my Situation lead me thus to moralize; and I hope the Goodness of your Heart will receive my Thoughts with Seriousness and improvement.

This morning, while Mamma and Sister were at the Abby, I was conducted by Mrs. Leigh to the Pump-Room. I went the sooner, partly, because when Church is over, there is a vast crowd of People assemble there, and, partly, because Mr. Chantor Snow made me an offer of Part of his Chaise, at half Hour after Twelve. For, this Offer I accepted of, and had a very agreeable Airing, five miles on the lower Bristol Road, in gentle weather, and the Chantor very sociable. There was but little Company in the Pump Room, as I wished; but one was Dr. Barnard, Bp. of Londonderry in Ireland. It is a neat Piece of Building, and has in it a marble Statue of Mr. Nash aforementioned, and a large handsome Clock. There are two Pumps in the Room,

tended by a man and woman, who pump Water into the Glasses,
(which the Gentlemen or Ladies call for) till they are warmed and filled
with Hot Water, the Degree of Heat so much as you would chuse to
drink a Draught. I shall go, as often as I can, to the Pump-Room, that
I may drink the Water as hot from the Pump as possible; for Mr.
Haviland tells me, the nearer it is drunk to the Spring, the more
efficacious it is. While I was at the Pump-Room, and on my Jaunt,
Mamma was at Church. She says, the Number of Communicants was
like that at Gluvias; as many Gentlemen as Ladies (that is uncommon
elsewhere,) some few poor Persons, and (what she was pleased to see)
one Footman with a Shoulder-Knot. I believe, the People frequent the
Churches, as well as the Assembly Rooms for I spoke with no less than
four this Day, who were at St. James's Church, and offered Money for
a Seat, but could not be admitted for Want of Room: tho' in this
Church, there is no Sermon mornings, only Prayers. – Your Mamma
hath had a Ticket presented to her, to gain admittance to Lady
Huntingdon's Chapel. [19] It is a Message-Card with this Inscription:
"Strait is the Gate and narrow is the Way which leadeth unto Life and
few there be that find it. Mat. 7. 14. This Ticket admits the Bearer to
a seat in my Chapel "S: Huntingdon. Seal. March 16. 1766." Texts at
the Abby, Morn: Psal. civ, 1, 2. by Dr. Saurin, an Irish Dean: Even. 1
John iv. 16, by Mr. Vivian of Cornwood. Fanny is gone to the Rooms
to drink Tea, that she may see the manner of it. What Entertainment
she meets with there, she herself must describe to you. We have had
Tea-Visiters this Evening Mr. and Mrs. Robinson; Mr. Billy Robinson, who is on a Visit to his Father from Oxon; Mr. Grills, and his
Son; and Mr. Glynn.

### Monday, Apr. 21.

I wish you all Joy of Fanny's Birth-day: I hope you will all drink her
Health, and pray that she may see many Returns of this Anniversary in
Happiness. – I have this morning seen three more Tickets to Lady
Huntingdon's Chapel. The Texts written on them differ; in all other
respects they are alike. The Text on one of them is, "Whosoever he be
of you that forsaketh not all that he hath, he cannot be my Disciple.
Luke 14.33." on another, "The Just shall live by Faith. Rom. 1.17."
on the third, "No man can say that Jesus is the Lord but by the Holy
Ghost. 1 Cor. 12.3." Mr. Vivian has heard from Devon, that Lady
Rogers is dead; he says, that, unless she has lately altered her Will, she
has left a large Legacy to the Poor of Penryn. If it be indeed a large

19   Built in 1765.

Legacy, I wish it may be made a perpetual Benefaction, somewhat in the Nature of Mr. Verran's Charity. To-day I received *The London Chronicle*, for the first Time: But the best News I read, and the best Papers I receive, are News from Penryn, and the welcome Letters of my dear Peggy and my other dear Children. Oh, how glad should I be to have a Sight of you! We have heard too from Mr. Hocker, and have the Pleasure to hear that his Reverence is well. Your Mamma and Fanny have been to Prior-Park, to see late Mr. Allen's fine Seat. Mamma was treated with a Chaise by Mr. Vivian: Fanny walked with him; and the young Gentlemen under his Charge with Billy Robinson came close after them. They were highly delighted with their Entertainment, are full of Prate about the charming Things they have seen, wish I had partaken of the fine Sight with them, and seem to have such an Impression made on their Minds that they will have many pretty Things to say to you when we come Home. If I could write you an Account of all they have seen, it would not be prudent so to do. For what Fools should we be of Travellers, who, when we return, have nothing to relate but what you know already? Just after the Ladies begun their Excursion, I went to the Pump-Room, stroled about the little Way my weak Feet would bear me, and came back to my Lodgings not long before Lord Edgcumbe did me the Honour of calling on me. His Lordship was extremely free, stayed with me half an Hour or more, gave me Directions where to find him, and desires me, when I write, to give his Compliments to his Penryn Friends. His Lordship is here for the Benefit of the Waters: My Lady could not leave the Child: and the Child could not be brought, because the Small-Pox have very lately been in Bath, perhaps at this Time are not totally ceased. I see a great many go the Street with spotted Faces. In the Afternoon I was at the Abby, the first Time of my being at any Place of public Worship, since I have been here. The Abby is a very venerable Structure, adorned without with Sculpture, and within with innumerable Monuments, the Walls and Pillars being lined with them. But I shall say more of this another Time, when I have made more Observations on it. I could not venture to look much around me now, for Fear of getting Cold. I shall only tell you, that in the West Front is a carving in Stone of Jacob's Ladder with the Angels ascending and descending on it, wretchedly executed, and atop of all is the Image of a venerable old man, designed (I am told) to represent God the Father, an execrable Design! and over the Communion Table, in the midst of the Altar Piece, which is all Marble, is a Painting of the Wise-men making their Offerings. From the Church I went to the Pump-Room, Mamma with me; thence Home, where Mrs. Leigh was so kind as to drink Tea with us. I only mention to you such as drink Tea here, or are new Visiters: But we are seldom free from Company, which sometimes greatly incommode me, when I would rather be scribbling to my dear Peggy, etc. It is now a Quarter past nine, and we have not begun supper.

Tuesday, Apr. 22.

I do not see, my dear Housekeeper, how you can be spared at present from the great Charge incumbent on you; but I would have you prepare, as well as you can, to set out for Bath immediately on our coming home: for you will do anything (I'm sure) for the Good of the Family; and what can be more so, than for you to set up here as a Nurse-keeper? They have a Guinea a Week. As you are so expert in that Profession, and can be so strongly recommended for Industry and Honesty, you will certainly make more of it. However, this is not forced upon you: you are left to your own Discretion and Choice. – In my last you had an Account of Cookery Expences: I now send you the Price of Washing and Ironing, the Cloths very well put out of hand, and the Laundress very civil. An Under-peticoat, 2d. – a Shift, 2d$\frac{1}{2}$ – a riding-Shirt, ditto – Pair of Stockings, 1d. – Pair of Pockets, 1d. – Handkerchief, $\frac{1}{2}$ – Cap, – $\frac{1}{2}$ – Band, $\frac{1}{2}$ – Shirt, 3d. – This Laundry-Article reasonable enough. –

There is now in Town to be seen, 3d. apiece, a remarkably large Ox, fatted on Hay alone, seventeen hands and half high. It cost the present Possessor forty pounds. He has made four pounds by shewing it. It is to be killed for next week's market, but not to be sold under sixpence per pound. This I had from a Clergyman, who saw it; and my curiosity is satisfied. This is News for Dr. Coode. Tell him also, that he would be delighted to see what Horses here are, both Saddle and Coach Horses. There is something in real Beauty, which strikes every Eye; insomuch that even I, who am no Connoisseur that way, cannot help looking on Numbers of them with great admiration.

Your Mamma's Knee continues to vex her, as it did; with walking more than usual, it is at present rather worse: But there is no Remedy, but Time and Patience. She consulted Mr. Haviland about the Trembling of her Nerves, whether it were best to use the Waters: his Advice was not to meddle with them, tho' some recommend them in Nervous Disorders as more kindly and beneficial than any Medicine known in Nature. Fanny has consulted him, whether she should drink the Waters. Why, what is the Matter with you? Nothing, Sir. Then endeavour to keep yourself well, while you are so. I am hindered to-day by rainy Weather from going to the Fountain-head for mine.

But holding up in the Afternoon, we went to Mr. Robinson's Lodgings, and drank Tea, and about six paraded it with Mr. Grills and Mrs. Robinson, under Conduct of Mr. Vivian, to Lady Huntingdon's Chapel. Would you think it? I walked, tho' half a mile; and was finely sweated, by the Time I got there. So I went into the Vestry, where was a Fire and an Elbow-Chair, and there I continued till Beginning of Sermon. The Chapel is exceedingly Decent. In the South Side are two handsome Doors: Four Windows in the West End, Five in each Side, i.e. North and South: and in the East End is an Alcove, with a Communion Table railed in: on one side of which is a Vestry, and on the other a little Room for Lady Huntingdon and friends. At the west End is a raised Gallery, about 3 or 4 steps ascending to it, the middle half whereof projects considerably before the rest, the whole having before it an handsome Iron Rail. At the South End of the Part projecting is a White Eagle, where the Reader stands: At the North End, is another, where the Clark stands, dressed in a Gown Tufted down the Shoulders, and a Band; a very decent Officer. In the midst, raised 3 Steps higher is the Preacher's Eagle, nearer to the Wall. Behind each Eagle is a Chair, covered with Scarlet, It looked to me like Damask. Inside the Rail sat several Ladies: the rest of the Congregation all on Forms. I believe the Number of People might be about, or near, three hundred. On the North and South Sides of the Chapel between the Windows were eight Branches, four on each side, and five Candles in each Branch: two others of the same were in the East End: and in the West End, on each side the Reader, on each side the Clark, on each side the Preacher, was a silver Branch on a fine mahogany stand holding three Candles: Behind the Preacher's Back, above his head, was another of the same: and at a distance, on each side this was another with five candles, such as were against the other walls. All the Candles were of Wax. The Prayers were read very well, three Hymns sung very sweetly, and had there been no Preaching nor extempore Prayer the whole had been much to my Satisfaction. But these I could not away with. The Preacher is a Swiss, beneficed in Shropshire, with a lank Face like Wesley, and true Methodistical Hair: in his manner (and he delivered himself off-hand) a mimic of Whitefield. His Text was Rev. iii. 20. His Matter in general pretty good, tho' some ridiculous Allusions were intermixed. His Manner theatrical, with such Vehemence of Voice and Gesture, as was enough to surfeit any one, not infected with Fanaticism or Enthusiasm. The same Discourse delivered in a more sober way would be much more affecting to all sober Persons. His Name Fletcher.[20] Against the wall,

20   Fletcher or de la Flechére, John William (1729–1785), born in Switzerland,

Lady Huntingdon's Chapel. Watercolour by J.C. Buckler circa 1830. The chapel was newly built in 1765 when John Penrose saw it.

where the Preacher stands, is written this Text from Rom. i. 16. "I am not ashamed of the Gospel of Christ: for it is the Power of God unto Salvation, to every one that believeth." I came home in a Sedan, price 1s. and am not sorry I went, tho' I probably shall go no more, unless I could hear Maddan or Whitefield. This Preacher's Rant is no other than a Burlesque upon Preaching. – I have seen two more Huntingdo-nian Tickets: the Text on one of them is, "Other Foundation can no man lay, than that is laid, which is Jesus Christ. 1 Cor. 3. 11." – on the other, "Beware lest any man spoil you thro' Philosophy and vain Deceit, after the Tradition of Men, after the Rudiments of the World, and not after Christ. Col. ii. 8." I shall conclude my scribble this Day with a Specimen or two of Mr. Fletcher's Rhetorick. – He told us, that, as Christ would not keep company with the Devil, whenever we open the Fore-door to let Christ into our Hearts, we must drive the Devil out at the Back-door: – That when Christ came unto his own, his own received him. Where? In a Stable. But we, worse than the Jews, will not admit Christ into the Stable, what Stable? The Stable of our Hearts. Our Hearts are a Stable, full of Dung and unclean Beasts:– That, having used many Motives to induce us to receive Christ, he had almost forgot the Argument from the Blood of Christ. This was a little out of Character for a Preacher of Christ, but good methodistical Jargon. The Text, you will see, if you look in the Bible, is concerning Christ's standing at the Door and Knocking: and he so often used the Word Knocking, that Mr. Grills says he could think of nothing all Sermon-Time but the Cock-lane Ghost.

### Wednesday, Apr. 23.

Remember us all with utmost affection to Mr. Coode, whom we congratulate on this Return of his Birthday, wishing him Health, long Life, and all Manner of Happiness. Remember us in like manner to the Doctor, Daughter Coode, and beautiful Molly. I am not at all the worse for my Walk yesterday; so I hope I am better, and purpose when the Weather permits to walk about again. Your Mamma hath bought a Bonnet for herself, and a Hat for me. What the Bonnet comes to, I don't know as yet: my Hat comes to a Guinea, and a Girdle and Buckle around the Poll costs ———[21] We were all at Church this morning. But it is now come in rainy. Dr. Stackhouse called in this

---

came to England as a tutor. Impressed with Methodism he was ordained deacon, then priest. He became very intimate with the Wesley brothers. In 1768 he was invited to take the superintendance of Lady Huntingdon's College at Trevecca in Wales.

21   See letter of 24th April. The cost was 1s.4d.

morning, and with him Miss Kitty Stackhouse, Miss Tremaine, and
Miss Coryton on a Visit to Fanny: he desires Fanny to accept of a
Ticket to the Play next Saturday, to drink Tea with the Ladies, and
away with them to the Theatre. Fanny was not in the least averse, that
I could see, to receive the Doctor's Favour. After Church I spent an
Hour with Arch-deacon Sleech at his Lodgings, which are near ours.
Mrs. Grant's Bill for the last week is as follows, viz:
Apr. 16. Roasting a Fowl, 2d. – The Fowl cost 1s.8d.
Apr. 17. Roasting Mutton – 4d. 18. Roasting Mutton, 4d. Mem.
It was a Loin, price 1s.9p. 19. Frying Beef-Stakes, 4d.

Apr. 20. Roasting Beef. – 6d. Mem: It was a Piece of Beef, (the
Stakes were cut off it) between the Loin and Rump, for which we have
no Name at Penryn, Meat not being cut there in the same manner.
This Beef served us cold the 21st with a good cut of Mutton Pye, sent
me for my Dinner a Present from Mrs. Leigh.

Apr. 22. Boiling Salmon, 4d. The Salmon was $1\frac{1}{4}$ lb. and cost 11d.
My Stomach is come again, and I am very hungry at meal-times, and
the Victuals begin to look and relish better. One week's Lodgings,
£1.5.0d. I hope, Peg, now you are a little acquainted with Household
Expences, you do not think us extravagant. If you do, speak.

Your welcome Pacquet came this morning in due time. Mrs.
Coode, and you, Mary and Jacky, have our Thanks for your Letters.
Mamma desires Mrs. Coode to excuse her Writing to her, because she
has nothing to communicate, but what my Letters to you contain. We
are very glad to hear from her, that Dolly continues very good, as we
supposed she would be: we don't doubt, but she will be very good at
Home, while Mrs. Coode is at Methleigh. I am sure we are much
obliged to Mrs. Coode, etc. for taking such care of her. I hope, they
have a pleasant Jaunt to Methleigh, and that dear Molly (if her cough
proceeds from a cold) will leave her cold there. Our Compliments wait
on good Mrs. Hearle.[22] We rejoice, that she is able go abroad. Desire
Mrs. Coode to let Mrs. Hearle know, yesterday added a shilling to my
Chair Expences. I think so far I have been frugal in that Point.
Eighteen pence a fortnight is not much. I am as saving for her, as I
should be for myself. – Mrs. Coode says you were disconcerted a little
about your marketing last Saturday. Don't be uneasy, honest Peg: do
the best you can, and then be satisfied, as we shall be. I wish Mr.
Evans, who is curious to a Proverb, would put what Questions he has a
mind to ask of Jacky, in Latin, and teach him to answer them in Latin:

22   Mrs. Hearle of Penryn seems to have undertaken to pay John Penrose's chair
     hire while he was at Bath.

then his Interrogatories might do him good, as well as gratifie his own impertinent Curiosity. Compliments to Mr. Crowgey and Mrs, Trevethick, etc. we are obliged to them for their civility to you, etc. Ld. Edgcumbe enquired after Mr. Crowgey, and asked me if Mrs. Trevethick were married again. When next you see Mrs. Hawkins at Church, present her with our Compliments, also Mrs. Cock, Mrs. Searle, and Mrs. Behenna. I fancy Mrs. Behenna, Mrs. Clies, and Miss Heame, as they are used to ranting enthusiastic Strains, would have heard Yesterday's frantic Preacher with great Glee. I don't think, if they had heard Mr. Harris, instead of Mr. Evans, they would have been so pleased, as they would have been to hear the Revd. Mr. Fletcher. – We wish Mrs. Giddy Joy of her Daughter: are glad to hear Redruth Church is to be rebuilt in earnest: (If need required, I reckon Mr. Pickering would give me any Assistance:) thank Sister for the Catalogue of the Sale to be at Falmouth, but want money to buy Dressing-Boxes, tho' much in vogue: Sister will want none; she will see the Vanity of this Place, and the Folly of it, but will come home the same honest girl she left Penryn: are glad the Doctor is better and wish him quite rid of his Head-Ach and Lowness of Spirits. Mr. Pender[23] must come to Bath: I hate for gouty folks to lie at home grunting, when so cheap a Remedy as Water is within 200 miles of them. Compliments to Miss Hearle, whose Disorder afflicts us, and to the younger Branches of that worthy Family. Mrs. Sewell better. John calls here every morning. This Paragraph is in answer to Mrs. Coode's kind Letter, and to Part of yours. Mrs. Coode is desired to continue her Correspondence, and accept of my answer in this manner.

Of all you write us, dear Peg, nothing gives us more Joy, than to hear that Jacky and Charles behave well at Church. This will draw down God's Blessing on them, and make them behave well at Home and every where else; and will, if possible, double our Love towards them. Give our Service to Mrs. and Miss Thompson, Mr. Davis, Mrs. Neville, Mr. Bath, all who enquire after us, all who are so kind as to take Notice of you. Let Mrs White know, that Aurelia is well.

I am very well satisfied with Jacky's doing the Business of the School, little as it is: only let him do every thing with the greatest care and exactness. If Time lies on his Hands, it is pity he should be idle: let him study what he likes best. If he reads English, I would recommend to him *Ovid's Metamorphoses,* or *Duncan's Caesar,* or, what is very entertaining *Plutarch's Lives.* Your Sister is answering Mary's

---

23  Perhaps Mr. Benjamin Pender, eldest son, by a previous marriage, of Mrs. Coode Senior. He died in 1769.

saucy Letter: so I have nothing to say to that Quarter.

I believe, next Post I shall write you again, just to change the Posts. For now you write us the Post you receive our Letters, and we write you the Post we receive yours. Now do you continue your usual course; and if I write next Post, both you and we shall have a clear Post to answer Letters in. This long one of mine will be so tedious, I fear; that I expect you to wish I would curtail them for the future. "Dear Papa, your Letters frighten us: they are as long as a Sermon: who d'ye think can read them thro'?" Let us know your Mind. In the mean while, "God bless you all"! is the sincere Prayer of your affectionate Mamma, and of your ever loving Father

### JOHN PENROSE

Fanny's Love.

Bath, Thursday, Apr. 24. 1766.

My dear Peggy,

And all the rest of my dear Children, By the Blessing of God I still am on the mending Hand, and hope I shall continue to mend. The Weather to-day being wet prevented my going to Church in the Morning: but in the afternoon, it holding up a little, I was enabled to go; and twice I have been at the Pump-Room. If it holds up ever so little, it is good walking here: for some of the Streets are all paved with flat Stones, as I told you the Parades are, and all of them have flat Stones on each side of them, from which the Wet soon wears off. We wish sometimes, that some of our neighbouring Clergy were to see how reverently and devoutly Prayers are read at the Abbey. There is a great Variety of Readers, the same Clergymen seldom reading Prayers two days together, and sometimes there are two Clergymen to officiate in the same day; yet all of them hitherto have officiated with remarkable Decency. The Church itself is past my Description. It is exceeding lofty and awful: is divided into two Parts: Between the two Parts is a fine Organ. In the outer Part is a very antique Stone Pulpit, never used. Divine Service is always celebrated in the inner Part. The Pulpit there is very handsome, and has a very finely carved Canopy: the Desk is under the Pulpit: the Clark's Desk under that: (By the way, he wears on Sundays a Gown and Band, and always tells what Day of the Month and what Psalm, which the Minister does every where else that I know of:) the Mayor and Magistrates sit opposite. The Pulpit stands on the North side of the Church, about midway between the Organ-Loft and Altar: behind it, is a Gallery; and fronting it, two

A perspective view of the Abbey Church of St Peter and Paul at Bath, 1750, engraved by George Vertue after the drawing by his brother James

galleries one over the other. The fine Velvet Cloth for the Communion Table, and fine Velvet Cushion for the Pulpit, (both Cloth and Cushion fringed with Gold) are only kept up Sundays. The Pulpit Cushion naturally introduces a Mention of that sent by Mr. Padgett by the caravan to Mr. Coode for Gluvias Church; which, I hope, is a very fine one, for it comes to a very fine price. I don't know, that I was ever more surprised, than when I read Mr. Padgett's Charge in the Letter herewith sent you, and which I desire you to deliver either to Mr. Coode, or to Mr. Bolitho. If I had thought, it would have cost half the money, I should have been loth to have had it this year. – To return again to Bath, and call another Subject. You cannot have a Turkey here under 7s.6d. and about a fortnight ago 15s. was asked for a Green Goose, not a meal for one Man. We shall be content without Goose or Turkey. All Poultry is excessive dear. I told you in my last, that the Buckle and Ribbon to my new Hat cost – and said not how much. I can now tell you, 1s.4d. But the Haberdasher bated 4d. on the whole. – The Streets here are so well illuminated in the night with Lamps, that you may walk about as well as by Day: this is of no great advantage indeed to us, who are no Night-walkers. In the Entry of our Lodgings, and of every House (I suppose) where there are Lodgers, there is a Lanthorn lighted with a Candle of six to the Pound (and we burn no other) which Candle is furnished by the several Lodgers in their Turn. As this is a Day, wherein we have had no notable Adventure, and I was willing to say something to you, I have given you this Prittle Prattle. Indeed this is the most leisure day we have had in Bath, tho' we were not without Company good Part of the morning, some Part of the Afternoon, and have been in the Evening to see Mr. Robinson, who has the Gout pretty smart in his left Hand. If you do not know it before, know it now, as a Piece of News from Helston, by way of Bath, that the famous Betty Fowler is there dead and buried. My sending to you by this Post instead of next will give you a clear Post between your Receipt of this and the Time of your writing to us: so you had best not leave writing till the Day you send your Letter, which will set you in a Hurry; but set things down as they occur to you. Remember us to all friends. You know, who are so, and who seem desirous of our Welfare. Remember us to them, tho' not named by me: for it is needless, and will take up too much Time and Paper, to name all by their Names, most of whom I have mentioned in my other Letters. – The Play, which Fanny is going to see next Saturday is one of Shakespeare's, *As you like it,* with a musical Entertainment, *The Chaplet.*

### Friday, April 25th.

This morning I took my Eight o'clock Draught of Water in the Pump-Room, the first Time I have been there in a morning. Mamma accompanied me. By the Way we looked into the Bath, and saw the People bathing, several Persons both Men and Women, and one Child in Arms. The usual Time of Bathing is between six and nine in the morning, when there is a fresh Supply of Water. For the Water, which rises one Day is discharged before the next Day, so that every morning there is clean wholesome Water. The Persons bathing have most of them a Person to go into the water with them, whom they call a Bath Guide: and the Water is deep enough to take one up to the Neck, unless a tall person. All round the Bath, and round a Building in the midst of it, called the Kitchen, are Seats for such as chuse to sit down covered all over with Water. They do not go into the Water naked (for both Sexes bathe in the same place, and that Place public) but in a canvas Dress prepared for the Purpose. Having looked a little while on the Bathing, we went to the Pump-Room, which is just by the Windows of it on the South-side looking into the Bath. There we staid about an Hour, and heard the Tweedle-dum and Tweedle-dee of ten Musicians, seated in a Music Gallery at the West End of the Room. A great Number of Gentlemen and Ladies were there who kept such a Prating that the Pleasure of the music was lost. The Clock in the Pump-Room is accounted the best in England. I told you formerly, there were two Pumps in it: I should have said a Marble pump with two Mouths, very ornamental. From thence we went home to Breakfast: where we found the Colonel's John, with Compliments from his Master, etc. and three Tickets for this evening's Ball. The Colonel has promised to send three Tickets every Ball Night. Fanny accepted one, intending to go this evening with Mrs. Robinson and Friends. She is not very fond of the Ball; but, when she was last there, her Company came away before Tea, and she with them; and now she has a mind to stay Tea, and see the whole Ceremony. The Day I put on my common Shoes, (having walked about in my Gouty ones till now:) And I think I have made good use of them; for I walked after morning Prayer from the Pump-Room, with your Mamma and Fanny, almost to North-gate first, and then almost to West-gate, to buy Ribbon, Snuff, and Sugar. After The Evening Service we went on a Tea-Visit to Mr. Arch-deacon Sleech and his Lady: but they were so late with the Tea, that Fanny was forced to go without any, that she might be Time enough at the Ball, and not make Mrs. Robinson wait. There she now is.

A view of the King and Queen's Bath, including the Great Pump Room at Bath, 1746. Engraving by William Elliott after the drawing by Thomas Robins made in 1747. John Penrose describes watching the bathers and the central feature known as the Kitchen.

You will remember the general Direction given before concerning Compliments to our Friends. But give them in a particular manner to Dr. Coode, and Mess. Evans, Osborne, Harris and Walmesley, when Opportunity offers, my very kind Assistants. Fanny's Love and Service wait on all as due. Your Mamma and I pray to God for a Blessing on our Son and Daughter Coode and pretty Molly, and on you, your Brothers and Sisters. Remember us to the Maids and George: we hope, they as well as the rest of your family, considering the Burden which lies on you, will do all they can to make it sit easy. You say the Clark gives his Duty to me, but do not say whether or no he goes abroad again. I want him to collect Money for you with the utmost Diligence: and I hope, in my next to send you for him some Lady-day Receipts. I am, my dear Peggy,

> Yours, and your Brothers and Sisters,
> Ever affectionate Father,
> JOHN PENROSE.

> Bath, Saturday, Apr. 26. 1766.

Dear Peggy,

And all the rest of my dear Children, the Blessing of God be with you and remain with you. I still continue pretty well, tho' rather weaker footed, than I was a day or two ago. I have walked To-day over the Parade, however; been twice at the Abbey, three times at the Pump-Room, and paid two little Bath Visits to Major Tucker and Mr. Robinson: the former bathed this morning, and so confines himself to his Room for Fear of getting Cold; the latter has the Gout in his Knee as well as Arm. Your Mamma is not very well, complains of Deafness and Colick, and has not been at Church this Afternoon, tho' there in the morning, and also at market. I saw this morning strawberries offered to Sale, at a shilling apiece. Fanny is gone to Dr. Stackhouse's to drink Tea, and from thence she is going to the Play. She was Home from the Ball last night before Ten o'clock. So, you see, good Hours are kept here: they are not such Rakes, as they are at Penryn Assembly. I was asked to go to the Ball by a reverend Doctor in Divinity, who offered to bear me Company: but it is quite out of my Way, and (as Mr. Baker phrases it) I would as soon sit in the Stocks. Indeed abundance of Clergy go there; even Mr. Vivian himself: but it doth not suit my Inclination. I am told by Mr. Vivian, that his wife has five hundred pounds left her by Lady Rogers. Tell Miss Harriet Hearle and

Miss Jenny Heame, that Miss Sleech remembers them at School with her at Chelsea. Miss Harriet seems to have been a favourite. Let Mrs. White know, that Aurelia dined with us this Day, and that Mrs. Sewell is still very ordinary, sometimes better, sometimes worse, that we cannot tell whether she is, or is not, better on the whole. I have not seen her yet, nor the Colonel this great while. – There is a Rumour here, in every Body's Mouth, that the Countess of Huntingdon is confined, or has run in Debt, and squandered away a great deal more than the Annuity upon Vagabond Preachers, and places for them to preach in. I cannot learn with any certainty, what the case really is: but there is something or another at the Bottom of this Rumour, which will soon be better known. I told you just now Mr. Vivian was at the Ball: I must tell you too, in Justice to him, that he only went to see the fine Sight, and did not tarry more than a Quarter of an Hour. The Cornish People, that I have seen at the Pump-Room, are, Mr. Mrs. and Masr. Robinson, Mr. and Masr. Grills, all of Helston; Mr. Mundy, of Redruth; Mr. Blake, of Truro; Mr. Carlyon, of St. Austle: Mr. Williams, of St. Ewe; Mr. Gregor, of Tregony; Dr. Stackhouse and Miss, of Probus; Misses Corryton and Tremayne, with Dr. Stackhouse. These, whom I have seen, with Mr. Sam Thomas of Truro, Miss Eliot who was lately at Mrs. Hawkins's, our three selves, and if we may reckon in Ld. Edgcumbe who lives the Cornwall side of the Tamar, and Mr. Vivian a native of Truro, make in all the Number of Twenty one. Cornwall has supplied it's Quota pretty well.

Since I wrote the above, your Mamma and I have taken a Turn or two on the Parade, and made an Observation that all under the Walk are Cellars, and that the Houses are two Stories under-ground, and three stories above-ground besides garrets: so that from the lowest Floor to the Top of the Roof is a vast Height. Before the under-ground Stories is a large Area, into which you look from the Street over a Stone Ballustrade. – Your Mamma's Bonnet is now paid for, 11s.6d. –

Past ten o'clock. Sister is returned from the Play, very well pleased with her Evening's Entertainment. – In reckoning up the Cornish People, I forgot to name Mr. Glynn of Helston.

### Sunday, Apr. 27.

Glorious Weather this Day. I have been three Times at the Pump-Room, twice at the Abbey, twice on the Parade with your Mamma (who has a great cold in her Head) and Fanny. The Gentleman, who preached in the Morning, was Dr. Goodall, a Gentleman possessed of several Ecclesiastical Dignities, but I know not where. His Text was Luke vii. 2,3,4,5. It was an occasional

Sermon for the Bath Hospital, which was erected between twenty and thirty years ago for the Reception of sick Poor from all Parts of the Kingdom, such whose Disorders are particularly Bath cases. The Building is capacious enough to admit upwards of an hundred Patients: but the Subscriptions and Benefactions will not maintain more than seventy; for which Reason the Governours do not think it adviseable at present to admit more than that number. A collection towards this useful Charity was made this Morning at the Abbey and all other Places of Public Worship in Bath, except Lady Huntingdon's Chapel. At the Abbey was collected £65; at Queen Square Chapel £36; at St. James's Church £30; at Cross Bath Chapel, £6. What at other Places I have not heard; nor what was gathered in the Afternoon at the Abbey; for there a collection was made both Parts of the Day. It was a very affecting Sight to see all the Patients ranged in two Lines, the men on one side, the Women on the other, making a Lane from the outer Door of the Abbey to the Door of the inner Part, where Service is performed, for the Mayor and Magistrates and all the Congregation to pass through. Eight Beadles, in an Uniform Dress, (Brown Great Coats, with yellow capes, and Sleeves turned up with Yellow,) with each a Staff in his Hand with a Brass Knob at the Top attended them. And when they went from Church, they all walked two and two very orderly, four Beadles with Staves preceding, then the Men Patients, then two more Beadles, then the Women Patients, then the other two Beadles closing the Procession. In the same manner we saw them come to Church in the Afternoon. The Substance of the Preacher's Discourse, which was an excellent one, and well adapted to the Occasion and the present circumstances of the Hospital, was, "The Character of the Centurion both in public and private Behaviour. His Goodness to his Servants, the Regularity of his Family, his Zeal for Religion, which Zeal influenced his conduct and was a good Motive to the other two Branches of his character, and therefore may probably be supposed to proceed from the Love of God as it's Principle: This Love of God, if it be in us, will make us consider God, who is Love, as the common Father of Mankind, and consequently all Mankind as our Brethren, whom consequently we should love, and, where the case requires it, be merciful as God is merciful: The Propriety of Beneficence to Objects of this Charity, and many Arguments and Motives to the rich to give plentifully, to the Poor to give gladly of their Little, pressed with a decent Freedom and a rational Strain of Eloquence." In the Afternoon Prayers were read by one Mr. Penrose, a Cornish Clergyman, who is here for the Benefit of the Waters: the Sermon was preached by Mr. Taylor, Reader at the Abbey; the Text was Matt. xxv.42. "Christ will judge Men according to their Works, with an especial Regard to their Charity or Want of it. This Charity must be founded on the Love of God, and proceed from Faith: The Nature of saving Faith set forth, and established by much Arguing against the Notions of a certain living Author, (I cannot tell who) not tending in the least to the Edification of the Audience." I believe, this Reverend Divine was right upon the whole, i.e. taking all the Sermon together from Beginning to End; but I cannot agree with him, when he says, "Faith is a simple Act of the mind," for I take it to be "Such a Belief of Things revealed in the Gospel, as makes us act accordingly." I do not like this Gentleman's Preaching so well as his Reading Prayers: for he reads Prayers with great Judgment and Exactness; not so he preaches.

We desire you will let us know, how you go on with the Psalms, and how Charles learns his Collects. It will be a concern to us, if we find there is among you a Neglect of any thing good, and on the contrary a proportional Pleasure to hear you all pursue the Things which are laudable, and tending to God's Glory, and your own Improvement in Religion and Virtue. May God, the Giver of every good Gift, assist you with his Grace!

We are now told concerning Lady Huntingdon,[24] that her Son has taken out a Statute of Lunacy against her: that Madness is incident to the family: and that she is Sister to that Lord Ferrers, who was hanged at Tyburn not long since for wilfully killing his Man. A Nephew of hers, Walter Shirley, who hath published a small Volume of methodist Sermons, is expected here soon in Succession to the enthusiast Fletcher mentioned in my former Letters, to serve her Chapel. This Shirley is Brother to the present Lord Ferrers. I do not find, that her Ladyship pays the Preachers in her Chapel; but gives the Liberty of it to such as she approves of; and when no such one is here as there is not one here always, the Chapel is shut up.

Miss Leigh and Mr. Cook drank Tea with us this Evening. Mr. and Mrs. Robinson are advised, and intend, to stay here a fortnight longer. We reckon, Penryn is now in all it's Glory. The Orchards hereabout are in as beautiful Blossom, as possibly can be. We hope, as the Spring is so late, it will be a plentiful year of Fruit. Are not the Apple Trees hanging out their Colours, for Joy that the Cyder Act is so altered? For my own Part, I wish it had all remained as it was, so selfish am I;

---

24    Selina, Countess of Huntingdon (1707–1791) was converted by her sister-in-law, Lady Margaret Hastings and became very intimate with the two brothers Wesley.    .

Portrait of Lady Huntingdon (1707–1791). Engraving by J. Fitter after R. Bowyer.

rather than pay sixteen shillings additional Window Tax, as I apprehend will be the case.

I forgot to tell you just now, that each of the Poor belonging to the Hospital wears on his or her Breast, in conspicuous manner, a circular Piece of brass, with the Words Bath Hospital, and a Number, on it: that Mr. Mayor was accompanied to Church by nine Magistrates, all in Black Gowns, preceded by two the grandest Maces I ever saw: that at one End of the North Gallery, next the Altar sat the Boarding School Misses, twenty six in all, with their Mistress and Teacher: that Mrs. Aylsworth, late Mistress of Chelsea School is here in Town; and that we hear an extreme good Character of the Lady who now keeps it: and that John was here this morning with Word that Mrs. Sewell is better.

The Churchwardens have a Seat to themselves, near the Communion Table, where two Rods of Office are stuck up and distinguish those great men.

### Monday, Apr. 28.

Very fine Weather to-day. Walked to the Pump-Room in the morning, took my Glass of Water, and hastened home with all Speed, to receive my welcome Pacquet from Penryn. The Western Post arrives here in the Evening, but the Letters are not delivered out till next Morning between eight and nine o'clock. Then they are sent round to the Persons, they are directed to, and we pay a half-penny a Letter: for the sake of which Half-penny, the Post-master will not deliver the Letters to any one, we send to the Office for them. Our little Servant has several Times gone to the Office, and been told the Letters were not sorted; and after waiting there a good while, been told that they were carried out. About nine however, we had the Pleasure, the greatest Pleasure we have here is this Place of Pleasures, to receive your Letters to Mamma and me, Jacky's to me, and Mary's to Fanny. For all these we heartily thank you, and approve of the contents of all of them, and think that our Absence from you Will be a Means of improving you in Epistolary Correspondence, which may hereafter be of Use to you.

Now, my dear Peggy, having read all your Letters again and again with great Satisfaction, I shall answer some Parts of them. And first I answer yours.

You are very kind to Fanny, to excuse her, tho' she should not write much, as she has so many Hindrances: and I do assure you, she writes as much as she can, and that is not a little, tho' it is not so much as she would. You find by my walking out, that I am greatly recovered: the Waters may probably have some Effect on me for Good, and I think they give me an Appetite. I am as hungry at Dinner-Time (and we now dine daily at Two) that could make a Meal on any Thing. But indeed, since Mamma has gone to Market herself, we have as fine Victuals as can possibly be. The Bread and Butter here is excellent. We have had no Asparagus as yet, they being eighteen pence a hundred. We do not grudge any expence, yet we would not be extravagant. We do very well upon the whole: and if I go on long at the Rate I do, Yet I don't think after all, I am the greatest Eater in Bath: for our little Servant eats twice as much as I do, and she assures us she has a very little Stomach. Jacky would make a poor figure here, according to her Account; I am sure, she would out-do him a deal. The Price of Butter here is very uncertain. The same day, it will sell from six pence half-penny to eight pence: it rises and falls like the Stocks. But after all I have said of my Stomach, I am told the Bath-Waters will be most serviceable hereafter, and that my Gout will probably be more regular, more painful indeed, but less crippling. – Mr. Vivian is a due Attendant at Lady Huntingdon's Chaple. He preached yesterday at Bradford, six miles hence: but came back soon enough to go to the Preaching. He was to have left Bath To-day, and gone to Bristol: but the Journey is delayed till To-morrow. He tells me, all the different Reports about Lady Huntingdon are groundless; that she is one of the most sensible Ladies in England; and that her Son is as kind to her, as can possibly be. He has not yet heard from Mrs. Vivian, since the Death of Lady Rogers; so that he cannot say, how she has disposed of her Effects: but he is informed in general, from pretty good Authority, that she has give away twenty thousand pounds from Sir John; and he says, if her Will has not lately been altered, there are a thousand pounds given to Penryn for charitable Uses, and three hundred pounds apiece to Jemmy Pellow's and Clear Frood's Wives. All this I shall be glad to have confirmed. She has, surely, left five hundred pounds Legacy to Mr. Vivian's Wife. – Remember our hearty Love to Brother, Sister, and Cousins at Falmouth. We are sorry his Eyes are bad, but hope they are growing better.[25] We are glad, Cos: Fanny likes London so well. What would she say, did she see Bath? Bath as far exceeds London, as London Penryn, or else I have forgot London. – You say, Mr. Evans hath preached a new Sermon. This News wants confirmation. – I am glad Mr. Harris is so well liked: he will probably do the more Good: and that consideration will make him like Budock. If Mr. Thomas is not free to officiate, it is not worth while to press him: for

25 John Penrose's brother Joseph, the tailor, was evidently suffering the eye-strain inevitable in that employment.

the Parishes will be well served without, to mine and their Satisfaction. – You cannot conceive, what Joy it is to us, to hear that Dolly and all the rest behave so well. Good Temper is it's own Reward; and, besides that, it shall always meet with due encouragement from us. – We are glad to hear the Maids intend to weed in the Garden. It will be an Amusement to them: and, as we are abroad, I think George should not hire any more than necessity obliges. – We wish Charles Joy of his new Hat, and desire he will take care of it: and we thank you for your care, that you would be at the Pains to go to Falmouth, rather than buy one too dear. But we would have you walk out sometimes. It will be beneficial to your Health. – I would have you write again to Mr. Michel, or one of the Family, to let them know, that we are all well, and desire them to accept our sincerest Love. – Write again to the same Purport to Mrs. Walker; and tell her, we fear Mr. Cook, our fellow Traveller, who was so kind and useful to us on the Road is Methodistically inclined; for he frequents Lady Huntingdon's Chapel, nay even on Sundays when there is Service at the Churches. – It was very kind of Mr. Coode to invite Mr. Hocker to Methleigh. I dare say, Mr. Hocker accepted the Invitation with all Thankfulness. Remember us affectionately to both, and all the Coode Family. You are in the Right not to shew our Letters to any but them, and such as we consented to, because we write a Pack of Trash, agreeable enough to you and particular Friends, but to others ridiculous. Any particular Passages which you think fit, in your usual Prudence, you have Liberty to read to any one. Let Mr. Coode know, that I have not been in a Coffee-house since I have been here; and, what he will think as strange, as I do of Mr. Evans's Preaching a new Sermon, that I have not been in a Booksellers's Shop; and, as well as I love Reading, that I have read scarce an Hundred Quarto Pages, put all together. I have not Time: and it is a Maxim universally received, that any Degree of Study, or Reading any thing but Trash, prevents the Efficacy of the Waters. – Mr. Street is welcome to see the Reviews. My Compliments to him. – If Mrs. Chenhall wants any Writing belonging to her in my Custody, let her tell what it is, and desire Mr. Coode to look it out for her. You will find it in one of the Bottom Drawers in the passage Letter-Case. Remember me to her, and I am sorry she is ill. I am sorry also for Padgy Adams's Misfortune. While I express Sorrow for the evil Accidents befalling others, I cannot be thankful enough to that good Providence which watches over all you and all us for Good; that no Misfortune has come near either Your or Our Dwellings – Remember us to George, who, I hope, will find me better, when next we meet, than when last we parted; and to the Maids, wishing Betty Trelease

Joy, that her Tooth ach hath left her, – Mrs. Sewell is better, but the Colonel complains of a Gout in his Foot, and Hands, and of being much disordered.

I now come to Jacky's Letter, which has given us a great deal of Pleasure. I like it exceeding well, and desire a continuation of his correspondence. His two Texts are translated right, except that in Luc. XVII. 17. he has twice put *illi*, which should not be at all. The Going on in the way, your Mamma set you in, of learning the Psalms etc. is very commendable. He is mistaken, if he thinks the Gentleman, he has made an Esquire of, wants a *Greek Bible*. No, he must mean a *Great Bible,* but I fancy there is none left. I am glad, you all shewed such Regard to your Sister by celebrating her Birth-day: I can assure you, she is now at the Play, to see a Comedy called *The Jealous Wife,* with the *Farce of The Honest Yorkshireman*. Miss Leigh is gone with her. She went this Evening, because next Saturday the Benefits begin, and then the House is so crouded, that the Scenes are commonly taken down, and Seats erected on the Stage, and it is not worth while to go. Otherwise, she would rather have defer'd going, till the Time of Departure hence is nearer approaching. – I am glad Jacky and you like our Letters. We write you every thing we can, and your ready Reception of them encourages us to persevere. His writing Day by Day is easiest to Him, and very entertaining to us. And I see, he writes with care: that I am very glad of, for his own Sake. He has told the Tale of the Gentleman with Mrs. Walker's Letter so well, that I was in Suspense at reading it: and wondered what the Event would be: *Quorsum hoc evaderet*. I congratulate him on his finshing the *Andria*. I hope, he met with his Master's Applause, as well as that of his School-fellows, and that he is now got into an Acquaintance with Terence's Style, so that the next Comedy he learns may be truly a Sport to him. *The Comedies of Terence* have such Resemblance to each other, that he, who knows one well, cannot be ignorant of the others. I hope, he is very exact in making his Exercise, and that he has got over the Difficulty of rendering the Greek Testament into Latin. I shall rejoice, when the Day comes of meeting him at Exon; and, Oh, How happy will it be, if it please God we all meet again at Vicarage in Health and Safety! What numberless Mercies do we receive at his Hands, and what Gratitude do they require from us, both in our Lips and Lives!

Your Mamma will answer your Letter to her, and Fanny will answer Mary's.

Along with your Letters we received one from Mr. Heard, Mrs. Barnett being indisposed with a cold: He writes, that she has been very active in our Affairs, and has in her Possession the Writings of the

The Circus at Bath, 1784. Aquatint by Thomas Malton.

Walden and Littlebury, not the Ewell-Fenn, Estates. He says he shall be at Bath the latter End of this, or the Beginning of next Week. From him we shall be able to determine, whether we shall go hence to London or no: By his Letter we rather think, that we shall not. But when we see him, he will inform us, what Steps have been already taken, and what are best to be pursued.

After reading these Letters, and having been to Breakfast, we set out in company of Mr. Vivian and Major Tucker to see the Circus and other grand Buildings in the Northern End of the Town. The Circus is reckoned one of the most elegant Piles of Building in Europe. It was begun building about twelve years ago, and is now finished except one House now in building. It is quite circular, and has three Openings for Streets leading to it. One street (Gay Street) is completed, very noble indeed: a great many Houses are built in the Street from the North-West: that from the North-East is not yet begun. The Circus consists of thirty two Houses, all quite uniform; three Stories and Garrets above the Level of the Street, two below, with a very wide Area between the underground Rooms and the Street. The Garret-Windows are hid by a Parapet Wall. Each Story has over it a grand Cornish, supported by Pillars of different Orders; the lowest Pillars of (I believe) the Tuscan Order; the middle ones, of the Ionic; the highest of the Corinthian. The whole Pile of Building, truly magnificent. Yet I think it would have added to the Beauty of it, had the Parapet on Top been so contrived as to have concealed the Roof. In the Centre of the Ground, which this circular Building surrounds, is a large Bason of Water, always full; round it a pretty Gravel-Walk, inclosed with Iron Palisades. From Description I had conceived a grand Idea of this Place, but the Sight proved beyond all conception. No House in the Circus, less than £100 per ann.

In the Way to the Circus, we visited the Square, commonly called Queen's Square. This is rather larger than the Circus, magnificently built, especially the North-Row of it. In the Inside of the Square, and comprehending all the Ground of it except a large grand Street before each Row of Houses, is a Garden with fine Gravel Walks, confined by a handsome Ballustrade of Stone, with four noble Iron Gates opening into it, and in the midst of all is a large circular Piece of Water, in whose centre is an Obelisk erected in Memory of the late Prince and present Princess Dowager of Wales, seventy foot high, which looks beautiful. I must now tell you, that among those houses, whether in the Square, Circus, or elsewhere, there are comparatively very few, over the Doors of which there is not a Tablet advertising Lodgings to be let: and all Rooms in Lodging Houses set at the same Price, whether such as we lodge in, which tho' very convenient, and I would not exchange it for any in Bath, makes no Appearance without worthy Notice; or those which I have described just now, and are pompous enough for Palaces for great Princes. I must also mention another circumstance, while it is in my Head, that over most Doors in the new elegant Streets is a small Plate of Brass, with an Inscription on it in neat black Letters, signifying the Name of the Occupant.

To return to the Square. On the East Side lodges Lord Edgcumbe, whom I called upon, but found him not at home. I left my name with his Gentleman, and some Covers which I wanted to have franked: and this Evening the Gentleman came to my Lodgings with Compliments and my Request granted. I see his Lordship every Morning at the Pump-Room, and sometimes have a little chat with him. He is exceeding free. On the West Side of the Square, is a very neat Chapel,[26] with a Portico before it very grand, the Roof supported by Pillars of the Doric Order. In the Inside the Pillars are of the Ionic, exactly like those in Gluvias Church: the Pulpit Canopy richly carved; the Pulpit itself carved round the pannels exactly like the Wood-work at Gluvias Altar; and the Altar-Piece painted white and the carvings and proper Members of the cornishes and Mouldings gilded, exactly as they are at Gluvias. You cannot think, how I was pleased to see in so many particulars, and in more than I have Time to mention, such a Similarity of Things near Home. The Windows are sashed; a double Row of them, as at Helston, but a narrow Gallery going all round within the Church separate them and makes the Place much handsomer and more Church-like. The Canopy of the Pulpit is supported by two small Pillars, in form like the rest. The Altar Piece very decent. I am informed, this Chapel is 57 foot long, and 48 broad, and 36 high. Here we attended Divine Service at 11 o'clock this Morning, before we visited the Circus. We returned home about one, I pretty well tired with my walk, but not the worst for it: calling at the Pump-Room in my Way for my Noon's Glass of Water. The Water, hot from the Pump, is extremely agreeable: I don't know any Liquor more so. The worst is, that when I go for it, or indeed when I go any where else, one is obliged to be dressed, best Coat and best Wig: My fine flower'd Night-gown would make a despicable Figure here. Within Door I sometimes have an opportunity of putting on my black

26  St. Mary's Chapel, begun in 1732 and opened for service on December 25th 1734, was the first of Bath's many proprietary chapels – John Wood was the architect.

Queen's Square at Bath, 1784. Aquatint by Thomas Malton.

Night-Gown. Oh, how comfortable it is! But it is a comfort I seldom enjoy.

After dinner I was within Door all Day, except that we were at the Abbey, and I went thence to the Pump-Room. Whom should I see at the Abbey, but Mr. Paul, who came thither in Hopes of seeing me there, that he might know where we Lodge. He would not drink Tea with us, as Mr. Vivian did, but he promised to breakfast here To-morrow morning.

Your Mamma is afraid my Letters are so long, that they will tire you out.

I forgot to tell you, that every House in the Circus has two Lamps before it. They must look very beautiful by Night, when lighted.

### Tuesday, Apr. 29.

Mr. Paul, according to Promise, broke Fast with us this Morning. We breakfast at nine: Because I take my second Glass of Water in the Pump-Room at eight, (my first Glass I take in Bed at seven,) and I stay an Hour, meeting my Friends, and conversing with them. Fanny breakfasted at Spring-Gardens,[27] with Mrs. and Miss Leigh, at the Invitation of Mr. Hutchinson, Capt. of an East-India-man. Spring Gardens are only separated from Bath by the River Avon. A Ferry-Boat conveys the People over. In these Gardens is a House, where you have Tea, Coffee, Chocolate, Sweetmeats, Music, Dancing. What Entertainment Fanny met with, let her herself set forth. She handles the Pen of a ready Writer. Do not you think, she is a great Rake, To Play last Night, and Dancing this Morning? But, like Lady Grace, she doth all these Things soberly. And to let you see, her Heart is not quite bent to Amusements, she was this Day invited to Tea in the Rooms next Sunday Evening with some Devonshire Ladies by Counsellor Short, an old Acquaintance of mine, but does not design to go. As soon as Mamma came back from Market, we went to Dr. Stackhouse's Lodgings, But the Doctor and Ladies were out an airing. Thence to Mr. Robinson's, Mr. Grills and his Son went away this morning. Mr. Vivian, Mess. Glynn and Rogers, before noon. We are come to a great Loss, especially in Mr. Vivian. At Eleven we went to the Abbey; afterwards I went to the Pump-Room: then Fanny and I took a Turn or two on the Grand Parade, from whence the View is terminated by a fine Chateau, built by late Mr. Allen, with a Grove of Trees on either side of it. Mr. Paul dined with us, on a fine Shoulder of

---

27   Spring Gardens were opened around 1760. Naturally they were closed during the winter, but in 1766 they opened for the summer season on 10th April.

Mutton. Your Mamma, whose Cold, thank God, is better, bought it
in the Market, where she saw eighteen pence given for a Lamb's
Appurtenance. The Morning was very fine, but it hath been a moist
Afternoon: yet I have been at the Abbey, where I read Prayers, and
afterwards (as usual) at the Pump-Room. I have drank more Water,
since I have been here, than in many Years before. I may have told you
so before, for what I know; for keeping no memorandum of what I
write, it is not unlikely but I may use Tautology. Last Sunday at
Church a Lady was brought in a Sedan, and placed before the Reading
Desk in the Alley, and remained in it all Service Time. This is no
uncommon thing. And this morning another Lady, the same; and,
after Prayers, was carried up to the Communion Table to be Churched
(for Women are Churched there) and did not come out of the Sedan at
all. Mrs. Leigh drank Tea with us this afternoon, and we expect her
and her Sister to sup with us on cold Shoulder of Mutton and Tarts
from the Pastry Cook's, who is no inconsiderable Person, but keeps a
Post-Chaise. While we were at Tea, the only Son of Late Dr. Young,
Author of *Night-Thoughts*,[28] coming to take Leave of her, we invited
him into our Rooms, and we had the Pleasure of seeing the only
Descendant of that great good Man. The Colonel's John has just now
been here; he says, the Colonel's Disorder is partly Gout, and partly
St. Antony's Fire, and, that if he is not better soon, he will be brought
to Town, for the sake of being nearer the Doctor. Mrs. Sewell is much
better. – Your Mamma has forgot, whether Dolly's Silk-Worms Eggs
were left out. If not, you may let Pellew open the Top of Dolly's
Bureau, and take them out: but he must take care to shut it again.

It is now between ten and eleven. Mrs. and Miss Leigh supped with
us, and have taken Leave, setting out for Oxford Tomorrow. We shall
come to a great Loss. No Ladies could behave with more Civility and
Kindness. They have made us a Present of the Remains of their
Householdstock, a little Salt, a little Vinegar, 2 large Pieces of
Candle, half a Lemon, some Ink, and a Pack of Cards. Pray God send
them a good Journey and an happy Sight of their Friends!

If you take Notice of my Account this Day, you will see we have had
Company at Breakfast, Dinner, Tea, and Supper.

## Wednesday, Apr. 30.

I will begin this Day's Memorandum with our last Week's Bill: viz.

---

28   Edward Young (1683–1765) Poet. Was a friend of Elizabeth Montagu and of
     Colley Cibber. His most famous work *The Complaint, or Night Thoughts on Life,
     Death and Immortality* was published between 1742 and 1745.

+    Apr. 23.    Roasting Veal, 4d.    + 24.    Roasting Veal, 4d.
     *    26.    Roasting Mutton, 4d. + 27.    Roasting Lamb, – 4d.
                                                 Stewing Spinage, 2d.
     *    28.    Roasting Mutton, 4d.ø 29.    Roasting Mutton, 4d.
                    One Week's Lodging, £1.5.0.


+ The Veal roasted Apr. 23 and 24 was a Breast, in Two Parts, 1s.6d.
Apr. 25. We had a Mutton-Pye from the Pastry-Cook's – 1s.6d.
* The Mutton, April. 26 and 28 was a Loin – 2s.1d.
+ The Lamb, Apr. 27. was a Loin – 1s. and the Spinage came to 1d.
(dressing it 2d.)
ø The Mutton, Apr. 29 was a Shoulder – 1s.10d.
All this Week's Provision prodigious fine Victuals, such as you never
saw in your Life. We had Potatos to eat with our Meat always, except
when we had the Spinage; but these your Mamma boiled herself.

Mr. Paul is set out again for Exon. By him I sent a Letter to Mr.
Pierce of Yendacot, another to his Brother at Topsham, and a third to
Mrs. Fleetwood at Dawlish, acquainting the last that, if it suits her
convenience, we will take a Bed at her House in our Way Home. I also
have sent her £5.17.0. an arrear due to her from Verian Sheaf. I have
told her also, that if Mrs. Hugo is ready with her Rent, she may pay it
to Mr. Coode, whom I have desired to receive it, and send a Bill for it.
Mrs. Fleetwood's Address, is at Dawlish, near Chudleigh, Devon. A
Letter for Mrs. Hugo comes herewith, which I desire you to send to
Verian, when you can. I have desired her to present my Service to Mr.
Michel, and let him know how I am.

Poor Fanny was up early this Morning, and waited on her obliging
Friends Mrs. and Miss Leigh to the Inn, and saw them in the Oxford
Coach. So they are gone. And soon after Breakfast Mrs. Hutchinson
came to take Leave. She sets out To-morrow. Many Families have left
Bath since our coming. The Leighs, at going away, gave a Guinea to
each of the Three Maids, with which we suppose them to be well
pleased; for they speak well of them: and the Ladies said, they had
made diligent Enquiry among their numerous Acquaintance, and
found seldom less was given. The Maids in Lodging Houses have no
Wages, and find their own Washing and Tea.

We went this Mornig to St. James's Church,[29] not the Abbey;
because we had a Mind to see it. It is an old Church, has been often

29    St. James' Church was rebuilt during 1768–73 by the architect John Palmer –
       It was destroyed in the second World War.

repaired and enlarged, and the Minister told me that in all Probability it would soon be taken down and rebuilt, built larger, for that it is not half big enough to contain the People who would be glad to attend there. This Church, like the Abbey, is lined all round, both Walls and Pillars, with monumental Inscriptions, which has a venerable Aspect. Our Lodgings are in St. James's Parish. There are only Prayers at this Church Sunday-mornings, no Sermon: and Prayers begin half an hour later than at the other Churches. I am told, the original Design of this, was, that Servants might go thither, setting out after and getting Home before their Masters and Mistresses, who went to the Abbey. The Minister told me, that there is now such a Resort of People to Bath, that in some Seasons here are ten thousand Persons Strangers. After Divine Service (But first I must tell you, the Sexton-Woman wears a Silk Cardinal and Bonnet, very genteel,) we went to the Pump-Room, where I had been before from Eight to Nine, and from thence through the Grove, now called Orange-Grove in Honour of the late Prince of Orange who was here for his Health, to whom an Obelisk is erected in the Centre, (Dr. Stackhouse lodges in this Grove, in a charming pleasant House) to the Bookseller's Shop for some Pens and Message Cards; then we took two Turns on the Parade, and came Home to meet Mr. Paul before he went, or we should have walked longer. Before Church, Your Mamma and Fanny went to Market, which they are charmed with the Plenty of, and the Richness of the Provisions. Geese are come cheap, only six shillings apiece; and you may have cucumbers, some at a shilling, some at only ten-pence, Dog-cheap!

In another cover, sent by this Post, you will find a Map of Bath, which I would have you pin up in the Parlour. You will see, what House we are in, by two Pin-Holes, if you look for them in Abbey-Green; and you will entertain yourselves sometimes, by looking in the Map for the Places we go to. We suppose, you keep our Letters: we shall be glad to revise them when we come Home, to refresh our Memories. Your Mamma's Cold is better, her Knee just as it was. I hope, I am better daily. I will tell you one good Sign, my Doctor has given me up, quite forsaken me.

I read Prayers again at the Abbey this Afternoon. Now I am found out, I expect full Employ. I thank God, I am able stand to do the Office. It is a very easy Church to speak in. After Prayers we all went together to the Pump-Room, and came home by a little circuit through Staul Street and Abbey Lane. I do not know, that I shall say any more to you about my Tours to the Pump-Room. I shall tell you once for all, that at seven in the morning I drink my Glass in Bed,

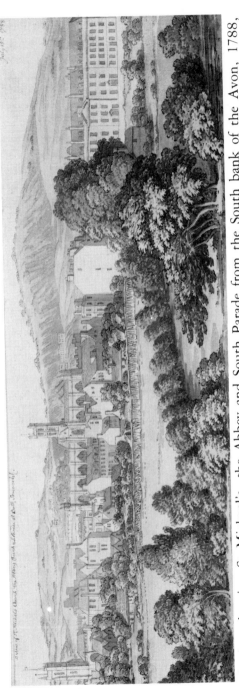

A view showing St Michael's, the Abbey and South Parade from the South bank of the Avon, 1788, by Samuel Grimm.

(That is Toping with a Witness;) at Eight I take a second in the Pump-Room; stay there an Hour with a multitude of Company, and usually there meet all my Acquaintance; at nine, Home to breakfast, excellent hot French Roll and Butter; at eleven to the Abbey; after Prayers, i.e. about Twelve, take my third Glass at the Pump-Room; dine at Two; To the Abbey, at four; To the Room again for my fourth Glass, after Prayers, i.e. about five, − Tea about six; Supper, about nine; Bed, as soon as we can after Ten. This is our regular course, which, you may presume, we always take, unless I tell you it is interrupted. The Time of our Bath Visits is between Twelve and Two. We walk as much as I can, without hurting my Feet, which still are weak and ache. − You must not imagine from my cracking, that I am so strong as Hercules. I bless God, Im so strong as I am, and for the good Prospect in my View.

Tho' it wants of six o'clock, I will even conclude my Epistle, which, thro' my Desire of giving you all the Intelligence I can, is swoln to an enormous Size: and if any thing occurs more this Evening, I will mention it in to-morrow's Letter. Remember us to all Friends. It is endless to name Names.

St. John says, in the Second Lesson for this Evening Service, "I have no greater Joy than to hear that my Children walk in Truth." God grant, I may ever have this Joy in you all! I am, dear Peggy, etc. your ever-loving Father,

JOHN PENROSE.

Bath, May 1st. 1766.

My dear Peggy,

And all the rest of my dear children! After I had finished my yesterday's Letter, which was accompanied, when sent to you, with two other Pacquets, enough to make you stare, Mr. and Mrs. and Mr Billy Robinson were so kind as to drink Tea with us, and afterwards take a few Turns on the Parade. You would be greatly diverted, if you were to see, how the Gentlemen walk up and down with Spectacles on, (themselves a mere Spectacle;) nay, Fanny saw one at Spring Gardens dance with Spectacles. Those, who don't wear Glasses on their Noses, carry them in their Hands, and constantly apply them to their Eyes: for it's quite the Fashion to be near-sighted. If Mary, who is a Fashion-monger, chuses to follow this Fashion, let Madamoiselle chuse a Pair for her, and your Mamma will not be against it. Without my calling Names, Mary guessed right about Sally.

The Colonel's John was here this morning. The Colonel better, and Mrs. Sewell prodigiously mended. So says also Mr. Haviland, who called here to-day, after a long Interval, and tells me that he never saw so great an Alteration before, in so short a Time, as in me. So well as I am I cannot venture out, but with a clear Sky. The Morning was wet, so I could not stir out till Church Time, when it held up. Sometime after Prayers, Sir Booth Williams, a Baronet of an honest and good Heart, but of a weak Head; a Lover of Religion, and of the Clergy, tho' like Sr. Francis Wronghead, "he wants it here;" came to our Lodgings, to invite me to dine with him. I excused myself from that, but promised to drink Tea with him this Even. He is always at the Abbey, where I am to read Prayers this Afternoon; and I promised to go with him from thence. It is now near Prayer-Time. Perhaps before Bed Time I may resume my Pen. –

Well, Peg, I have been at Sr. Booth's[30] But I have put Mrs. Hearle to the Expence of a shilling Chair-Hire, in being carried first from the Abbey to Sr. Booth's near the Cross-Bath, and afterwards from thence to Abbey-Green. I was very genteely entertained with Tea and Coffee. Sr. Booth smoked his Pipe, and drank Port pretty plentifully. He had it all to himself: for neither I, nor any other of the Company, who were five of us in all, besides him and Lady Williams, partook of either. One of the Company was a Clergyman, called Wroughton, related to Mr. Wroughton of Penzance, Attorney at Law, and Coroner for the County of Cornwall, and to Mrs. Penneck of Gulval: another was Mr. Roberts, Minister of this Parish, St. James's, who desired me to preach a Sermon Sunday next at this Church on a Collection to be made for the Charity Schools, but I begged to be excused. – When I came to the Abbey this Afternoon to read Prayers, the Vestry was locked, and Miss Sexton gone away, no body knew where, with the Key: so that after waiting, and keeping the Congregation waiting, a Quarter of an Hour, I was forced to desire the Clark to go to a neighbouring Church to borrow a Surplice. This was a singular adventure. – Yesterday, you know, we lost two Ladies, Lodgers in this House; and To-day Mr. Snow and his Lady went away for London. We are now the only Lodgers remaining here, except a single Gentleman, who is here always. All is Peace and Quietness, whereas there did not use a Quarter of an Hour to pass, without some one or other coming in, and calling out aloud, "Mrs. Leigh's Servant!" "Mr. Snow's Servant!" For this is the Method observed here, when you want to speak with any one in a House where are several Lodgers: you must call aloud for the

30  Sir Booth Williams.

Person's Servant, then the Servant will let the Gentleman or Lady you want know you are there, or introduce you to them, or take your Message. – Mr. Garrick and his Lady also left Bath To-day: we saw them take Coach just before our Lodgings, – This being May-day, a great many Boys go about the Streets with Garlands of Flowers round their Hats, and beg money towards a May-pole. I fancy, Charles would have liked to see the Garlands.

Friday, May 2.

One of the first Things I think upon in the Morning, when your Pacquet is expected, is of your Pacquet: and the first Opportunity I have of putting Pen to Paper (for I have many and many Impediments) is readily employed in answering it. This Morning with great Joy we received your and your Brother's and Sisters most agreeable Present: which Joy was heightened, when we read the contents, and found (thro' God's great Goodness) all is well among you, and such strong Expressions of Tenderness and Duty towards us: and what heightens the Joy still more, that from long Experience of your Honesty (and Mary says, she and all the rest of you are as honest as you) we have all the Reason in the World to think those Expressions sincere.

It was a great Misfortune to us, and no small Uneasiness (I presume) to you, that you dined abroad the Day you were to write us: tho' it was exceeding kind in Mr. Heame to invite you, and I dare say everything was done, that could be, to make your being there agreeable to you. You will not be so straitened again in Time, because you will not answer our Letters till the next Post: nor need you have been so straitened now, if you did, as I do, set down every Day the Occurences of the Day, on a Supposition that sufficient for every Day is the Business of it. We all desire you will take the first Opportunity of giving our Compliments to Mr. Heame and all his good Family, and let him know we entertain a grateful Sense of our obligation to him for his taking such Notice of you.

If we do not go to London, I hope we shall be at home before the Visitation, even tho' we should stay at Bath a Week or Fortnight beyond the Time proposed: for if I receive Benefit from the Waters in six weeks, I might receive a more than proportionable Benefit in Two Months. Be this as it will, George must appoint the Visitation-Dinner where it used to be: at Biggs's now, as I suppose the Court will be held at Penryn.

Your Mamma or Fanny will answer Daughter Coode's very kind Letter: She is worth you all for News. Let *me* say to her, that if she cannot express Molly's Language, she might give us an History of her

Progress in Tricks: I reckon, she has almost as many new Tricks, as we have been absent Days. We thought Mr. Hocker had spent more Time at Methleigh; are very glad, he saw my Letter: and desire to be remembered to him, when you have Opportunity, with an unfeigned affection. Mrs. Coode could not do otherwise, than she did, with Respect to shewing your Sister's Letter. However, you have had our Directions how to proceed for the future in like circumstances. And when you let any one know we send Compliments to them, and their Names are mentioned expressly, as Mr. Heame's is above, it will be more respectful to them, if you have the Letter about you, to read the words, wherein the Compliments are conveyed. We are heartily sorry, Victuals are so dear with you. Poor Peg! you have commenced House-keeper in an uncomfortable Time. What can the Poor do? No one need rob them, as Jacky says some one has at Milor. The Prospect of a plentiful Season, from the Fineness of the Spring; and the Cheapness of Mackarel and other Fish; administer some Consolation: yet I heartily commiserate their case, and wish to God it were in my Power to alleviate their Distress. Sorry are we all from the Bottom of our Hearts for the Doctor's Disorder continuing so to afflict him. If Doctor Peters is eminent in his Profession, he will advise him to try the Virtue of Bath Waters. We are studying his case, and we are all of Opinion, that Bath will do him good: and we are told here, that May and June are the two best months of the Year; that these Waters are then most efficacious. Tell the Doctor, that I will not have my Apothecary abused, no not in any Degree; and that, tho' no Graduate in any University, he is universally allowed to be as skilful in his Way, as any Physician in or out of the College. I am concerned, tho' I was not acquainted with Mr. Glover, to hear of his being such a Drinker of Brandy. Two hundred Quarts in three months exceeds all Belief. Before I left Cornwall, it was said, he had almost drank up all his Drink: but it seems, there was a good Quantity left, tho' but little Time left to drink it in. He must have been an enemy to himself, and no Friend to the Function. But he, that is perfect, cast the first Stone.

I know nothing of Lord Fleming: but Miss Foss may say of herself, she might have been a Lady, if she would. Did she but enjoy her Fortune, or do that Good with it, which a Person ought to do, whom Providence has entrusted with such an abundant Measure of good Things, in my Judgment she would be much happier, than to throw away her Riches upon one, who probably has no Regard to her Person. I wish his Lordship, if ever there be a War, may be more successful in Battle, than now in his Amour; and gain a greater Fortune by his Valour, than is now refused to his Love.

I wish Mess. Johns and Polglaze good Speed in their Buildings. May the former erect an House suitable to his Wealth, and the Situation he is to build upon! It is provoking to see such a pitiful Dwelling as Gill's in the most conspicuous Part of so pretty a Town. Miss Foss was more overseen in permitting that, than in rejecting Lord Fleming.

Your Sister Coode had no occasion to apologize for the Length of her Letter. It has been very entertaining to us. I am sure, it is a very sensible one, and the Writing very good. All your letters are entirely to my Satisfaction: your's very honest: Mary's very smart; Jacky's an Imitation of mine, so I must needs like that. A little use will greatly improve Mary, whose Pen is already fluent and lively to a great Degree. She has diverted us much, and made us laugh heartily; a very comical Hussy! I am forced to call her sawcy, and humble her now and then with some slighting expressions: for if she was to know, how well I think of her Writing, both as to Matter and Manner, I am afraid she would grow conceited. Do only let her know, that I read her Letter, and called her Hussy: that's all.

I thought my changing the Post would be convenient to you: therefore I did it. And I am very glad you are able amongst you to pick out my meaning. I reckon, when you are reading to your little Audience, you are like Cato in his little Senate, and they all hang with utmost Attention on your Tongue. I know, I see, my Writing is a most miserable Scrawl: but I have such a multitude of Interruptions, that if I do not write away as fast as I can, my Letters would be too short, to give you the Amusement I wish to give you.

Jacky's Account, where he hath been, and what he hath had, is entertaining. I approve of his Latin Texts. Only instead of *Epistola*, he should have written *Epistolæ*, the latter of two substantives, and *capite* understood in the former: for the whole, if wrote in Words, would run thus, *"Primæ Epistolæ Johannis capite tertio et verribus vicesime & vicesimo primo."* I desire you will remember me to Mess. Evans, and Osborn, and such Clergy, as are so kind as to help me in my absence. It is great Pleasure to us, to hear that Dolly, and Jacky, and Charles, behave themselves so well. It is not expressly said, but I think it may be inferred from Mrs. Coode's Letter, that Dolly is again with her, since the Return from Methleigh.

I have now answered such Part of your several Letters, as Time will permit; and now return to give Account of ourselves and our Proceedings here. This Day we have been a Month from Home, without any cross accident to any of us, either in Cornwall, or at Bath. My Gout on the Journey, I hope, hath been for the best. Things for

the present not joyous, but grievous, sometimes yield peaceable
Fruits. Mr. Burroughs, who saw me at Bridgewater, and was much
affected with the Sight, (I was then in doleful Dumps) desired a
Gentleman, a next Door neighbour to him, who was coming to Bath,
to call and enquire after my Health; which he did this morning, and I
thank God that I could send back by him so good account of my
change for the better.

When I sent you a List of Cornish People at Bath, I did not know
that Mr. Mundy and Mr. Carlyon have each a Lady, Daughter, and
servant with them, which add six more to the Number. Two new
Lodgers have taken the Rooms over our head, which Mrs. and Miss
Leigh had. They are Ladies from London; one of them a married Lady,
the other her Neice; the former called Marsh, or some such Name, the
latter's Name I have not heard. They have a genteel coach with them,
and two Servants, viz. a Man and Woman, who are Husband and
Wife.

Mr., Mrs. and Miss Grant, and a fine old Lady, hearty and sociable,
drank Tea with us this Afternoon. Tea Visiters don't come till six
o'clock, and make very short stay. Mr, Grant however stayed with me
till past eight. He is a very sensible man, has read a great deal, has a
good Head to retain what he has read, and I believe a good digesting
Faculty. I was well pleased with his Company, and, when it does not
interfere with my Correspondence with you, I shall be glad to have
more of it.

You, according to Custom, had Asparagus Fanny's Birth-day. We
could not afford so expensive a Dish. But To-day, the Price being
fallen, and come so low as fourteen pence a hundred, we had half an
hundred to eat with some Veal. From Garden-Stuff, we are led to
enquire about Charles's Garden, How it goes on, and desire you to
charge him by no means to stir out without an Hat.

The sociable old Lady mentioned above, is Mrs. Grant's Mother.

### Saturday, May 3.

Dear Peg, That unlucky circumstance of your and your sisters
staying so long with Miss Heame, by which means you had not Time
to finish your Letters, hath deprived us (we suppose) of a good deal of
News, which you have been treasuring up in your Stores. Pray, what is
become of Mr. Bath? We often think of him, and wonder you never
say, he enquires after us. Be as concise as you please in answering my
Letters, rather than omit any thing, which concerns your Neighbourhood at Penryn. – The Colonel is better, Mrs. Sewell almost well; but
they are not well enough to see Company: for, as soon as they are,

which we hope will be next week, we intend to walk and see them, if I can walk so far. – This morning your Mamma and sister sent up a Ticket to Mrs. Marsh and Miss Graham (that is the Neice's Name) welcoming them to Bath, and with a Compliment of waiting on them, if agreeable: they sent for Answer, that Mrs. Marsh was at present disordered with Lowness of Spirits; that, when she is a little better, she shall be glad to see them. – I was applied to to-day to read Prayers to-morrow at St. Michael's Church; but begged to be excused, because I have a Mind to hear Dr. Frampton at the Abbey, a famous extempore Preacher. Arch-deacon Sleech was to have set out for London Yesterday, but has postponed his Journey to Monday, through the same curiosity. – Consult your Sister Coode about your speaking to Molly Barry concerning Potting Butter. Your Mamma used to speak to her in May. But now Butter is eight pence a pound, too high a Price for Potting. Consult your Sister about it, and when she thinks it best to speak about it, then speak. – I have herewith sent you twelve Receipts for Tithes, etc. due Lady-day last. You do not let us know, whether you have received any money, nor whether the Clark be dead or living. If the Clark be able go abroad, I desire he will be diligent in collecting for you.

You have seen in the News-papers, that the foundation Stone is laid of an Octagon Chapel to be built here in Milsom-Street: and it is but need. Bath is so enlarged, that the Places of Public Worship will not contain a Tythe of the Inhabitants, and Strangers resorting hither. At the Chapel in Queen-Square, a Stranger cannot get a sitting under half a crown a Time, or a Guinea for the Season: the Inhabitants themselves, to have a Seat, must pay a Guinea a year each Person. So numerous as the People here are, of some Sort or other, here is no Place of Burial but in the Churches; or none worth mentioning: and the Fees for Breaking Ground in Churches monstrous high, Ten Pounds at the Abbey. So all the Poor, and middling People, nay all except the rich and great, are carried, when dead to the Church-yards of Widcombe or chiefly at Bathwicke, two neighbouring Parishes the other side the river Avon, which is crossed in a Ferry-Boat; and four or five shillings are paid as a Fee for breaking the ground. – We suppose, as the Wind is westerly or south-west, you have a good deal of Rain. The Weather here is mixt, sometimes drizzling Rain, sometimes a Glimpse of Sun-shine; too bad to walk out in, unless to Church and for my Water; which are not far off. – Among the Octavos in my Study is a Book called *The Project of Peace.* You must look for it under P. *Project.* In the Margin of some of the first Leaves in it, is, I believe, what we called at School *A Bill of the School*, i.e. the Names of the Scholars. If this List be

there, as I suppose, let Jacky copy it, and send me. Let him write it in
different Columns, the Margin of one page in one column, the margin
of another page in another column: or if he cannot well do that, let
him at least leave a space between the Names of the several Pages. If
there are any Marks before or after Names, such as + + +, he need
take no notice of them. This Evening I received a Letter from the
Colonel, wherein he says, that "Thanks to Heaven's Blessing on Mr.
Haviland's Endeavours, he is now able to tell us, he is so well recovered as
to hope we will take a commons at Lincomb next Wednesday." A Line
from me, thankfully accepting the Invitation, will go to him by John To-
morrow morning. He proposed "Dining at any Hour we should name":
and I have wrote him Word, that His usual Hour of Dining will be most
agreeable to us, which we presume is not before Two, our usual Hour.
The Colonel "hopes, I shall hear Mr. Frampton To-morrow" – *cui mens
divinior atque os Magna sonaturum* – Jacky will see, I have a Love for him,
by my giving him this sweet Bone to pick. –

Sunday, May 4.

Well, this morning I heard the famous Frampton: his Text 1 Cor. XIII.
13: the Occasion, a Collection to be made for the Charity Schools: a very
suitable Discourse, and peculiarly adapted to these particular Schools. In
his Discourse he paid a very genteel compliment to the Memory of Mr.
Nelson, Author of the *Fasts and Festivals*, who was principally concerned
in raising a Subscription towards founding these Schools. Fifty Boys and
twenty Girls are cloathed and instructed in them: the Boys are taught
Reading, Writing, Arithmetic; the Girls, Reading and the use of the
Needle. I should not forget to mention, that among other Things they
are taught to sing (the Thing of least Importance which they are
taught) and one of the Boys in the Front of the Organ-Loft, between
the two Services in the Morning, and before Sermon in the Afternoon,
sung solo an Hymn, a copy whereof is herewith sent you, all joining in
the Hallelujah. He sung exceeding well, and the Chorus too was sung
well. They were all ranged along the Abbey, before and after Service,
the Boys on one side, the Girls on the other, forming a Lane for the
Congregation to pass through. They were all new cloathed, in blue,
with white stockings; the Boys with Bands, and caps, with a white
woollen Tuft on the Top, and a woollen Ribbon on the side; the Girls
with a white whiff round the Neck; and all of them with a Nose-gay of
Flowers in the Bosom. They made a decent appearance, and I was
much affected with the Sight. The Preacher observed in his Sermon,
that the late Mr. Wood, Architect, of great Skill and Judgment, equal
to most, who was the Occasion of building Queen-Square and many

Streets contiguous, the two Parades, and the Streets which connect them, and laid out the Plan of the Circus, beautiful beyond Description, had his Education in these Schools. Under the several Descriptions of Faith, Hope, and Charity, he had a Fling at enthusiasts of whatever denomination, expressed with Judgment of Thought, but in too angry a Manner. I believe, I told you before, that he is an extempore Preacher: but I find by his well connected Discourse, that he is rather a memorizer Preacher (i.e. he composes his Sermon, and gets it by Heart.) He affects the Orator, and fancies himself a fine one: but Mr. Garrick, who heard him lately, says he is none nor has any Notion of Oratory. Mr. Garrick is indisputably a Judge. My Opinion of him is, that he is like an Actor on the Stage, that so over-acts his Part, that no Audience in Great Britain, but would hiss him off it. So that I like his Matter extremely well, but think his Manner extremely ill. But he is a popular Declaimer, and pleases the Million. He, and I, and Mr. Taylor the Reader, assisted Mr. Arch-deacon Sleech in the administration of the Sacrament. Mr. Taylor preached in the Afternoon on the same Occasion, and made a very sensible useful Sermon. His Text was Heb. XIII. 16. I prefer *his* still small Voice, to the Thunder-Storm of Mr. Frampton. I read Prayers; and was forced to have a chair to put me home, taking the Pump-Room in my way, because of the Rain. Six pence more added to my Chair-Hire Account. What Sum was collected, I cannot yet tell. But this Day se'nnight, was collected (I now know for certain) for the General Hospital, at

| | | |
|---|---|---|
| The Abbey Church — | 63. 5. 2½ | Where Dr. Goodall preached, A-deacon of Suffolk. |
| St. James's Church — | 34. 1. 4. | |
| St. Michael's Church — | 20.14. 2½ | |
| Walcot Church — | 6.13. 3. | |
| Chapel in the Square — | 36.17. 7. | Where Arch-deacon Sleech preached. |
| St. John's Chapel — | 1.17. 0. | Mr. Chapman's. |
| Revd. Mr. Franks's Collection — | 14. 7. 3. | Presbyterians. |
| Bell Tree House Collection — | 12. 7. 6. | Members of the Church of Rome. |
| To be added to the Collection — | 5.14. 6. | |
| | 195. 7. 7. | a very good collection. |

This Evening Fanny was invited by Counsellor Short to meet some Exeter and Devonshire Ladies in the Public Room, which she did not chuse to do, but went with her Mamma and me to drink Tea with Mrs. Marsh and Mrs. Graham (not her Niece, but Cousin) upon their Invitation. I can tell you no more of Mrs. Marsh, but that she is come here to try the Waters for a bilious complaint, and has an Husband and two children in London. She is one of Clapham in Surry, and has been married four years.

Monday, May 5th.

This morning for the first Time I drank my first Glass (which I used to take in Bed) in the Pump-Room: and hope to continue the Practice. At Breakfast Time we had the Pleasure of hearing Mr. Hocker is well; and a Letter came from Bristol from Mr. Vivian, who hath had a Letter from Mrs. Vivian, wherein she does not say a Word about Lady Roger's Benefaction to Penryn, but that "Sr. John told her she has a Legacy of £500, and Mrs. Walker (James Walker's wife) £100, and all her poor Relations £200 each." Farther this Deponent saith not. Mr. Blake of Truro went hence this morning. If he had communicated his Intentions to me, we would have sent Compliments and a Line to Mrs. M. Walker. – About eleven, Mrs. Marsh made me an Offer of an Airing in her Coach with her and her Cousin, which I gladly accepted of. We went about four or five miles in the higher Bristol Road. For the Satisfaction of your tracing my Route in the Map; we went thro' Abbey Lane, up Staul Street, through Westgate Street, Monmouth Street, and Bristol Road, and returned the same way. We returned about a quarter after one, so I did not lose my Glass. Coming from the Pump-Room, I met Mamma and Sister in the Church-Yard. They had been strolling with Mrs. Robinson to the Cross Bath and that neighbourhood. In the Church-yard I also met with Mr. Taylor, who desired me to preach at the Abbey, next Sunday Even., which, if able, I think to do; tho' I begged to be excused, and told him I would much rather read Prayers, and hear him. – In the Way home we went to see the Duke of Kingston's private Baths and Sweating-Room. They are constructed on the left hand of the way, as we come homeward from the Church-yard, where in the Map there are Gardens pictured. The Water of these Baths, five in number, is from the same Springs which supply the King's and Queen's Baths: they are small, that one can but just turn round in them and five shillings a time is the Price for the Use of them. They have only been opened since we came here. Some use them for Privacy's sake, and for the sake of bathing naked.

All that I have learnt farther concerning Mrs. Marsh is, that her

Husband lives in Thread-needle Street, and that she knew Capt. Lemon and his Lady very well, and Capt. Williams, Mrs. Lemon's Brother: and concerning Mrs. (or Miss, for I know not whether,) Graham, that she comes from the West Riding of Yorkshire. They know Mr. Venn very well (he was minister at Clapham) and should have liked him very well, if he had kept his Pulpit to himself, but he was always introducing Jones, or some methodist or other, which made the Claphamites glad to be rid of him.

Mr. Grant, the Gentleman of the House we lodge in, has a Son at Latin School near Devizes in Wiltshire, who is just now come home to keep the Tide: a very fine Lad, about Jacky's Size, six months older. He learns Homer, Virgil, Terence, and Horace; and has been at Latin School from five years of Age. –

Before Evening Prayers, we took a little walk, terminating in a call upon Dr. Stackhouse. His Lodgings, in Orange Grove, are exceeding noble and pleasant. Just under his Dining-Room Windows flows the River Avon, with a Water-Fall making a pleasing awful Noise, of great Length: on the other side the River are Spring-Gardens, of which he has a full Prospect, and of all the Company going to them.

I had forgot to tell you, that chilly Fanny, when in the Duke of Kingston's Sweating Room, did not care to come out again: and, when in a former Letter, I reckon'd up the Cases, which the Bath Waters are most efficacious in, I did not know, that Miss Eliot bathes, in Hopes they will make her grow; so Shortness of Stature was not reckoned among them.

Your Sister has wrote this Post to Mrs. Coode, and is under great concern, that she cannot write Mary. I hope Mary will excuse it: for, indeed, Fanny has no Time lying on her Hands, and she must make an Apron to wear next Wednesday to Col. Sewell's. Your Mamma and I were both very fine yesterday: she had on a new Mob, *not* alamode de Bath; and I, a new Pair of black ribbed stockings. We can have Stockings here big enough for me, which we cannot have at Penryn, 6s. per Pair. The Taylor's Bill was paid to-day, for my new Coat, £2.6.0. –

You cannot imagine, and will scarce believe, what a mongril Kind of Animals Bath Methodists are. So far from being straight-laced, as they are in Cornwall, they can reconcile the Difference between the Tabernacle and the Theatre. One of the chief Musicians at the Play-house is Lady Huntingdon's Right-hand man, and a great Stickler for her Chapel; the same Boy, that lights the Candles in her Chapel, has an Employment under the Actors; and you cannot know them by the Looks, as you can at Penryn. The Penryn Methodists, tho' more starch, are more consistent. I don't like this dividing the Matter between God and Belial. But the Methodists here, are Whitefieldians; who are not so precise as the Wesleyans.

Send the inclosed to Ensign Smith with all the Diligence you can. George may convey it by some safe hand to my Brother for him, unless he knows a more expeditious way, equally safe.

Our Blessing, Your Mamma's and mine, be on you! That God will protect you from all Evil, and crown you with all the Blessings of Time and Eternity is our daily Prayer. Your Sister's Love to you all. Remember us all to all friends as due, especially to my Brother and his family, and to Dr. Coode and his. You know, who shew you Respect, and whom we have complimented in former Letters: Remember us to them all. And I desire, George will tell my Parishioners of Budock on Sunday next, that tho' I am at a great Distance from them, I remember them in my Prayers.

I am, my dear Peggy, and all you my dear Children,
        Your ever affectionate Father,
        JOHN PENROSE.


Bath, Tuesday, May 6th 1766.

Dear Peggy,

And all the rest of my dear Children, you cannot be more willing to hear from us, than I am ready to write you, and communicate such little Occurrences, as come in our way. Many Things I write are trifling, but "Trifles, light as air", become of imaginary Importance, when communicated by them who are dear to us.

To my Account of Yesterday must be added Mr. Pitt's coming to Town. I was in Hope to have seen him this morning at the Pump-Room; but, it seems, he never comes thither, always sending for his Water. Perhaps he thinks he shall be revered the more, by not making himself cheap, "and keeps like Asian Monarchs from our sight:" or perhaps, being conversant with Kings and Princes, he chuses not to mix with the Herd at Bath, who would not in their carriage distinguish between Him and lesser Men: for Bath, like "Caesar's Arms, doth throw down all Distinction;" and unless you are acquainted with a Person, however eminent, you pass him by without shewing any Token of Respect.

I don't suppose Your Mamma or Sister will meet with any the least Reverence more than common, for all they have each got a new Gauze Apron, striped very pretty: nor do I, tho' I wear a Cassock and Band,

and am the only one so habited except Dr. Potter Arch-deacon of Wells. – Many Clergy wear Cassocks under their Coats, but wear no Bands. But poor Country Parsons pass by the side of a Bishop, without any compliment to his Episcopal Order.

Are you rich, my honest Peg, can you honour my Draught, if I should draw upon you for a round Sum of Money? What Cash we brought away with us, is almost exhausted; so that this day we were forced to convert into Cash the Bill we brought with us. The Colonel's John was our Negotiator, who has been useful to us on many Occasions, and is truly obliging.

At eleven o'clock, we went to St. Michael's Chapel, commonly called St. John's Chapel, because it is near St. John's Hospital or Alms-house. In this Hospital are comfortably supported six aged poor men, and as many aged poor women, with each a separate Lodging. The Person, who looks after them, is Minister of the aforesaid Chapel, who has an handsome Revenue, and reads Prayers, himself or his Curate, twice every day. Mr. Chapman is the present Chaplain, who resides at present near Melksham in Wiltshire; his Curate, one Grigg, a Cornishman, educated at Lanceston. The Chapel is a pretty little Room, quite plain, but not decently kept, being overhung with cobwebs of long standing, which I pointed out to the Curate with a Mark of Reprobation. My country-man, who wants to make an Excursion into the Country, has taken me in for a Sermon Whitsunday in the morning. He will get some one else to read Prayers, and help at the Communion, because of the Aching of my Feet and Ancles. Near this Chapel is the Cross Bath, so called from a Cross on Top of a Monument erected in the middle of it, from whence the Chapel is commonly called The Cross-Bath Chapel. I drank the Waters from this Bath, at my first coming.

From Chapel we walked to Chandois Buildings, to pay a Bath Visit to Mr. and Mrs. Mundy, who lodge there. Mr. Mundy had taken Physic, so we saw him not; but we saw Mrs. and Miss Mundy, and Mrs. Carlyon, who lodges in the same House, and Miss Carlyon. The Esquire himself was rode out an Airing with Dr. Stackhouse. Mrs. Carlyon asked kindly for Mrs. Hearle. Mess. Carlyon and Mundy join their two families together, and keep but one Table betwixt them.

From Chandois Buildings we passed by (2) West-gate, through Saw-Close, by (Y) the Charity School, cross Trim Street, through John Street, and Wood Street, into the Square. I called at Ld. Edgecumbe's, who has not been to the Pump-Room several mornings; but his Lordship was gone an Airing, so I left my Name on a Card with his Servant, and rejoined my Company. We then took a Turn in the

Garden, went up Barton Street, turned into George Street, and there called at Mr. Gregor's Lodgings. Him too I have missed several mornings. But he being walked out, I also left my Name on a Card with his Servant. Then we went thro' Edgar Street (a very fine Row of Buildings) and Foss Lane, then down Broad Street and High-Street, and through Wade's Passage to (C) the Pump-Room. We rested there near half an Hour, and about half past one got home, not a little wearied for my own particular.

If there be a Pleasure in Variety, we have very pleasant Weather, for I am sure it is very various: good, bad, and indifferent, chequering almost every day. This Morning was glorious, or I had not so far deambulated: this Afternoon so foul, that we could not go to Church. I was carried to the Pump-Room in a chair. Ah! Poor Mrs. Hearle, what expence do I put you to! At the Pump-Room I was told a Gentleman had been enquiring not five minutes before, where I lodged; and not getting Information there, was gone to the Post-Office to make Inquiry. This Gentleman was at my Lodgings before me, and proved to be Mr. Heard from London. He was but just arrived, had taken no Place to board in, so hurried away again in a few minutes, promising to let us see him to-morrow morning. Before he was gone out of Door, came Dr. Stackhouse, with the three Ladies under his charge, Miss Kitty, Miss Coryton, and Miss Tremayne, brought in four chairs. We drank Tea immediately, and immediately after away they went again, in four chairs, to the Ball. The Young Ladies were tossed off to the Life. The Doctor desires us to drink Tea with him one day; and to breakfast with him next Friday, if the Weather permit, at Spring-Gardens, where the Doctor gives a Breakfast to all the Cornish Gentlemen and Ladies now at Bath. Not expecting any more Company for the Evening, unless such as would excuse my Night-Gown and the Ladies Dishabille, we begun to unrig as soon as the Coast was clear: for 'tis very disagreeable to be all day dressed in form. Company indeed we had, such as I expected, which stayed with us till the Chimes went Nine: cheap, as you call it, with Respect to Pecuniary Expence, but very expensive with Respect to Time. I have told you before, that Visiters here, except very particular Acquaintance, such as Major Tucker, etc. make very short Visits: they bounce into the Room, and shew themselves, and away; and being generally well-dressed, they make me compare them to Jupiter, when he came in his Glory to Semela: they are glorious in their Apparel, make a Noise like Thunder, and are gone again quick as Lightning. If this Simile will not hold good, let it pass for a Squib.

## Wednesday, May 7th.

Lo, for your Entertainment, another week's Bill: the first thing offering itself this morning.

Apr. 30. Boiling a Lamb's Head, 3d. – Price 6d.

May 1. Roasting Veal   –   4 ⎫
     2. Roasting Veal   –   4 ⎬ a Breast, price 2s.

Boiling Asparagus   –   3. Price 7d.

     3. We had a Mutton-Pie, price 1s.

     4. Roasting Lamb   –   4d. ⎫
     5. Roasting Lamb   –   4. ⎬ a Fore-quarter, price 2s.6d.

     6. Roasting 3 Hearts   –   4   Sheep's Hearts, price 6d.

One Week's Lodging   –   £1.5s.0d.

The next thing offering itself this morning, was Mr. Heard, who was here, when your Letters came; before he went away, Mr. Robinson etc. came in, and stayed till Church-Time; immediately after Church the Colonel's John was waiting to conduct us to Lyncomb-Spaw; from whence it was Night e're we got home: and till this time we had no opportunity of giving your Letters a fair Reading; we could only half run them over, or snatch a Word here and there: a Mortification this almost past enduring. These Letters of your I shall review by and by, and say a Word or two perhaps to some Particulars in them: but at present, let me give you a brief Account of Mr. Heard's conversation.

Mr. Heard is a very agreeable young Gentleman, born at Ottery St. Mary in Devon, has been a great Traveller, resided many Years in Spain, Italy, and other Parts of Europe, and before he was Twenty had been in all four Quarters of the World. I do not find by him the Necessity or Usefulness of our going to London: our Business can as well be done, we being at Penryn. The Trouble and Expence of sending Writings to and fro will make all the Difference, which are trifling in comparison with a London Journey, even from hence: and were we to go from hence, we cannot sell the Estates without a Purchaser. He has Reason to think, the Earl of Bristol will gladly purchase, and give a good Price, because our Premises lie intermixed with his: Mr. Pennystone thinks, that a separate Sale of the Premises, Parcel to one, Parcel to another, as they lie contiguous to other Owners, may bring in most money: No way is yet pitcht upon, as most eligible. But Mr. Pennystone promises to lose no Time in Enquiry, what way it will be best for us to pursue for our advantage, and to assist us to the utmost of his Power. Mr. Heard has seen Mr. Pennystone, and is of Opinion that he is one of the amiable and honestest of Men. I told him, that in Mr. Barnett's Illness, I had made an offer of a certain Sum for his Moiety, by which might be known the Value I set upon the Estate: he told me, he knew it, and the Reasons I produced, why I would offer no more, which he thought were sufficient ones in my Case, but that he was very well satisfied, it will yield a Sum much greater. He says, he has seen late Lord Suffolk's Marriage-Settlement, and took a judicious Friend with him, who was clearly of Opinion that the £3000 belongs to us, or £150 Pounds per ann. He mentioned it to Mr. Austen, the Steward, who told him, that at first sight it would so appear to any one; but that the Estates, which Ld. Suffolk had bound to the Payment of it, were entailed Estates which he had no Power to bind. Now I have a copy of the Entails belonging to the Family, in which I can see, when I know what the Estates are, whether they are entailed or no: for, if they are not entailed, they belong to the Heirs at Law; and I think, if they were entailed, and so not liable to make good Ld. Suffolk's Obligation, the present Possessors would take the advantage of their Right, and refuse to pay his surviving Lady the Annuity. Mr. Heard will have a copy taken of all that Part of the Settlement, which relates to this matter (which he may have for a Fee to Mr. Austen's Clark, and Ld. Falkland has ordered the Steward to let us have a Copy if desired,) and send to me at Penryn. Then we may take the Advice of Friends, as well as Mr. Heard; and I have promised to send Mr. Heard a Copy of the Entails. We both think it worth while to examine into this affair; and he assures me, both he and his Sister will leave no Stone unturned, till it clearly appear whether our Suppositions are justly or unjustly founded. You see now, that, as I told you above, we shall not go to London: but we cannot tell you, when we shall leave Bath, till I speak with Mr. Haviland. We intended to stay here six weeks, whereof four weeks elapsed last Tuesday: but I am advised by many to stay a week or fortnight longer. I shall consult Mr. Haviland about it, and, I believe, follow his Direction. He can have no Interest in keeping me here; for he seldom calls upon me; I take no Physic; and, if I stay a fortnight longer than my first Design, my Fee for his Advice will be just the same as if I go sooner. So much for Mr. Heard; let us now proceed to

Another Head of Discourse, our Walk to Lyncomb. Our Way to it was over the Grand Parade, through Duke Street, and Part of the South Parade, across the Ferry (12), then down to the Crane for loading Barges with Free-stone (7).[31] So far level Ground, and pleasant

---

31   This crane was constructed by John Padmore, a Bristol engineer, for the purpose of handling Ralph Allen's freestone. It is curious that John Penrose does not mention the railway – also constructed by Padmore – which brought the stone down.

Walking, but from thence to Lyncomb, the longer half way, or rather two thirds almost of the Way, an uphill and downhill, very rugged and uneven. However we got to Lyncomb in good Season. I was much tired, sweating as if in a Bagnio, was glad of a Glass of Wine, yet recovered my self so well before Dinner came in, that I made a most excellent Meal. The Colonel's Lodgings, on the side we entred the House, is two Pair of Stairs up; on the opposite Side, but one Pair, that side being under Ground. It is a very pleasant Situation, in the midst of Variety of rural Scenes, not the less pleasing for being rural. Mrs. Sewell received us with her usual Address, and is well recovered from her late dangerous Indisposition. The Colonel was on his Couch, looking like a Corpse, but is bettering daily. He talked of coming to Bath this Week, but the Doctor would have him stay where he is one Week longer. They were both glad to see us, and we had all the Reason imaginable to think we had a sincere and friendly Welcome. The servants were rejoiced at our coming; and I supposed rejoiced at our going, for we gave them Half a Crown apiece. They merited it for the Civilities and ready Services done us at our coming, and every Day since John has been so kind as to come in and offer his Assistance, which, when we need it, we freely accept of. Our Dinner was a large flat Fish, called a Brill, as solid as Turbot, boiled; with two little Soals fried. The fish cost 3s. There was Shrimp-Sauce. This was the first Course. The second was an excessive fat fore-quarter of House-Lamb, worth at least five shillings: the victuals here are so fine, that no Description can convey an Idea to you, so I aim at none. After the Lamb, a bread Pudding (Oh, when did we see Pudding before?) and Cheese. A very good Dinner, (and to use Mary'a Phrase) don't you think it is? After Dinner Wine, as usual. We chatted away the afternoon, till Tea-Time; and Tea being over, (we had Coffee too,) Mr. John again conducted us to Town. But we did not return the same Way we went, but came along the Road from Claverton Downs to the Bridge, up Horse Street, Stall-Street, to Abbey Lane, etc. Don't you think I was finely tired by the Time I got home? I freely confessed it. How Mamma's Knee was affected, she alone could feel: but you know, she makes the best of every thing, and rarely complains. Yet I was not so much tired, as I expected to be, and I hope I shall not be the worse for it.

I must postpone answering your Letters to To-morrow. I hope, you will excuse me. I don't mean it out of Disrespect, but you see how it is with me. Two or three trifling memorandums shall conclude this Evening's Scrawl. In the first Place, I must ask Pardon of Mr. Pitt for speaking of him from Report. He was twice this Day at the

Pump-Room, but not when I was there. He was brought in a Sedan, drank his Water, and made no Stay. In the next Place, Mr. Short, who invited Fanny with his Devonshire Friends to last Sunday Evening's Tea, had seventy to treat. Thirdly, it is computed, that there is not less than ten thousand pounds weekly spent in Bath. Fourthly, and lastly, Your Sister had this morning a most obliging Letter from Mrs. Leigh, who with her Sister arrived safely at Oxford, which she intends answering To-morrow by Mr. Billy Robinson, who sets out for Oxford early next friday.

I must write one word more, to tell you, that tho' I have proceeded to Fourthly before conclude, it is quite out of fashion to have more than 3 Heads of Application or Inference to any Discourse. Oh me, what shall I do? I am to preach at the Abby next Sunday, and my Discourse has no fewer than twice three Inferences, and all so practical that I must in Conscience be out of fashion.

### Thursday, May 8th.

By and By, for your Letters. But I have had a busy Day, and shall forget some-thing or other, if I do not set down directly the Occurrences of it. I got up very late, because I sweat so prodigiously after yesterday's fatigue. I had my first Glass in Bed. But when up, my Feet were quite easy; a little Weakness in my Knees, and a slight Pain in my Calves: my right Calf was crampt in the Bed a little, and made me cry Oh! At the Abbey was a Sermon, it being Ascension-Day. Dr. Grant preached, and that very well. It was a good sensible Church of England Discourse, well adapted to the Festival: the Text Heb. ii.9. I dined with Sir Booth Williams; Gentlemen there besides me, Mr. Roberts, Curate of St. James's, Mr. Taylor Reader at the Abbey, the famous Mr. Frampton, and one of Exeter, I don't know what, Mr. Townsend. For Dinner was, a Dish of Mackerel, a monstrous large Neat's Tongue, a Dish of Spinnage and Carrots, and a Dish of stewed Pigeons, with plain Butter, Butter and Fennel, and Gooseberry Sauce: Second Course, a beautiful Hind Quarter of Lamb, a large Dish of Asparagus, a Dish of Radishes, a Various Sallad, and a creamed Apple-Pye. Here was an expensive Dinner: don't you think it was? We had variety of Wines, Tea, etc. and with our Tea Cambridge-Cakes buttered. We have had these too ourselves. They are round thick Cakes, a penny apiece, hardly an Ounce weight; look like Dow, all white and soft: these we toast a little by the fire, just to warm them through, and then butter them; they eat exceeding well. While I am upon the Article of Hot-bread, I must tell you, that so many speak against the Use of it, we were afraid for me to breakfast on it any more;

so to-day I mortified on Bread and Butter: but this Evening I met with Mr. Haviland. How do you do, Mr. Haviland? How do you do, Mr. Penrose? Pray Mr. Haviland, as I am fortunate enough to meet you, let me ask you, do you approve of my eating hot Bread for Breakfast? How much do you eat? – an half-penny Roll. – How does it settle in your stomach? – Very Well. – Then eat it. – But many advise me against it. – Pugh! – Ah! my dear Peg, Mr. Haviland is one of Ten Thousand.

This evening new Lodgers are come into Mr. Snow's Room: a Clergyman and his Wife. I know no more of them.

I omitted telling you, that an hard Shower obliged me to be carried to Sir Booth's in a Chair. Six pence more added to the Chair-hire Account.

We are very sorry Jacky's Teeth have ached. If they should ache again, he had best have Recourse to Mrs. Williams, and apply the same Medicine which gave him Ease. We are obliged to Mrs. Coode for her great Goodness to you all: it was exceeding good in her to commiserate the Case of her poor distressed Brothers and Sisters, and give them a comfortable Meal. By Dolly's Account they are in most miserable condition. Oh, fy, Peggy, keep a better House. Your Mamma says, you don't live extravagantly. Better let the Rats live, than starve the Family.

Mary's Scheme, about your advertising your Drugs, is a very good one. But I do not think, it is worth while to do it, unless you affix a Price to each Article. Then indeed you will not get, as she thinks, enough by your Trade to maintain the family: unless she reckons this way, that by fixing a Price you will lose all your Custom, and a Penny saved is a Penny got.

The two last Paragraphs are in Answer to Mary's and partly to Mrs. Coode's Letters. To Mrs. Coode say, that I am obliged to Mr. Coode for his minding Mrs. Hingston's Debt to me for Tithes: I have not her Account with me. But it will be soon enough to distrain her, both for the Church-Rates and Tithes, when we come home. For should we stay here eight weeks, instead of six, as we proposed, we should set out hence June 2d, and get Home about June 13th which is ten Days before the Visitation. – We are charmed to hear the good Account given of Dolly, and hope by the Time we return she will be so confirmed in good Tempers, that she never more will have an angry Word. She can be excellent Company, if she will; and she will gain the Approbation and Admiration of all, when once she has gained the Mastery of her Resentful Temper. – We have bought a Paper of Rat Powder for Mrs. Coode, which shall be sent next Monday by Mr.

Robinson, to be left at Mrs. Penrose's in Helston. If it answers to Mrs. Coode, and our Rats get the better of Your Frugality, my Peggy, we will send for a Paper too. They say at the Plough, where we bought it, that it may be had of the Sherborne News-Man. Remember us to Mr. and Mrs. Coode, the Doctor and Molly, as due. We should be exceedingly rejoiced to hear, that the Doctor's Health was throughly established; but fancy he must come to Bath first. You cannot conceive, unless you were to see me, how stout I am. I wish, when Mr. Robinson is home, Mr. Coode could see him, to have his Report concerning me. I pray God, my Strength may continue: and if my better State be owing to these Waters, as the Cause of it, (which Time will shew, and Time only; for many other Causes may possibly concur towards it, tho' here the Waters alone run away with the credit) I shall not repent of my Journey hither.

Remember our Love to Brother, Sister, and Cousins at Falmouth. We are glad, that they, and Fanny and Billy are all well. I hope, they and all other friends will excuse my not writing to them. It is impossible, I can write to any but you, and be so particular to you as I wish to be. But you may shew you Uncle etc. at Falmouth our Letters, as you do to Mr. Coode, etc.

Charles's Letter is very pretty, and conveys a Piece of Intelligence, which we should not have known, if it had not been for him, and yet it concerns our own family; I mean the Account of the Bantam Hen and the four Chicken, which we congratulate him upon the News of. It is very kind of Mary to propose Teaching him to write. I am sure, he will be a good Boy, and bring credit to his Teacher. The being well reported of, as an able Mistress of her Pen, will be an Advantage to Mary, when she settles at Verian, as she will put into her own Pocket, what else would be paid to a master.

It is exceeding kind in Mr. Evans to give his scholars so many Holidays, as we learn from Jacky's Letter. I wonder, he does not advertise it in the Public Papers, that at his School all imaginable care is taken that Jack shall not be a dull Boy. Oh, how would the Boys dislike all other Schools, and teaze their Parents to Death to put them to him, when they hear of a half-holiday almost every Afternoon, and not above half an hour's Business to do in a morning! Some Parents, covetous Wretches, do not care if their children work like Negros, rather than not have all they can for their pitiful Stipend of Two annual Guineas: but Mr. Evans is more judicious, he understands the capacities of children, and hath more Sense than to endeavour to pour an Hogshead of Learning, into a Head that will hold scarce a pint. He would certainly love me dearly, if he knew how I plead for him.

Jacky's Latin wants a little correction, tho' I give him my Applause. *Gaudio* for *Gaudeo* is wrong, and *Ad ministrum magistrum* should have been *Ad reverendum dominum,* and *Ad Bathoniam* should have been *Bathoniæ* or *Apud Bathoniam.* Else I am very well pleased with his Letter, tho' we are sorry for those Parts of the Contents concerning his Tooth-Ach and Mrs. Gideon's Illness.

Now, my honest Peg, I come to your Epistle, which is very entertaining, and gives many evident Marks of your Skill in Huswifry, and Regard to the Good of the Family. Be as frugal as you can, consistently with every one's having their sufficient Allowance in due Season; and starve the Rats if you can, never mind Dolly, – We shall be glad to have it confirmed, that Mr. Sam Enys has some lucrative Employment, tho' it should fall short of £300 per ann. but there is some mistake in the Name you give, when you call him "Inspector over the Pacquets at Plymouth and Cornwall;" for there is no such Officer, nor at Plymouth any Pacquets. – Tell Dr. Williams, we sincerely condole with Mrs. Williams and him at the unfortunate Disaster, which has befaln the youngest child. Mr. and Mrs. Sewell have a great Respect for the Doctor. Tell him, he has a great advantage in Point of Honour by living in Cornwall: why, was he resident here, he would be degraded to an Apothecary. – We are very sorry, Things continue so dear with you, notwithstanding the Fineness of the Spring. In one Sense, your Provisions are much dearer than ours: for if the noble Provisions, which are in Bath Market, were exposed to sale at Penryn, they would deservedly fetch a much higher Price than the best you ever saw. – Mr. Paynter is a Person of much Zeal and little Knowledge, of great Conceit in proportion to his Understanding. Had he more Sense, he would think such ill-grounded censure a sure Token of Defect in Grace. Would he and his Intimates study to be quiet and mind their own Business, and leave their Neighbours to stand or fall to their own Master, they would bring more Glory to God, and more Credit to the Christian Profession, than by a random scattering of Firebrands and Death, with Solomon's fool, and then saying Am I not a Saint? – I hope e're this, you have the Licenses. The Carrier does not come every week: therefore I desired Mr. Geare to send them by the Caravan. Which if he had done, you would have had them sooner. But you say he wrote George they were sent by the Carrier. This caused the Delay.

At length I have answered your Letters, all of them very entertaining.

Friday, May 9th.

We this morning were most elegantly regaled with a Breakfast at Spring Gardens, with all the other Cornish Gentlemen and Ladies now in Town, excepting Mr. Gregor who is a little out of Order, and Mr. Sam Thomas who absented himself we know not why, at the polite Invitation and Expence of Dr. Stackhouse. We all assembled in the Pump-Room about a Quarter before Ten, and were ferried cross the Avon from Orange Grove. Spring Gardens lie along the opposite side of the River. The Passage Boat would hold thirty People, covered over the Head and Sides, a shelter against every thing which might incommode. The Gardens are a most delightful Spot, laid out in Gravel and Grass Walks, some strait, others serpentine, with a fine Canal in one place, and a fine Pond in another, with the greatest Variety of Shrubs, Trees, and other Vegetables that the most curious could desire. In these Gardens is a large handsome Building, wherein is a Breakfast Room capacious enough to hold many Sets of Company, having six windows in the side, (so you see it must be long) and proportionably wide. There were three Companies there this morning; seventeen in Dr. Stackhouse's; about ten in another; and a noble Lord, I can't tell his Title, sat solus. It was said by a wise man of antiquity, that he was "never less alone than when alone:" this must justifie my calling his single Lordship a third Company. But after all, I am afraid I must cry *"Peccavi,"* in supposing his Lordship to be so contemplatively disposed: and I do not know, but I should ask Pardon of the whole Order, in comparing any of them, without a thorough Acquaintance with him, to a wise man of antiquity. When we entered the Room, the Tables were spread with singular Neatness. Upon a Cloth white as Snow were ranged Coffee Cups, Tea Dishes of different sizes, Chocolate Cups, Tea Pots, and every Thing belonging to the Equipage of the Tea Table, with French Rolls, Pots of Butter, all in decent order, and interspersed with sweet Briar, which had a pretty Effect both on the Sight and Smell. At the Word of Command were set on the Table Chocolate, Coffee, Tea, Hot Rolls buttered, buttered hot cakes. What should hinder one from making a good Breakfast? Yet I was so moderate, and had such a philosophical command of my appetite, that in the midst of all this Plenty, I eat but one Roll and one Cake, and drank but one cup of Chocolate, two of Coffee, and two of Tea. From filling we proceed to Emptying. (Filling and Emptying in Jacky's Grammar come under the same Rule.) Every one's Eyes in search of a Fro. As Need required, we found Two. Over the Door of one was written "for the Ladies only;" over that of the other, "For the

William Pitt the elder (1708–1778). Engraved portrait by R. Houston after a painting by William Hoare.

Gentlemen only." Against the Wall, within the Gentlemen's was written with a Pencil, "Whosoever comes into the Place, is desired to be cleanly, to let down the Lid, and shut the Door." I hope, now Mary and Dolly will be satisfied. Whatever relates to the Ladies Fro, must be kept an inviolable Secret. – Being now a little lightened we walk about the Gardens; and enjoy the enchanting Scene. Nor did we land the Bath-side till near Twelve. A Proposal was then made to go see a curious Shrubbery in King's Mead Street, but a little Sprinkling of Rain made us all take Refuge in the Pump-Room. There between one and two we saw a Cedar, tall as the Cedars of Lebanon, which made full amends for the Loss of the Sight of the Shrubbery. This tall Cedar was the Great Commoner, Mr. Pit,[32] whom we saw distinctly, and viewed him cap-a-pe. He is exactly like his Prints, only his Prints are much younger; for he has marks of age in his whole Countenance. For my Part, I was extremely glad to see *him,* whose Fame so loudly resounds throughout Europe, Asia, Africa, and America. I had seen him once before, viz: this morning between Eight and Nine, when the Pump-Room was crouded with Company expecting him. As soon as he entred the Room, the Music stopt the Tune then playing, and struck up "Britons, strike home." His Stay in the Room was short: in the morning he exchanged a few words with a Lady, and at Noon he talked two or three minutes with the Sardinian Envoy. Lord Edgcumbe was again at the Pump-Room this morning, after a week's absence, and desired me if I wrote to Penryn to present his compliments to Mr. Heame.

My dear Peggy, you will be careful to make our Obeisance to Mrs. Hearle's, and Mr. Heame's two families, and to all such others, as they come in your Way, as you think will take it kind. To you yourselves, and the Servants, our Blessing and Love, as respectively due. Aurelia's Duty to Mrs. White. May God keep you, and all our Gluvias, Penryn, and Budock friends under his watchful Protection! I am, dear Peggy, and all my dear children,

Your ever affectionate Father,
JOHN PENROSE.

Bath, Saturday, May 10th. 1766.

My dear Peggy, and the rest of my dear Children,

All Grace and Peace be with you! – As I find my Diary is

---

32  William Pitt (1708–1788) suffered from gout all his adult life, and had already
    made a visit to Bath in 1765 – He was to be made Lord Chatham in July 1766.

entertaining to you and our Friends at Penryn, I proceed as usual to particularize our Bath Adventures. The first Thing to be mentioned is an Occurrence of yesterday, which was too late to be inserted in yesterday's Letter, and That is, we saw a Funeral Procession pass before our Window, a Hearse preceded by men carrying Streamers, and followed by two mourning Coaches. Fanny had never seen a mourning Coach before, That is one remarkable Thing; another is, that no Mob attended the Procession, no not so much as one rude Boy, whereas such a Scene at Penryn would have alarmed the whole Town; and whereas at Penryn, on such an Occasion, it would have been known e're this to every Body, who was buried, what his family, what his Faults, etc. a third thing remarkable, is, that we cannot learn by much Inquiry, who was buried, tho' buried in the Abbey, not above two Stone's cast off. – Let me now mention another Thing which slipt my memory this day se'nnight, which is, that the best Pieces of the great Ox, mentioned in my former Letters, sold for ten pence a Pound: the Tongue 10s.6d.

To-day having a slight cold, attended with a little Hoarseness, I lay abed till Eleven o'clock: as I was getting up, Mr. Heard came in, and Mrs. Carlyon, Mrs. Mundy, and their two Daughters; unseasonably enough, for it hindred all of us from going to Church; tho', I believe, I should not have gone, had they not come in. These, Mr. Robinson and Mrs. Robinson, and lastly Dr. Grant, never left us one moment to ourselves till Dinner was ready. I made an Apology for going to the Pump-Room, and returned immediately. All here is Hurry, Hurry. Yet we had a quiet Afternoon, which is a great Rarity: and after Prayers, we made a Tea Visit to Mr. and Mrs. Robinson, who will set out for Helston next Monday. He is greatly recovered, and I wish he may take care of himself. We stayed with them till near Nine, a long Visit for this Place; and immediately on our coming Home, I gladly embraced the Opportunity of writing to you.

It was my full Design, if the Weather proved dry and warm, and my Strength would permit, to copy those Inscriptions on the Monuments in the Abby, which relate to Devonshire and Cornish Families. But Mr. Heard says, he will save me this Trouble. For he has a copy in London of all the Inscriptions in the Abbey, and has promised to send me a copy of those I intended to take. Which Copy shall be Peggy's Property, and serve as a Supplement to our Bath Memoirs.

### Sunday, May 11th.

My cold still continues, tho' you will see it is but a slight one, by

my assisting with the Bread this morning at the Administration of the
Sacrament, and, what is more, preaching this afternoon at the Abbey.
I held out very well, considering that Preaching is a Thing new to me,
considering too my cold, and weak Feet. I expected my Voice to fail,
but my Hoarseness rather abated as I went on: my Ancles I found most
affected. But all is very well. My Text was Luke XXIV. 50,51. The
morning Preacher is called Pote, Chaplain to Lord Camden, son to one
Pote a famous Stationer at Eton: His Text, Matt. XXIV. 44. a very
good Discourse on the Nature and Necessity of Watchfulness,
particularly enforced from the Consideration of the Uncertainty of our
Lord's Coming, and a Word or two towards the Conclusion concerning
the Manner of his Appearance, viz. in like manner as the Apostles saw
him ascend into Heaven, in order to adapt it to the present Season. – I
took my first Glass in Bed, the other three in the Pump-Room, where
after Evening-Prayer I saw Mr. Morshead and his Son, whom the
Father is going to place at Oriel College in Oxford, a College at this
Time of great Repute. I should not have known Mr. Morshead, if he
had not first spoke to me: so I thanked him for the Honour done me in
taking notice of me. I am grown vastly polite; why, we are all so here;
but I fear I shall lose all my Politeness again by the time I cross the
Tamar. – From the Pump-Room I went to our Lodgings, and staid
while your Mamma and Sister went to see Mrs. Mundy, Carlyon, etc.
and wish them a good Journey, the former to London for which they
set out to-morrow, the latter to Cornwall. These go in Company with
Mr. and Mrs. Robinson, whom we all three went to this Evening to
wish them a prosperous Journey, and happy sight of their Friends in
the West. They have the Rat-Powder for Mr. Coode. In our Way to
Mr. Robinson's we paid a Tea-visit to Major Tucker and his Lady. She
and their Neice, one Miss Eliot, were very finely dressed, for
Simpson's Rooms. They never go to Church, nor a multitude besides
them, for Fear of catching Cold; but between five and six o'clock they
adorn themselves as richly as they can, and away to the Public Room.
We came by the End of the Parade, as we came from Mr. Robinson's;
and it is incredible what a crowd of People are taking their Pleasure
there this Sunday Evening. – Sir John Glanvil was at the Pump-Room
with Mr. Morshead, but I did not know him. – Mr. Robinson desires
his Name may be added to the List of Clergymen, who would assist in
my absence if wanted. – As you do not say a Word about it, I don't
know whether the Friendly Society are to have a Sermon or not the
Tuesday in Whitsun-week. But as I spoke to Mr. Harris about it, he
must have Notice, whether there be a Sermon or no Sermon. –

### Monday, May 12th.

I am tolerably well recovered from my Weariness yesterday, and had good Spirits given me by your most agreeable Pacquet received this morning. I received also a most obliging Letter from Yendacot; in which Mr. Pierce expresses great Joy at my bettering, "and flatters himself that he shall see us return all in high Spirits, not muffled up as I was like an old Friar. Mr. Tom Pierce is confined to his Bed in the Gout." A very kind Letter from Mrs. Fleetwood "invites us to Dawlish in our Return, and desires we will not think of staying so little a while as one Night: assuring me and my good Company of a sincere Welcome. She complains, as usual of an ill State of Health, but hopes she shall grow better as the Weather comes warmer. Miss Weston is well, and in good Spirits, and hath entred into Business, following the example of her Cousin Grant, with a Prospect of good Success, she giving her mind to it, and being very diligent. Mrs. Fleetwood concluding with her best Wishes for my Recovery, and our good Journey to Dawlish."

Pray give my best Compliments to Doctor Coode, and thank him most heartily for his Intelligence concerning Mess. Peter and Harris. I hope, their differences will not affect the Service of my Churches. I am confident, if Mr. Harris (before my Return) should be out of Employ, he will be very ready to assist me, where his assistance can be of most Service: and Mr. Walmesley, residing at Mawnan, will be as ready to supply Budock then, as Mabe now. All this is Selfishness. Yet I am truly sorry any difficulty should arise to discompose my good Neighbours. I ought to respect them all, having ever found them well disposed to serve me in Time of Need. We are heartily sorry, the Doctor's Arm continues weak: and are sensible, he writes with Difficulty, which doubles the Obligation he has laid us under by his writing, as it is no slight Obligation laid on us that he wrote at all. The Colonel and Mrs. Sewell intend coming to Bath next Wednesday. They have a great Respect for the Doctor, and all the family. We sent them your and the Coodes Compliments this day by John.

It is very kind of Mrs. Coode to continue her Correspondence, tho' her Mamma, doing all she possibly can, cannot keep it up on her side. It is kind to take the Will for the Deed; and I will be responsible for it, the Will is not wanting. Your Mamma's Cold is gone, but her Knee is just as it was. I reckon, it was a great Satisfaction to you all, to have an Account from Mr. Grylls who had lateley seen me, and again from Mr. Vivian to Mr. Conon, that I was pretty well. Indeed I am so, and various Causes may operate towards it: the Benefit from the Bath

Water is chiefly to be expected hereafter. We hope Mrs. Coode's Cold
hath left her, as she calls it a slight one: but, poor little dear Molly! it
is grievous to hear of a Cough tearing her dear little Sides. As to her
Briskness at Intervals, it is no more than we might expect from her
Sweetness of Temper. We hope our next Advice from Cornwall will
give us the welcome News of her being quite free of her Cough, and
that Mrs. Coode and all that Family enjoy perfect Health. It was very
obliging in Mr. Michel to visit you in our Absence: It was very kind in
Mr. Coode to invite him to Dinner. His Refusing the generous
Invitations to a feast of fat things, in order to fast with my
Rat-starving Peggy, was a singular Proof that the Compliment in
visiting Vicarage was only meant to Vicarage Family. You did well in
sending Mrs. Hugo's Letter by him, and I suppose you told him of my
Request to you to write him.

Charles's Letter made us all laugh several Times. He is a very
diverting correspondent, and we shall always be very glad to hear from
him. We are obliged to him for writing so many Articles of News.
That Particular of his being "exceeding good indeed," is not reckoned
by us as a Piece of News; because we apprehend, he has been so ever
since we came away, and we don't question but he will always
continue so to be, especially as he goes on learning the Collects.

Jacky's Willingness to write me, and that in Latin and Greek,
without being ordered so to do, shews a Love of Learning, which it is
very happy when young minds are endowed with. I have returned it to
him, (that he may see, wherein he was mistaken,) with a few
Emendations. Let him not be discouraged: for I assure him, it hath
given me no small Pleasure.

As you, my honest Peg, had an Engagement on your hand, you
acted with your usual Prudence, in beginning your Letter the Tuesday:
had you delayed writing, as some giddy Girls of your Age probably
would, you would have been hurried beyond all Patience, and we
should have lost a Treasure of inestimable Value, for such we one and
all esteem your Favours to be. Our Account of our Adventures being so
agreeable to you all, encourages us to proceed as formerly. Mr.
Robinson, etc. went off To-day, as I told you they designed. We shall
have more Time probably on that Account, but the Time of our going
away, and turning our faces homeward, seems now to be pretty well
fixed; and the nearer that draws, the more Business will it bring with
it. After Morning Prayers we all took a Walk to Mr. Haviland's. He
lives (near Letter Z) in Cross-Bath-Lane. He being abroad, we went
through West-Gate (2), and had a Sight of the Colonel's Bath-

Lodgings. Mrs. Betty[33] was there, getting them prepared for her Master's coming. They are in the Corner-House in King's Mead Square, next King's Mead Street. There we begged three or four Pens, which makes my Writing something more legible, tho' not much. To avoid passing through Avon-Street, a Street of ill Fame, we went through an Inn at the South-West corner of the Square into King's Mead, then down to the River, along the Key to the Bridge. You know our Way home from thence. Don't you think, I took a fine Walk, I that was grunting so about aching Feet? Sweating pretty much, I took a Glass of Wine, and I hope received no Detriment. While we are at Dinner, in comes Mr. Haviland. We consulted him about my Case; told him, I shall have been here six weeks next Tuesday; and asked Leave to go Home. He advised, that as I was out, so far from Home, and found Benefit by the Waters, so much Benefit as he never saw a like Instance, we should stay a fortnight longer. So I have been advised by many others; but his Advice has Weight with me. Dr. Coode will tell you, it ought to have. So we are thinking to take Place in the Exeter Stage-Coach for this Day three weeks, June 2. If Mary is not packed up, and sent away by this Time, (I hope, you have made sufficient air-holes in the Box, she is put up in) she had best not think of coming. You may depend on it, we will have the Box from the Carrier as soon as ever it comes; and Sally shall enquire for it at the Inn next Wednesday, the Day the Carrier comes in. As Jacky will be so kind, as to meet Mary and us at Exeter, your Mamma thinks it best for his Hair to be cut short. All the Boys here have it short. And that he may not catch Cold, if it can be helped, we would have it cut immediately on your Receipt of this, not so short as it should be; and an handkerchief put about his Neck, and then cut again as soon as he is sure of the Time of setting out to meet us. Whatever is done by Jacky's Hair, the same may be done by Charles's. What I am now going to write, I write with much concern. Oh, how my hand shakes, my Pen trembles! Fanny says, it will cost ten pounds to fit out Mary, who is a gay young Lady, and very dressy, so as to make a decent appearance here; and advises us, as soon as the Box comes, not to open it, but to alter the Direction, and send it back again. There is great Sagacity in this Scheme of Fanny's and if Mary has so great a Regard to the Good of the Family, as you, my honest Peg, she will be horsed back again rejoicing. However, we will reconsider this Scheme between this and Wednesday. − To return to your Letter. I am glad, the Map amuses you: If the Peaches be so thick, and so large, it is high Time to thin them, that the Fruit to be left on the Trees may have the more

33  Presumably another of the Colonel's servants.

Nourishment. We like your management, as Mother of a Family.
You'll be married years the sooner for being so good a Housewife. You
are equal to the gravest Matrons. I remember Mr. Evans's preaching
the Sermon you mention, in Mrs. Busvine's Time. Mrs. Busvine took
it to herself, as Mr. Paynter and the Methodists may now: but I have a
Reason, that, when the Sermon was composed, the pious Author had
neither of them in his Eye. Your Mamma could scarce refrain from
Tears of Joy, at reading the Regard expressed in your Letter for a
religious Observance of the Lord's Day. May that reverent Regard for
the Sabbath encrease more and more! Lord Chief Justice Hale, and
many pious Tradesmen, have left their Testimony on Record, that the
more religiously Sunday was observed, the more prosperous were their
Affairs in the rest of the Week. Godliness has the Promise of the Life
that now is: but it's having the Promise of the Life, which is to come,
is the strongest Motive, that can be, to it's Express is God's Command
to hallow the Sabbath. – We are sorry for Mademoiselle's Indisposition. If you can do any thing to comfort her, I know you will do it. –
I'll see to get a couple of Franks for you, which will be enough for you
during our Stay here: and a couple more, directed to me at Exeter. – I
have now answered such Parts of Your Letter, as required an Answer,
except one or two things which my last Letter obviates; and as for the
other Parts of it, they are such as we would have you write, and are
agreeable to us to read, but to take Notice of them in particular would
be tedious, rather than amusing.

Mary's Letters to her Mamma and Sister are very good ones. If she
had not been sent away, I would have desired you to afford her a
Fairing extraordinary. I know, you will be kind enough to keep a
Taste for us all against we come home. And we shall get home all
together, unless Fanny's Scheme about sending her back unpackt
should take place: then she will be come before us: but I think we shall
not be so hard-hearted as to do it. – All that we yet know, concerning
the new Lodgers in Mr. Snow's Apartments, is, that their Name is
Backhouse, and that they live in Bedfordshire.– We are sorry, Mary
has had a Cold; but hope it is removed: and are also sorry for Mrs.
Rawling. – Betty must be the more careful of the little cat; as I
apprehend the House is free from Mice and such like Vermin, and the
Cat can have no meat but what is hand-delivered to it. – As we are
pretty well resolved about the Time of setting out, George had best
give our Compliments to Mr. Hearle and Dr. Coode, and put them in
mind of the Horses we are promised by them, Nacker for Jacky, and
Miss Hearle's for George, to meet us at Exeter, and help us home. – I
suppose, Charles was proud enough of being Mademoiselle's Usher.

He now experiences the Benefit of being able to read; and will be more diligent in his Learning. – I don't know, whether it may be worth while for Mary to print Fanny's Letters, because they are written hastily: but many a Joke at first, becomes Earnest at last, and I don't know but Mary herself may one day turn Authoress. I observe, though, a little Slut, how she fishes for Praise. "Find what fault you please, and I'll try to mend." To be sure, she expected a Compliment, like Sr. Samuel Garth's, "Thou hast no Fault, or I no Fault can spy: Thou art all Beauty, or all Blindness I." But I'll humble her Pride; and if I can find no other Fault, I'll rip up her Spelling: I'll rather play a small Game, than stand out. Then I am sure, if Impudence be a Fault, and what can be a greater in a Girl of her Age? she hath said enough of "a little man and a little woman," (I know who she means) to draw a whole House upon her Back; and if once they come there, she'll find it hard work to claw them off; they'll stick like a Bur. "Why, how now, sawcy Jade?" a song for you or rather for her. – I have taken some Notice of all your Letters, except Dolly's. Her's is lost in carriage. I hope, she has kept a copy; and that when she writes next, she will give also the contents of the Letter which is lost. Give our Blessing and Love to all your Brothers and Sisters, and Service to all friends, among whom we rank in the first Place Dr. Coode, and (whom we presume you will see to-morrow) Mr. Hocker. You will all be so glad to see him, that you need not be told to take care of him. We take it for granted, he will give you as much as he can of his Company, and that Jacky and He will be Bed-fellows. –

Poor Madamoiselle's Ilness owing to too much Pye-crust eaten! For the future you must not make it so rich. Go to surfeit Folks! Was it not partly owing to Want of Vicarage Ale? That has an Effect upon others, besides Madamoiselle. Mamma stints herself to a Penn'orth a Night, hath none at Noon; and, in sober Sadness, a Penn'orth is scarce the third Part of a Pint. I drink two Glasses of Wine after Dinner, two more (sometimes three) after supper; good Table-Beer with my Victuals; three dishes of Tea for Breakfast, ditto in the Afternoon; and four Glasses of Water, by order of my Apothecary, daily: and now you have a full and true Account of my Drinking. As for Eating, I do really play a good Knife and Fork, and I do not why I should turn my Back to any man. I will not even yield to Sally. – and that's a bold Word. If I knock under to any one, it shall be to my Clark of Budock: he is eminent in his Way, and next to *"Tempus, edax rerum;"* Time, the Devourer of all things. –

Inclosed I have transmitted to you a few Lines of high Compliment from Bladud, King of the Britons, before Christ 863 years, to Mr.

William Pit, the Great Commoner now at Bath. This Bladud is said to
have been the Discoverer of the mineral Waters at Bath, and of their
medicinal Virtues. You see it written in the old black English Print,
because it comes from a Prince of great Antiquity. I would have you
preserve it, as a curiosity: yet for fear of an Accident, I'll give you a
copy.

Kynge Bladyd to W – P – sendethe greetynge.
Much wond'rous Goode dothe Baia's founte dispense.
More wond'rous farre dothe flowe Thyne eloquence;
My Springes may aide some palsyed Lymbe to free:
Thy myghtier cure – must not comparede be:
Britannia's Self restor'd – to Libertie. –

Ye Kyndrede Streams, O! keepe your wontede course:
Let Ages prove your uncorruptede Source.
May humble Crutche bedecke poore Bladyd's Shryne:
Britannia's Hearte be offerede uppe at Thyne.

As the Author of these Lines is unknown, who can say but they
come from King Bladud, whose Name they bear? All can be said, is,
that a great Number of Copies, printed as you see, were brought to the
Gentleman that serves the Water at the Pump-Room, with a Desire
that he would distribute them gratis to Gentlemen and Ladies. By this
means, I had one. –

When you give our Compliments to Mrs. Hearle and the Ladies, I
desire you to tell Mrs. Hearle, (what you from Home tell me,) that so
many People have asked after her, as are too many to name: and say,
that we are as much obliged to her for her very kind offer of
recommending us to Mr. Ramsay, in case of our going to London, as if
we had actually been recommended by her, and received from him the
highest Civilities.

As Mary seems delighted with the Account of Spring-Gardens, you
may tell her, that by Desire of many Ladies and Gentlemen, there is
public Breakfasting and Music there every Monday and Thursday
during the Season. It begun to-day. Every Person pays eighteen pence
a Breakfast; and the Music continues playing till Two o'clock, for such
as chuse to dance.

### Tuesday, May 13.

If I had not promised to communicate to you all our Adventures,
the following one hath something so terrible in it, that I should have
suppressed it. But out it shall come, and it shall be faithfully related. I
consider, you will receive my Letter in the Morning; so you will have

the whole Day to recover from your Fright. Oh, had the Post not come in till Evening, how you would cuddle in together round the Fire! Last Night then, after I had dropt my Pen, who should come in but my worthy Friend Major Tucker? The Major is full of Stories, and in the Course of his Narrations he fell upon a wonderful Tale relating to Apparitions; then he went on to another, and so from Tale to Tale, till it was no Wonder had our Imaginations formed ever so many frightful Images, and we had all night dreamt of Spirits and Hobgoblins. Yet do not think, the Tale, I am about to tell, is a Work of Fancy, but a serious Truth, plainly set forth without the least Aggravation. Listen now with all your Attention. Last Night, about eleven o'clock, a solemn Hour, we heard, as we lay in Bed, a Noise very uncommon, unlike any Noise we had heard before, which greatly alarmed us. It seemed, as if some-body was knocking was [with] violence upon our Parlour Floor. I do not much mind Spirits; as they come, they may go. But your Mamma was resolved to know the Out of it, so she goes out of Bed, opens the Door leading to the Parlour; and in the middle of the Parlour (it was no illusion, I am persuaded now) she saw a Person, of a very tall erect figure, all in white, as if it were a Woman in her shift. Fanny heard the same Noise, and was alarmed as her Mamma was, (It is in the Power of Spirits to affect different Persons, in the same manner, at the same Instant) and came out of her Bed, (amazing this courage in timorous Fanny!) and saw a Person, all in white, exactly such as your Mamma describes, standing in the Parlour. Neither of them saw more than one: yet, strange! the Spectre seemed to be to them in different parts of the Room; Fanny says, It was here, Mamma says It was there; in all other Points they agree. Well, they being two of them had the courage to speak, your Mamma spoke, and had an Answer in a distinct Voice; Fanny spoke, and was distinctly answered too. When they knew the Mood of the Apparition, they went each of them, more composed than one would expect, to her Chamber, and the Apparition disappeared. One Thing here was vastly remarkable, It seemed to Fanny to go into our Room, to your Mamma to go into Fanny's. However we heard no more of it. I have no Commission from them to tell the Secrets they were let into; but your Mamma trembled all the night afterwards. Tho' I am not myself very anxious about Spirits, yet I ought to have some concern for my dear companions, who would not by choice live in an haunted House. So this morning away trudged Fanny and I to the Lamb Inn in Staul Street, a little below Abbey Lane, the other side of the Way, where the Exeter Machine puts up, and took Places for Monday the second of June. I warrant, Mary thinks of Tinsel and Mrs. Abigail: "Where are you going, Sir? says I. To Town, Child, says he. For to tell you truly, child, says he, I don't care to live in the same House with the Devil, says he." Dear Papa, how can you quote a Passage from a Comedy, after so tragical a Circumstance; an ungodly Play-book, after so serious an Affair? Why, I'll tell you, my dear Peg; the whole Mystery is now unriddled. Parson Backhouse and his Wife had been at the Play, and when he came home rapped very loud against the Floor of the Entry with his Cane. Fanny hearing the Raps, fancied them to be made in our Room; that your Mamma was out of Order, and I was not able rise to ring the Bell, which is in her Room, the String of it in ours: Your Mamma fancied the Rapping to be in Fanny's Room, and was confirmed in it, when she heard Fanny's Door open. So the double Spectre proves at last to be no other than their two selves: and this accounts very well, for it's seeming to be here to one, and there to another, and making it's Exit at one time at different Doors. I am glad I know the Truth of the Matter: that this wonderful Scene was only a Farce, after Parson Backhouse's Play. Being now quite composed, I come to Business.

Your Mamma would have you get some Samphire pickled, not a great deal. May is the Time for pickling it. – We have read the *New Bath Guide*,[34] a Series of Poetical Epistles, describing the Manners and Humours of the People. Some of it is very well, but upon the whole scarce worth the Price it is sold at, five shillings. But it is the Fashion to read it: and, who would be out of the Fashion? – We have had Thunder to-day. I hope, it will clear the Air, and occasion a little settled Fair-Weather. Almost every Day, since we have been here, has had more or less of Rain. – I was desired my Mr. Grigg, Curate at St. John's (or Cross-Bath) Chapel, to preach for him next Sunday morning, whilst he officiated at Bath-wicke, a little country Church of his own. Which I promised to do. But Mr. Taylor, of the Abbey Church, presses me to preach at the Abbey next Sunday morning, and assist at the Sacrament: and Mr. Grigg will excuse me till Trinity Sunday. – Last Night I sent a Ticket to Lord Edgcumbe for two more Franks directed to me at Bath, three to me at Exon, and one to Mr. Robinson, for whom I have two Letters, which came by the Post after he went away: and this Day His Lordship was so kind as to send them me, according to my desire. – I could not go to Church this Evening, because it rained. But the Rain did not prevent our going a visiting. Our Visit was not far off, under the same Roof, to Dr. and Mrs.

---

34   Christopher Anstey's satirical poem was, from the very moment it was published, a huge success.

Grant. You know, it has been usual with us, when we go a visiting, to have Company come to see us; and so it happened now. We had but just done Tea, (which by the way is made as soon as ever your Visiters come in,) when Mr. Loscombe of Bristol, Mrs. Richard's Father, very obligingly came to us at Dr. Grant's, and gave us a kind Invitation to Bristol, with offer of a Bed; telling us, that he soon expects Mr. & Mrs. Crowgey, and Miss Carthew who has been much out of Order. I desire you will some how or other give our Compliments to Mr. Richards, and tell him how sensible we are of Mr. Loscombe's Civility, and that we fully intend to wait on Mrs. Richards and Him before we leave this Neighbourhood. Soon after him, in came Major Tucker, who (according to Custom) did not go from our Lodgings (for he came hither with us from our Visit) till nine o'clock. It is now high Time to conclude this Day's Task: so may you all, and we, lay us down, and take our Rest, bearing it on our Minds, that it is the Lord only which maketh us dwell in Safety!

### Wednesday, May 14th.

What lies will People tell! Why, some will have it, that your Mamma and Fanny saw no Spirit; that it was too dark, to discern anything; not considering, that Spirits are as timorous, as mortals, and never walk abroad without a Light. But let them say, what they will, we all know now the Truth of the case, and need not disturb ourselves about it.

Dear Peg, I have now a Case of Importance to consult you about, which will make you rouse up all your Skill and Casuistry in culinary and domestic affairs to answer. Query then, suppose you, my careful Housewife, had a Cook-maid; a married woman, or a widow, with a family; and she, out of Love to her children, and understanding her Business, should cut off a little raw Meat sometimes from a Joint to be roasted, provided it was not wasted, and the remaining Part would roast the better; or suppose, you had a Maid-servant, who had a poor Mother; and she, out of filial Love and Duty, should cut off a slice or two of cold victuals, provided she took care it should not be thrown away, but fairly eaten; and suppose, it was the Custom of the Place to do so, and Custom had so reconciled them to these Practices, that it became matter of conscience, and a thing of ill Fame, not to cheat and plunder, if you can: what would you say, or do, in this case? I am for being light-hearted as may be, and apologize thus for them:

It signifies nothing to make any Pother;
For one hath a Daughter, and one hath a Mother,
And they both deal by us, as they would by a Brother.

Let not this my Judgment prejudice yours: but give us your sage Opinion.

Last evening Dr. Stackhouse and the Ladies would fain have gone to Lady Huntingdon's Chapel; but the Preacher decampt last Monday, and no Successor yet come. – This morning, a Stranger broke Fast with us, the Revd. Mr. Noah Neel Newcome, one Mr. Michell knows well, an old Acquaintance of your Mamma's; at least she was acquainted with him, if he was not with her; one that she has hardly seen before, since she rocked him in the Cradle; a Son to Dr. Newcome, late Dean of Gloucester. He has two Livings in Wales, but his Health will not permit him to reside on either; so he dwells at Bristol. He has given us an Invitation to Bristol, and proposes to go thither with us whenever we go, which we propose to do, weather favouring, some time in the Beginning of next week. He had heard with Grief of Heart, that Mr. Michell is a Methodist; but I wiped off that Aspersion from his character, and satisfied him of the contrary. Breakfast ended, and our Guest gone, Your Mamma paid Mrs. Grant's Bill: (May 7th we dined at Lincomb.)

May 8th Boiling Mutton, 4d – crag-end of the Neck, the whole Neck cost 1s.11d. This was the Day I dined at Sr. Booth's.

May 9th. Boiling Salmon, 4d. – one pound and half, price 9d. Shrimp sauce, 2d.

May 10th. Roasting Mutton. 4d. – the remainder of the Neck.

May 11th Roasting Veal, 4d. – Part of a Loin, which cost 3s.4d.$\frac{1}{2}$ – Boiling Asparagus, 3d. Price 8d.

May 12th. Roasting Veal – 4d. $\left.\right\}$Remainder of the Loin
May 13th. Roasting Veal – 4d.

One Week's Lodging – £1. 5. 0.

Besides what is here mentioned, we had a Lobster, 8d. and Potatos often, Noon and Night, but these we boil or roast ourselves; and one Night, Broth from a Bone of Mutton, our own cookery. You will not think us extravagant, when I tell you, that a single Tart (where Mrs. Sewell dined) cost fifteen shillings; and as much Turtle, as would barely afford a Taste to nine Persons, cost thirty. The Colonel and Mrs. Sewell came to Bath this Morning. After Prayers we went to congratulate them on their Arrival: the Col. was walked out, but his Lady was at Home, looking very well. – Having mentioned the Dearness of victuals, I must mention the cheapness of some sort of Physic: and I am credibly informed, that your Mamma bought senna enough for a Penny to serve her and Fanny six or seven Times. – No Laughing.

But yes, you may laugh, if you will; not at what is passed, but at what follows. Here is one Miss – what's her Name? No great Matter for the Name of one, who is ashamed to shew her Face. Oh, now I know, Miss Buncomb. This Lady, when an Infant, was very pretty, but Mamma thought Art preferable to Nature, and painted her even in those first Years. As she grew up, still she was painted, painted, painted; and for some years past, hath had her Face enamelled. Twice in a year her face wants to be new done, and she humbly submits to be six weeks in every half year laid before the fire, and dawbed, and plaistered, and varnished, that for twenty weeks to come, she may look like a London Doll. Her cheeks are so stiff, she cannot laugh; or if she could, she would stifle every Emotion of Joy, rather then crack the Enamel of her Face; and for the like Reason she doth but dare open her Eyes. Oh pretty creature! take all this Care of herself, and yet grow old without ever being married! The Fool did not consider, that the Gentlemen would like her much better in *puris naturalibus*, in her natural state, than if she were plaistered as thick as Thisbe's Wall. What I have written, is true; Mrs. Sewell, who knows her, my author. [informant] – Mr. Sewell has sent hither a *Delphin Horace,* which through mistake he carried away with him from Penryn, desiring me to restore it to Mr. Coode it's Owner. Now this Book weighs two or three pounds, and will cost two–pence per lb. carriage. Nevertheless, I'll bring home the Book; and if he'll pay me my Expences, he shall have it, otherwise I'll give it to Jacky to keep in Pledge. Sharp's the Word.

I read Prayers at the Abbey both Parts of this Day, and after Evening Service baptised a Child. The Baptismal Font is [in] a side Isle, quite removed from the Place where Prayers are read; so that the office of Baptism is never read in the Public Congregation. The Godfathers and Godmothers were all Mutes.

Tell Mrs. Neville, that we are all very much hers; and that this Evening I saw her old Friend, the great Pulpit Orator, Dr. Ashton: he was in a Chair, brought to the Pump-Room for his Water. He looks old, but venerable.

Fanny will not tell me, which way she got up this morning: but I guess by Dr. Stackhouse's giving her a Ticket for the Public Breakfast at Spring Gardens to morrow. She will go with his Ladies: and if Mary comes To-night she shall go to [too]. It draws now towards six, and I will send Sally directly to enquire of the carrier, whether she be come.

Mr. Heard hath been here, and complimented me with a Schedule from the Heralds Office,[35] containing the Genealogical Table of the

35  A copy of the Heralds' Visitation of Cornwall, made in 1620.

Penrose Family, nine Generations before 1620. The six first in the Table are Bernard P- John P- John P- Geoffrey P- John P- Richard P- all of Methela (Metheley) in Cornwall. The next in Order are John P- of Penrose, Bernard P- of Penrose Metheley, Thomas Penrose, ditto, who was alive in 1620, and John P- aged 9, grandson of the said Th. P (his father John being dead 1617.) I think this Genealogy is for the Penrose and Kestle Families. But it is evident hence, that Methleigh and Penrose have been united before now, and that it is a natural Union. I shall preserve this Schedule with all care.

I would not have you think, that, because so many of our West-Country Acquaintance are gone, we are forlorn; we have as many Acquaintance now, as ever.

One Sett goeth, and another cometh:
One Groupe unto another still succeeds,
And the last Groupe as num'rous as the former.
Mrs. Sewell says, that John told her, he believed Mr. and Mrs. Penrose had a deal of Company: and John had great Reason to say as he did.

Well, my dear Peg, Sally has been to the Packhorse in Walcot Street where the Western Carrier quarters, to enquire for the Box Mary was to come in, but there is nothing for us: So now we conclude, the Scheme did not take Effect.

Jacky's last Letter to me, and two Franks directed to me at Bath, are sent inclosed in a Cover, under a Frank, to Mr. Robinson of Helston, whom I have desired to transmit them to you the first opportunity. I was afraid, had I sent them, as I designed, in the same Cover with this Letter, they would have made it exceed two Ounces.

To you, and all your Brothers and Sisters, and all friends at Falmouth, Penryn, etc. Our Blessing, Love and Service, as severally due, must conclude this long, too long, Epistle, from

Your most affectionate Father,
JOHN PENROSE.


Bath, Thursday, May 15th, 1766.

My dear Peggy,

And all the rest of my dear Children, were I corresponding with any one less dear to me, or to whom I am less dear, I should not wonder to hear it said, after so many Pages sent from Bath, What will this Babler say? However, what I am now going to write you, will not be accounted Babbling, because they are very pretty Verses, except the vain Swearing in the last Stanza: and because they relate to a Western Beauty, a Cornish Beauty, some say Miss Kitty Stackhouse.

### Advice to Bath.

Listen, Bath, and the Voice of an Oracle hear,
Nor fancy the Poet in Jest:
Alarm'd for all Nature, I bid thee beware
Of a fair One that flames in the West.

From her cheek tho' pale Sickness has rifled the Rose,
And robb'd of it's Lightning her Eye;
Lo, with Graces sufficient the Virgin still glows,
A Legion of Nymphs to supply.

To recall those lost charms, to thy Fountain she wings,
But forbid her to taste it, or lave:
For, Woe to the World, shouldst thou grant her thy Springs,
And Health be the Fruit of thy Wave.

Fulfill'd would the Prophesy rise, (by my Soul)
By which poor Mankind must expire,
Which declares that the Globe shall be burnt like a Scroll,
That an Angel shall set it on Fire.

Who wrote these Lines I cannot tell you, only that it is a Cornishman, who composed them at Plymouth, when the young Lady, thus celebrated, was there taking Advice of Dr. Huxham.

This Morning I took half a Post-Chaise with Mr. Thomas of Tregolls near Truro, and went an Airing three or four miles on Lansdown in the Oxford Road. We went so far as the Monument erected to the Memory of Sir Bevil Granville, who was killed in that Spot in the Time of the Great Rebellion, in K. Charles 1st Reign. The Inscription on it is effaced; but what it was formerly is preserved in a little sixpenny Book, called *The Bath Guide*, wherein in [*sic*] is a fuller Account of those Places I have seen, than I have Time to write you. This little Book we shall bring home with us, and it will hereafter afford Entertainment both to us and you. When I went away on this Airing, your Sister was regaling herself at Spring Gardens. Ah poor Mamma! how cruel it was to leave her by herself! Why, my dears, it is impossible here to be long by yourself. The Colonel took care to prevent her pining away in Solitude, and stayed so long that he hindered her going to Church. Mrs. Sewell came in before Dinner, and engaged us to Tea in King's Mead Square this afternoon. They both are to drink Tea with us next Sunday Evening, when, Ld. Edgcumbe

Granville's Monument, Lansdown, 1793, by T. Cadell. John Penrose saw the monument on one of his "airings".

told me, this morning at the Pump-Room, he should be glad to take a Dish of Tea with your Mamma, if she will give him Leave. I thanked His Lordship for the Honour done us, and told him we should expect him.

As we shall not go to London, I desire you will present my Compliments to Mr. Baker, and tell him so: and as you know the Time when we purpose (D.G.) to be at Exeter, the 3rd of June, we desire you to look to it, as well as you can, that Jacky may have every thing ready for him meet us then, and make a decent appearance. Tell Mr. Coode, remembring our Love to him, his Spouse, the Doctor, and Molly, that if a man deserves his *Horace*, who pays the Carriage of it from Bath to Penryn, the Colonel thinks he equally deserves it for paying the carriage from Penryn to Bath: so he has again laid his Hands upon it, I dare say with consent of all Parties. The Colonel is become brisk again, tho' he complains of Weakness, and has Heats in his Face; and is as fine as fine can be. He had on To-day a very handsome scarlet Cloth Coat, with Gold Buttons, and broad gold Holes.

I was mistaken in saying the Colonel hindred your Mamma from going to Church. It was Miss Eliot hindred her. The Colonel did not come till about the Time Prayers must be over.

### Friday, May 16th.

We had barely Time to read your Letters over, before Prayers; so many Hindrances. We went to Church at St. Michael's a very pretty Church, and new, being built from the Ground since I first went to Oxford. On one side of the Commandments at the Eastern End is a Painting of Christ, with a Cross in one hand and pointing to Heaven with the other; on the other side, is a Painting of Moses, with the Two Tables of the Law, on which he is leaning his left hand, and pointing to them with his Right. They are said to be very fine Paintings. I am no Connoisseur. But I was a little disgusted to see Moses's Drapery, from his Legs upwards, such we see on modern Portraits. From St. Michael's Church we went to see the Town Hall, which is a very large handsome Room, with four Brass Candlesticks, such as in Gluvias Church, depending. All round are hung the Pictures of the Corporation of Bath, as drawn a good many (perhaps 40) years ago, and continued to this Time: Of uniform size and Framing. Adjoining to the Hall is the Council Room, decorated with Pictures the same as the Hall is. At the upper End of the Hall is a whole Length Portrait of the late Prince Frederic, and another of the present Princess Dowager; both presented by the late Prince to the Corporation: we were shewed a

magnificent silver Cup and Salver, gilt, a Present also from the same
Prince. At the opposite End, are two whole Lengths, one of Gen.
Wade, who was Member for Bath, and made the Corporation a Present
of all the Pictures round the Hall, etc. and the other of the present
Lord Camden. Over the Door of the Hall, as you come in, you see a
Picture of late Mr. Nash, and over the Door of the Council Room, you
see a Bust of the same Gentleman. You are also shewed in the Hall, a
curious Head of (Minerva they say, but in reality of) Apollo, dug up
some years ago near a House in Staul Street. I was very well pleased
both with the Church and Hall. And I cannot help wondering, that we
should hear every day, that People are afraid to go to Church, because
the Churches are cold; when in that we have now been at, and in the
Square Chapel all Things are contrived, as it were on purpose, for the
sake of Warmth. Two Hours between this and Dinner-Time I spent
with Major Tucker, who bathed to-day: in the mean while, your
Mamma and Sister went to the Colonel's. He was gone an Airing, but
they saw Mrs. Sewell. Fanny had a Ticket of her to go this night to the
Ball, where is to be a public Tea at the Expence of the Earl of
Hoptoun. Lord Edgcumbe sent her two Tickets; but she was provided
before. Mr. Grylls of Helston, was a Subscriber to the Rooms: when he
went away, he complimented Fanny with his Tickets, three for each
Ball Night during the Season. To-day we sent for them, and
complimented our friends. Mr. Arch-deacon Sleech and his family set
out for Exon this morning. I am sorry to part with him, who has been
very sociable and friendly. It is now between three and four o'clock. I
am by and by to read Prayers at the Abbey: we are all to drink Tea at
Dr. Stackhouse's: Fanny is to go with them to the Ball, to drink some
of Ld. Hoptoun's Tea. If any thing else occurs to-day, to-morrow I'll
write it to you. The Remainder of our Time this Day, shall be
dedicated to answering your most agreeable Pacquet, for which each
Scribe has our Thanks. I must, however, tell you in this Place, the two
or three following Particulars, as they have Relation to some Things
going before; that there is never any Sermon at St. Michael's Church[36]
Sunday Mornings, but Prayers only, unless when a Collection is to be
made for the Charity Schools or General Hospital; that the Clark of the
Abbey is Clark of the other two Churches, serving them by Deputies,
as the Rector serves them by Curates; and that at each Door of St.
Michael's Church is an Advertisement in large white Letters on a black
Tablet, signifying that "all Persons are forbid by the Church Wardens
not to come into the Church with Pattins"; as much as to say, that it is

---

36   St. Michael's Church, rebuilt in 1742 by John Harvey, a stonemason.

The Old Market Place, Bath, 1772. Watercolour by Edmund Eyre showing the Guildhall.

insisted upon, every one that comes there to Church, must come in
Pattins.[37] Excessively stupid and ridiculous! *Risum Teneatis, amici?*
    Now for your Letters, for which again our Thanks.
    In answer to your sister Coode's. Tell her, we are much obliged to
her for the welcome news of Mrs. Hearle's being able walk to Church;
and desire her to make our Compliments to all that Family: tell her,
we are sorry for the continuance of Mrs. Rawling's Illness: tell her,
that the Report of the Colonel's coming to Castle is utterly groundless,
and that Mrs. Sewell is much surprised such a Rumour should arise.
Mr. and Mrs. Sewell send their Compliments to Dr. Mr. and Mrs.
Coode, and thank them for their Congratulations on their late
Recovery, and depend upon her farther Enquiry about Cravats. Mr.
Loscombe told us, he expected Miss Carthew, with Mr. and Mrs.
Crowgey at Bristol next Tuesday, perhaps a Monday. Now we think of
going to Bristol next Tuesday, possibly we may see them. Mr.
Loscombe said, he could make four Beds, and Mr. Noah Newcome
said he can make one; so that we should not want Lodgings; yet we
think to have a Post-Chaise, and return the same Day. It is but two
Hours Drive. If we go the Monday, you will lose a Day in this Letter:
if we stay there till Wednesday, we shall not receive your Letters till
many hours later than if we are at Bath: so between our Respect to you
on one hand, and to ourselves on the other, we think to come back the
Evening of the Day we set out. – I have heard both Mr. Philipps's and
Mr. Langdon's reciprocal Complaints: but a more skilful Judge, that I
am, must decide between them. I am glad Mrs. Coode likes Mr.
Powell's Sermon. I would have everybody like my assistant Preachers.
You will pass for a Conjurer indeed, if you let your Discoveries be
known: be sure you conceal them from tell-tale Dr. and Mr. Coode. –
We heard of Mrs. Gwatkin's being gone to Roskrow, by Mr.
Loscombe: had she been at Bristol, when we go there, we should have
just waited on her. I don't suppose, she will have any Objection to the
Match between Dr. Jackson and Molly Dyer, and I fancy £1500, if she
has no more, will answer the Doctor's Scruples. But what a deal of
Money this is, to earn in so few years Service, especially as no one
doubts of her coming by it very honestly! – Mrs. Coode says, you are
quite a Beau, and admired by every one: as to the former Particular, I
can hardly credit it; the latter Particular I knew before I set out on my
Journey. Don't mind them, honest Peg; brisk up, and let them see,
that you have Philosophy enough not be disturbed in the midst of so

37   Pattens. Wooden soles with an instep-band, mounted on an iron ring for
     raising the wearer's shoes above the mud.

many Cares; but that you are rather like the Palm-Tree, which grows the faster and taller with a Weight upon it. *Crescit sub pondere virtus.* When any Latin intervenes, let Jacky be your Interpreter: when any hard English Word, *Johnson.* – We are glad to hear Molly's Cold is better, and that Dolly is a good Girl. Mamma excuses Dolly's not writing, upon your intercession; tho' she did expect a Line from her.

To Mary's. We are glad, you had so agreeable a Day at Milor. By what we can find, your Days are all Feasting and Jollity. You live so luxuriously, that you are all almost glutted upon what would be to us a great Rarity: for we have not tasted that delicate Joint, a Leg of Mutton, since we have been at Bath. – Neither have we tasted Cabbage. There are little Things they call Cabbages, exposed to sale in the Market; but we suppose, yield a Price only the Great can afford. – You were in the right, not to think of meeting Mr. Hocker at Mrs. Bath's, as you knew her to be so near her Time: This Thought was so prudent, that I suppose it to be a child of your Brain. But there, if you had determined otherwise her Lying-in the Saturday would have frustrated your Scheme: tho' Mrs. Bath recovers Strength faster than other women, and is as well in two or three days as others in so many weeks. We hope, she will now recover as speedily as ever she did, and desire you to wish the whole Family joy in our Names. There is no one, not nearly related to us, for whom we have greater Respect, or to whom we more sincerely wish Happiness, than Mr. Bath and his family. – We are obliged to Mary for her little Anecdote, how dear little Molly improves. Mary fears, she doth not express herself sufficiently clear: But she does; and methinks I see the dear little Hand held up, and hear the sweet Tongue say How, How. Let us hear some more of her. –

I cannot say much of the Sociableness of Mrs. Marsh and Mrs. Graham. The chief, almost the only Communication we have with each other, is, that I lend them my *London Chronicle,* and they lend me their *Daily Gazetteer.* The other Lodgers, Mr. and Mrs. Backhouse, we never exchanged a Word with till this Evening, when he came in, and was very sociable: she came in too a Quarter before Nine, being run away from the Ball in a Hurry, because the Public Tea prevented a Party being formed in the Card-Room; for this Parson's Wife, tho' no young Woman, is desperately fond of Dress and Pleasures, and Cards are the very Life of her. This Evening other Lodgers are come into this House, Relations to Mrs. Graham: so we expect no Society with them. They are Mrs. Foster and her Man, Lady Simpson and her Maid: so much I hear of them, and as yet no more. If they are disposed to be sociable, no Bar shall be on our Side; if not, they may have their

Humour; I am sure, we have more Acquaintance, than we have Time
to enjoy it. – When any of Mr. Heame's Family comes in your Way,
say that we are very glad Mr. Heame is rid of his Indisposition. We
shall always be sincerely grieved at any Thing, which may illy affect
him, or any of the Family. – Mr. Powell did Philip Taskes great
Honour in not venturing to attack him without an Arch-bishop on his
Side. He had better have despised the anonymous Letter, than so
publickly have answered it. It will only make Taskes and others more
impertinent. I am obliged to Mr. Powell for his kind Offer of Service,
tho' I hope I shall not want it: and I wish Mr. Langdon a good Cornish
Curacy, as he chuses it; but I wonder at his choice, as he has a Living
in Devon, and a Sweet-heart in Somerset, two powerful Motives to
draw his Attention Eastward. Whatever be his Fault towards Mr.
Phillips (for I suspect Fault in both of them) I take him to be a
good-natured man, I am sure I have found him so, and I wish him
Success equal to his Desire. – Mr. Coode, etc. drinking Tea at
Vicarage last Sunday was a Favour for which you all ought to reckon
yourselves under Obligation. They have been very kind to you all, as
well as to Dolly, so much that we cannot requite them. – I am glad,
Coz: Fanny is so well pleased with London. I hope her whole Tour will
prove agreeable. If her Envy of your Philosophy, be a friendly
Emulation, I wish she may succeed. It will prove of more real Service
to her in her future Life, than if she were to learn all the vain Airs of all
the fine Ladies in London and Westminster. Mr. Bath and Mary may
club their heads together in conspiracy against someone's Peace: but
their contrivances will prove abortive, and I would advise them to
consult their own Peace, to study to be quiet, and mind their own
Business.

For Jacky's. I trembled at the Thought of his riding the Chaise
Horse, as he had played such dangerous Tricks with me, and George
was not with him. Jacky's Letter was very diverting, and tho' there is
not much in it, that requires an Answer, yet we were very well pleased
with it, and like his correspondence. I wonder he lets non-sen-si-cal
people scribble scandal at the Foot of his Page.

For Charles's. An impudent young rogue! to expect me to write him
a separate Letter, when he knows I write to no Body but you!
However, as he is a young Gentleman, I would not willingly
disoblige, I have inclosed a Line to him in Answer to his. I assure you,
he writes very pretty Letters, all Nature without Art, Beauty without
Paint, not alamode de Bath. –

For Peggy's last. Tho' last, not least doth my honest Peg deserve
Regard.

O thou, whatever Title please thine ear,
Housekeeper, Butler, Nurse, or Conjurer,
Accept our Thanks for your Labours in every capacity. We are glad to hear the Maids weed in the Garden, and that they as well as you are all well, and agree so lovingly together. All things succeeding so well at home, will do me as much good as the Bath Waters, which have surely an Effect upon me. I am now better, than I have been for a great while, but I never drink the Water without feeling directly an Emptiness or Craving in my Stomach. – You did extremely well in writing to Mr. Geare. I hope, you received some Licenses from him, before you had another Demand. – If Mr. Hocker was this Week upon the Commission at Falmouth, it might save him Trouble, but you would lose a good deal of Pleasure, which we expected you would have in his company. Your Correspondence with him, and us, and others on my account, will be a great Improvement to you. I see a considerable Improvement already. I fancy you love to correspond with us; yet would rather converse with us tete a tete. Let Charles interpret, when any French comes in your Way. – Oh my dear Peg, my scheme of early rising was soon broke thro': my first Glass finds me generally in Bed. I think to try again next Monday, to get up before seven: but dare not form a Resolution. Lazy Lawrence comes slily into my Bed mornings, lies upon my shirt, glews together my Eye-lids, pinions my Arms, and disables me from doing what in Reason I should do. – *video meliora, proboque: Deteriora sequor.* – I'll lay sixpence, you are up before me next Monday; and I will not lie abed the longer for having waged. – When we give Orders to George to set out to meet us, he must brew two or three days before, so as to tun the Drink before he sets out. – We all hope in God, as you do, that it will not be long before we all have an happy Meeting; that the same Providence, which has kept you in Safety at Home, and in Safety brought us hither, will continue to keep us under his Protection; and that we shall have cause to praise the Lord for his Goodness in bringing us to the Haven where we would be. – Mr. Tresidder was the oldest man in Budock. Mr. Nic. Tresidder comes to a Loss in him; Tregenvar, which is £60 per ann. falling off at his Death. – If Mrs. Rawling should die, and have a Funeral Sermon with a chosen Text, as Mr. Rawling and his Aunt had, I am afraid you will be put to Difficulties for a Preacher, unless it be a common Text, which Mess. Evans or Osborn chance to have a Sermon on. You may look in the *Cruel Book,* and if there be any Sermon on the Text, and in my possession, I dare say Mr. Osborn would take out sufficient for the Purpose, and do the Business. But I hope, she will recover. I should be very sorry for her. – I hope the Clark will be as diligent as he can. Put

him in mind often, how great your Expences are. Mr. Rock, if he had
asked him, would have told him he had not paid me: I desired him to
pay the Clark. – We are sorry for Mr. Tresidder, Jane Hosking, and
Mrs. Bonnell tho' unknown to us, for Mr. Allen's Fainting, and Mr.
Bath's Necessity of having Recourse to a Doctor; and George's Father's
Ilness:

I am a Man; and all calamities,
That touch humanity, come home to me.
        or thus
I am a Man, and feel for all mankind.

I want Jacky's Opinion, which of these is the better Translation of
Terence's

*Homo sum; humani nihil a me alienum puto.*

I wish Mr. Osborn Joy of his being appointed Representative of so
learned and respectable a Body as the Clergy of the Deanry of Kerrier.
I beg the Favour of him to pay my Subscription, £1.1.0. Mrs. Jane
Hawkins's of Tremough, £1.1.0. which I have received, and for John
Enys of Enys, Esqr. £2.2.0 which he told me to lay out annually
(unless forbidden) and he would repay me.

Your Letters being all answered, God bless you all! To morrow
morning I'll resume my Pen. This phrase is alamode de Gluvias.

## Saturday, May 17th

Fanny herself will acquaint you, how she was entertained at
yester-night's Ball: how she there saw the Revd. Mr. Fothergill, Lady,
and Son: how they enquired after Mr. and Mrs. Usticke of Breage, and
Mr. Coode: how she was quite tired with her amusement: how it was
eleven o'clock almost, when she was brought Home: how good was
Lady Hoptoun's Tea, and Bread and Butter, and Cake, and Negus,[38])
and what a Multitude of Gentlemen and Ladies were Partakers of
them. I shall only tell you she came home with such Dislike to the
Hurry of so many in company and the tedious Fatigue of Idleness, that
a single Word from us would have drawn a Promise from her to
forswear Balls from henceforth. But what should we do then for a Rake
in our little family? It is necessary there should be one to rake, as well
as so many to scatter. What is the Matter with me, I trow? I am fallen
a Punning. Will you not think, we are all Rakes? Why, we all went
this morning to Simpson's Rooms. Mrs. Sewell put us there. Indeed it
was only to see them, after Prayers were over: and they are worthy the

---

38  A beverage of wine, hot water, sugar and spices. Col Francis Negus, its
    inventor, died in 1732.

Sight. The great Room is said to be long 90 feet, broad 36, high 30, the Ceiling highly finished, and is by far the finest and most elegant Room I ever saw, or perhaps any Body else. Mrs. Sewell also went to several Shops with us, that we might see the fine Things. I suppose there is nothing in the Kingdom curious or valuable, but you might serve yourself of it here. Mrs. Sewell made Fanny a very handsome Present of a Basket of Eggs. What will she do with it? Why, hang it up to her Watch. Was ever such a Thing seen? Oh, my dear Peg, 'tis only a pretty four shilling Toy, with a Seal at the Bottom. Among other Places we went to Mrs. Smith's, a Shop where artificial Flowers are made and sold: There we saw a made Auricula, which gained the Florist's Prize. The curious in Flowers were invited by a Prize proposed to see who could raise the finest Auricula. The Judges were set, the Flowers produced by their several Rearers, and this Flower by the Maker as the Production of Nature. So much in this Instance Art exceeded Nature, the Judges gave the Preference to this artificial Auricula, imagining it to be a true one. The Maker obtained the Prize, and was afterwards threatened with a Prosecution of the Imposture, unless the Prize was returned: but the Thing dropt, and Ingenuity had it's Reward. That the best Judges may sometimes take Art for Nature is evident from an antient story of two Grecian Painters, (if I mistake not,) Zeuxes and Apelles. You will probably find the Story I mean, under one or other of these Names in Ainsworth's *Dictionary*, or in Collier's *Historical Dictionary*, which lies in the corner near the Chimney in my Study. We also saw an artifical Wasp, so natural, that you would dread to put your finger near it, for fear of being stung, even after you were told it is not a live Insect. – Mrs. Backhouse, mentioned in my last, has been inoculated since Easter last for the Small-Pox, by a Doctor in Hertfordshire, who has an House fitted up for the Reception of Patients, and has inoculated thousands without ever one failing under his Hands. His Price is five Guineas. For which he finds them Meat, Drink, Washing, Lodging, and whatever he thinks they ought to have. He keeps them upon a very spare Diet; brings a Person with the Small-Pox upon him into the Room where the Party to be inoculated is, to take the Infection from; gives them Water to drink; will not suffer them if sick, to lie down, as long as they can possibly stand; absolutely prohibits their approaching any Fire; lets them go out in Cold, Rain, Wind, Snow, any Weather, by Night as well as by Day, nay absolutely forces them out, if they complain of sickness. It is a common Thing for such as are not past the Small-Pox, to make a Party of three, four, or more, to go to this Doctor's for inoculation, as for Ladies to make a Party of Pleasure.

Mrs. Backhouse is our Informer. She went away from her Husband in
Easter-Week from their Home in Bedfordshire: and they saw no more
of one another, till she was recovered of her Disorder, and came to him
here at Bath. –

We would have Jacky and George set out to meet us on Saturday the
last Day of this month, as early as they can in the morning, and sleep
(you must not say lie for the World,) at my Uncle's: they had best get
there as early as they can in the Evening, because Uncle's People know
not of their Coming. The Sunday morning they may go to Church at
Broadoak or Boconnock, and in the Afternoon go to the Bridge over
the Tamar (I don't know, whether it is Horse-Bridge or New-Bridge),
or, if they can, to Lydford. But this must be left to themselves. I
would not have Jacky over-heated. But he can speak to George, if he
wants any thing: and I can depend upon George's Care. This I desire,
they will be at Yendacot as soon as they can conveniently the Monday.
There I would have George examine my Chaise narrowly, and grease
the Wheels, and oil the Leathers, and let me have it at Exeter the
Tuesday. They may be at Exeter the Tuesday, as early as they will: I
suppose, Jacky will like be there early. We shall dine there at Mr.
Pauls, and go to Yendacot that Evening. How we shall proceed
afterwards, must be settled, when we get there.

The Colonel and Mrs. Sewell are civil beyond compare. They have
both been here To-day, and this Evening we drank Tea with them,
and spent there two Hours and a half. Sewell[39] came home from
Greenwich this Evening, to the inexpressible Joy of the Colonel. He is
grown, not excessively, but more genteel; as wild, as ever. He says,
Mr. Ben Heame was very well last week, and went to London to Mr.
Fletcher's. They both dined at the Inn with Mr. Crowgey, with whom
the Colonel is mightily pleased for taking Notice of Sewell. Mrs.
Aurelia would be glad to hear from Mrs. White, her Mother.

Poor Fanny has been much out of Order, all Day: I hope,
To-morrow she will be better. I have wrote this Evening to Mr. Pierce
of Yendacot, and to Mr. Paul.

Mr. Morshead is returned from Oxford. He has entred his Son at
Oriel. He did not see Mr. Billy Robinson, who is of the same College.
– Mr. Taylor of Denbury hath been to Eton with little Piercy. He left
him very well. – These two Gentlemen, Mess. Morshead and Taylor I
saw this morning at the Pump-Room.

Dr. Stackhouse sat half an hour with us this Evening. He says a
Lady, who had Lodgings in the same House with him, is just now

39   The Colonel's grandson.

gone, and has given the Servants of the House, to one six, to another five guineas, enough to spoil them and make them discontented with others, who judging more justly give less; of consequence has done an Injury to every Person of small Fortune, or less Profuseness. She gave amongst the Servants, in the whole, twenty Guineas. She had better have given it to the General Hospital.

### Sunday, May 18. Whitsunday.

Fanny somewhat better. I preached this Morning at the Abbey on John XIV. 16, 17. and afterwards assisted at the Communion, with Mess. Saurin and Mr. Taylor administer'd. There were between 200 and 300 Communicants, yet I held out pretty well, but not well enough to do any Part of the Afternoon Duty as I was solicited. The Mayor and Aldermen made a pompous Show in their scarlet Gowns. Seven pair of Banns were published; and one Gentleman, and twelve men and ten women belonging the General Hospital, returned public Thanks for Benefit received by the Bath-Waters. Mr. Taylor preached at Evening Service, a very good Discourse on Eph. IV.8. – When the Communion-Service was ended, it was too late for my Water, so I lost my Noon-Glass. After Evening Service Lord Edgcumbe and Mr. Heard drank Tea with us: the Colonel, and Mrs. Sewell, and little Sewell, were to have drank Tea here, but the Colonel complains, he is not able to walk by a sore-foot, so desires to be excused. Mrs. Sewell was at Church in the Morning, but could not leave the Colonel in the Evening. – Misses Stackhouse, Coryton, Tremayne, were here before Dinner, to take Leave. They set out, and the Doctor, To-morrow. I shall send a Line by him to Mr. Paul, with one inclosed for Mr. Sam. Pierce, acquainting them when we hope to be with them. With these Letters we shall wait on the Doctor a little before Night, when the Coast may be clear at his Lodgings; to wish him and the Ladies a good Journey, and an happy Sight of their Friends in Cornwall. – To entertain Lord Edgecumbe, we had a Twelve-penny frosted Cake: and we should be very glad, if you among you had the Remainder.

### Monday, May 19.

When Lord Edgcumbe was here, he told us he had been a week ago to Lady Huntingdon's Chapel, and repeated a great many ridiculous Things Mr. Fletcher said in his Sermon, and acted him to the Life: he then told us, that he was well assured, that these Preachers endeavour to suit their Sermons so to their congregations, that they deliver themselves with more care than common, when they know there are any men of Sense in the Audience; and that Mr. Whitefield one day, finding the Audience consisted wholly of true Methodists, begun a Sermon on these Words "God is no Respecter of Persons" in this manner, "Good News for you, Tag, Rag, and Bob-tail."

Mr. Heard left with me a Paper he received from a Friend in London, who inspected Lord Suffolk's Marriage Articles, which he gave me Leave to copy; so I'll copy it here. As the very Words of the Settlement are not taken, Mr. Heard thinks, as well as I, that it is the best Way to have a true copy of it tho' it will be attended with some Expence. "Upon inspecting the Settlement made upon the Marriage of Henry late Earl of Suffolk with Miss Irwen, it appears that Ld. Suffolk (among other Things) covenanted, that he would purchase a Mansion House built upon Lands of Inheritance, and furnish the same suitable to his Lady's Rank, and settle it so furnished upon her Ladyship for her Life, in case she survived him: Or, in Default thereof, that his Executors or Administrators should pay her Ladyship a certain annual Sum during her Life. No such House was purchased; and his Lordship having died intestate, his Administrators pay the said annual sum to Lady Suffolk for her Life, and insist upon that being a full Discharge of his Lordship's covenants, as his Lordship had a Right of Election either to purchase such an House, or leave his Assets charged with the above-mentioned annual Sum." As we have Leave to have a Copy of the Settlement, we will (as I said) be at the Expence, and then we shall be certain how the case stands.

Both Glasses this morning at the P.R. where your Mamma and Fanny were also an Hour. It is the hardest Work, that can be, to have their company there, because of Dressing, which they do not like so early in the morning. You wondered, what they would do for Morning Mobs and Morning Aprons. There are no such Things in Use here:
        "But now Sunday's Jacket goes ev'ry Day on."

This Line often runs in your Mamma's Mind. It is in an old Song, which she had not thought of before for many years. – There are now two Clergymen, who wear Cassocks and Bands, here, besides me. – We think of going to Bristol to-morrow. If we do, I shall bespeak a Pair of Shoes of Mr. Allison. The Soles of these, I have, are worn through to the very Cork. That I wear out Shoes, is very good News. I have sent you a *Bath Guide*, by Dr. Stackhouse. It will entertain you a good deal. Tell the Clark, that the Clark here is a very decent Person, and stays at Sacrament every Sunday; the Churchwardens collect the offerings; and tell Dr. Coode, that the Mayor and all his Bretheren staid yesterday at Sacrament. I did not see one Person in that large Congregation (and I made my Observation) that did not repeat the

Athanasian Creed. I fancy the Gentlemen abroad are not so conceited, such critical coxcombs, as our Western Esquires, and some others of lower Rank. And tell Dr. Coode, it is not the Fashion here to preach less than from 35 to 45 minutes: all except one, since we have been here, out-preach me in Length. – There is an Act of Parliament passed this Session, to enable the Corporation of Bath to make great Alterations for the Beauty and Convenience of this City: Particularly all the Houses are to pulled down, that are between Staul and Milsom Streets, and a grand Street to be built from the higher End of the former to the lower End of the latter. So many other alterations are to be made, that beautiful as Bath now is, it will be much more so in very few Years. – After morning prayers we went to the Colonel's, who was gone out in a Coach with Gen. Warburton. When your Mamma and Fanny went home, I went to dine at Sir Booth Williams's. Company there besides me, were Mess. Taylor and Grant. Our Dinner was, First Course, Scotch-Collops, Fricasee of Rabbits, Saddle of Mutton, Sallad: Second Course, Bullock's Tongue roasted, Dish of Asparagus, Dish of Radishes, Gooseberry Pie. Weather forbid me to go to Church, but cleared up an hour afterwards so that I drank my Water, and returned to Sir Booth's to Tea. Writing detained Fanny at Home.

If you have not broke in upon the Ten pounds in the Purse, desire Mr. Heame to give you a London Bill for it. If you have, ask Mr. Coode or Mr. Heame, with our Compliments; and one or other will be so good as to let me have a ten pound Bill upon Credit, and I shall be obliged to them. We may possibly have Money enough with us; but if we have, it will so barely do, that we think it best to have a little more, as a Corps de Reserve.

My dear, dear Peg, and all the rest of my equally dear Children, it is my earnest Desire and Prayer to God, and that of your most loving Mamma and Sister, that the Grace of our Lord Jesus Christ, and the Love of God, and the Fellowship of the Holy Ghost may be with you all evermore. Amen.

So concludes your ever affectionate Father,<br>JOHN PENROSE.

P.S. Our Pacquet was made up, and sealed; but being more than Weight, we were forced to open it again, and take out a Sheet Letter of Fanny's to Mrs. Coode: which shall be sent next Time. Upon Recollection, we have some Franks directed to Mr. Coode, we have sent Fanny's Letter this Post, and with it a Letter from the Colonel to Mr. Coode.

Bath, Tuesday, May 20th.

My dear, dear Peggy, and all the rest of my equally dear Children, it is
with Pleasure I now and always sit down to write you an Account of
our little Adventures. The Weather this morning being very unprom-
ising, a drizzling cold Rain almost deterring from a Bristol Journey, as
we had designed, we staid so long shall I, shall I, that we set out later
than we could wish by near an Hour. However out we set, in a
Post-Chaise with two good Horses and civil Rider, Fanny upon a
Stool, and without any Accident or Let arrived at Bristol. We did not
go directly to Mr. Loscombe's, where we purposed to dine, but went
out of our way to see the celebrated Radcliffe Church, of which I had
formed very high Expectations, having many Times heard it spoken of
as the finest Church, at least the finest Parish Church, in Britain: and I
found it exceed my Ideas, it being in Truth, a most magnificent and
venerable Pile. The Congregation were assembled, and Mr. Robinson,
one of the best Bristol Preachers, was in the Pulpit, speaking very
well, and the little I heard very good Matter: but my Business was
Curiosity solely, I had nothing to do with Sermons. So we walked up
the North Aile, to take a View of the Paintings at the Altar End,
which were extremely fine and had a wonderful Effect upon us when
first we looked toward them. There is a Painting over the Table, and
another on each Side Wall. The side-Pictures, if I remember, were the
Burial and Resurrection, of Jesus. I had but just Time to see that there
were Pictures there at all. The middle Piece I observed more narrowly,
the Ascension of Christ, painted by the famous Hogarth at the Price of
400 Guineas.[40] I believe the Painting to be very beautiful. But I always
find fault with Scripture-Paintings: the Painters always forsake the
History to follow their own fancy. Christ is pictured, as just received
into the Cloud, and the Disciples should have been drawn standing
gazing up into Heaven: but the Disciples here are drawn in various
Attitudes, some kneeling, some looking towards the Ground or one
another. This did not please me. I own I am no Connoisseur; but it is
all the fashion now, for Persons to criticize what they do not
understand. Do not all do so in Religion, Politics, etc. Why shall not
I do so in Painting? But enough of this. We must leave descriptions,
till we come face to face. From Radcliffe Church we went by the side of
the shipping, a long Way, (It was very entertaining to see such a
multitude of Vessels, as it were, in the middle of a long Street) to Mr.
Allison's. We just stept into his House, and eat a Bit of Bread and

---

40    This painting by Hogarth is now to be seen in St. Nicholas Church Museum,
      Bristol.

Butter, and drank a Glass of Wine (It is a little neat House, in a nasty Street, and his Wife a neat Woman) and then away to Mr. Loscombe's who with Mrs. Richards received us with great Courtesy, and gave us all the Reason, that could be, to think we had a hearty Welcome. They used importunity to prevail with us to stay the Night, by which means we should have seen Bristol more perfectly.

> But fix'd before and well resolv'd were we.
> As you, who know us, know we're wont to be,

and accordingly we returned to Bath this Evening. But what had we for Dinner at Bristol? At the higher end of the Table two boil'd Chicken, at the lower end a Fore-quarter of Lamb, in the middle a Sallad, on one side Asparagus and Goose-berries sugar'd, on the other Bacon with Cabbage, and a Goose-berry Tart. All served in China, with surprising Elegance. Mr. Loscombe's House is a Palace, a Court before it laid with broad Stones, an Iron Gate very grand before the Court, as neat a Garden as the Sun sees in it's Circuit under the Windows of the Room we dined in; the dirtiest Part of the House (for we saw the Whole) as nice as the cleanest Room in King George's Palace: But, why should I say the dirtiest Part? I need ask Mr. Loscombe's Pardon: for there is not a Speck of Dirt, I might almost say a Particle of Dust, in the whole House, nor a Weed in the whole Garden. Then the House *is rus in urbe*, the last in the City that Way, so that from every window you have a rural Prospect, and from the upper ones a View very extensive, and richly diversified. So you think in this exquisitely neat abode we took up our Rest, and saw nothing of Bristol, but what we saw as we passed through in our Chaise. No, my dears, Mr. Loscombe and Mrs. Richards were so kind as before Dinner to take us out with them a walking, me a walking over Pavement, rugged and rough, not like the smooth Streets of Bath: they led us through St. James's Churchyard where Bristol Fair is usually held, through Bridewell Court, before the Guild and Town Halls to the Exchange; to the Exchange-Coffee-House, reckoned the handsomest in England, where Mr. Loscombe treated us each with a Glass of Capillaire:[41] We went over the Market-place, which is vastly commodious, and when we came to St. Nicolas's Church, (a new church which we would have seen, but it being Holiday the Workmen were gone off with the Keys,) then turn again Whittington. If you meet with any one, that knows how far it is from Stokes-Croft to St. Nicolas's Church, he may tell you how far I walk'd, so far and back again. I was glad to return, for tho' I went out very stoutly, and was very stout

41   An infusion of Maiden-hair syrup flavoured with orange-flower water.

most of the Way back; yet I was beginning to complain of my Ancles, and was very glad to sit down. In the afternoon, I only went round the Garden, not large: but Mamma and Fanny walked Miles; they went into King's Square, and away to the College-Green: they came back wearied, drank Coffee and Tea, took Chaise immediately and me with them; and we came to Bath in very good Season, neither Day nor Night. When at Mr. Allison's Your Mamma and I were both measured for Shoes. Mem: I charged him again and again, and he promised again and again, not to make mine too narrow or too short; but I am afraid he will fail in both Respects: What say you, conjuring Peg?

Speak, for you know, how will he make my Shoes?

Omitted in my Account of Mr. Loscombe's Dinner, a Dish of Custards, and, to answer it, Butter, and Butter and Parsley. Let Mr. Richards know, with our respectful Compliments, when we saw his Bristol Relations; and that they were well: we promised Mrs. Richards, that Charles should make a visit to her female Cousin at Penryn, and invite her to Vicarage.

## Wednesday, May 21st.

All a little fatigued last night, and I, like Solomon the wise, loth to rise this morning. However I got to the P.R. between eight and nine. While I was in the Room, a melancholy Accident happened. One Mr. Croxton, a Gentleman of Chester, who was here for his Health, as he was sitting on a Bench near the Window, was seized with a Fit. His Lady and Daughter were standing by him: the former fainted, and was carried out of the Room; the latter ran out, as one distracted. No Surgeon was in the Room, but one was sent for. Mr. Croxton was carried out into the Air, a vein pricked, but he died. He spoke not one Word, from his first Seizure: and from the Time of his Seizure, to his being pronounced dead, was less than five minutes. How the poor Ladies are, I have not heard. From my Heart I pity them.

After Breakfast we received your welcome Pacquet, and are sorry you had not more Franks, that we might have received the whole you were so kind as to write: but we hope to receive the whole by Jacky and George, at Exon. Before we had read the Letters, the Bell tolled for Prayers: so away we hurried, but we might have staid longer, for Prayers did not begin till near twelve. This is the annual Feast of the Wiltshire Gentlemen living in or near Bath. They meet in the Town-Hall, and go in Procession to the Abbey-Church, where a Sermon is preached on the Occasion, and after dinner a Collection is made for apprenticing poor Wiltshire Children. Ten pounds apiece is generally given with them. We saw the Procession, or rather I saw

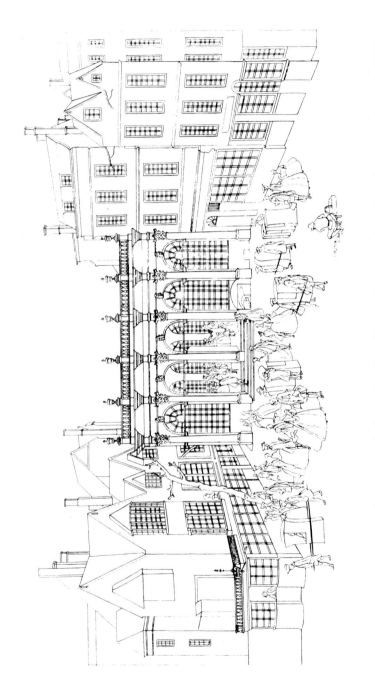

The Pump Room, 1754, engraved for a fan by George Speren, showing the extension of 1751.

something of it, and your Mamma and Fanny were in the Mob, which saw more than any of us. First preceded a Wiltshire Shepherd, in the common Dress, worn in the Plains, when keeping the Flock; upon one shoulder he had his Crook, at which hung a little caj, and in one hand was a string, by which he led his Dog. He had a Blanket over his Shoulders, and Wads of Straw wrapt round his Legs. Next him went sixteen Boys, now Apprentices from this Charity, with every one a long white Rod in his Hand, as great as Mr. Apparitor: then six musicians, playing on their several Instruments: then sixty Gentlemen, all in pairs, as were the musicians and Boys. The organ played them into Church. The President of the Society sat in the Mayor's Seat, the rest in the Magistrates and other seats; and the Boys in the Boarding-school Misses Gallery. The Sermon was preached by one Mr. Robins, now of Bristol, lately an Apothecary in this Town; a very good Sermon, and well delivered. The Preacher had his Book before him, but did not look in it. The Text, Matt. XXV.40. After the Second Lesson a man in the Organ Loft sung an Anthem, out of Psalm LXVIII. 32, etc. extremely well indeed. I am told, his Name is Anna Ford, and that he is going to be admitted into the Choir of Bristol. The Mr. Robins, who preached the Sermon to-day, is the same Clergyman, who was preaching yesterday when we at Radcliffe-Church.

Mrs. Grant's Bill, last Week.

| May 15. Roasting Pork | – 4d.a little chine of $3\frac{1}{2}$ lb., cost 14d. |
|---|---|
| 16. Boiling Salmon | – 4. $1\frac{1}{2}$ lb. at 6d per lb. |
| 17. Frying Tripe | – 4. price 9d. |
| 18. Roasting Mutton | – 4. shoulder, ls.10d. |
| One week's Lodging | – £1.5.0. |

May 14. We had a twelve-penny mutton Pie, to help out cold meat.

19. Cold Mutton. I dined at Sr. Booth's.[42]

20. We were at Bristol.

Potatos every day dressed by ourselves, as usual.

I left a Blank in the letter you received from me last Pacquet for a Clergyman's Name: which Blank may be supplied with Tatton.

This afternoon Major Tucker, his Lady, their Neice Miss Elliot, and Revd. Mr. Newcombe, drank Tea with us, and staid longer than Bath Visiters usually stay, from half hour past five to a little after Eight. The Major has fixed on next Friday for the Day of his leaving Bath. I

42  Sir Booth Williams.

shall lose an excellent old Friend, and the most entertaining Companion. – Fanny had a Ticket sent her by Mrs. Sewell for tomorrow's Play, *The Committee, or The faithful Irishman,* with the *Farce of the Guardian:* and this Evening she has been taking a Walk in Simpson's Walks, which are very fine and pleasant, but she must be left to describe these herself, and point out their several Pleasures.

I now come to answer Your Letter, and Mary's to Fanny, some Particulars.

First for my honest Peg. We approve of her conduct on Fair-Day and all other Times. We are glad Mrs. Tabois is better. We believe poor Peg hath too much both of Gadding and Visiters, and that she will be glad to have us home, were it only to enjoy her Needle in Peace; tho' a little Walking will be beneficial to her. We are glad to hear that after making, like a Book-worm, one Epistolary Meal, she thinks her Appetite will soon be prepared for another: this does not look like a Surfeit, which sometimes a Glut occasions. I continue, thank God, exceeding well, only an Aching in my Feet, and that only after a long Walk. We are much obliged to the Neighbours, that are kind to you, and that enquire after us: we should be overjoyed to be at Home again, but I hope I shall not return without my reward. But you must not think, that I am able run a Race, or ever shall be able walk without making a Zig-zag, as if I was marking out with my Feet a Chinese Pattern; nor, you must not think, that I shall be rid of my Gout. No, if the Blessing of God upon my Journey and these Waters shall legitimate my bastard Gout, and I shall come to have a regular Fit now and then, with some Length of Interval, you will have Reason to bless God, as we shall, and think the End of this long, troublesome, expensive Journey well answered. If the Event should prove better than Expectation, we must reckon on it as clear gain, and be thankful: if worse, it is God's Will, and we must be contented, and all will see that I have used the Means, and I can do no more. But I hope the best. – I am glad, you are so rich: my last acquainted you with our Necessities. – You will have seen by my last, that I preached at the Abbey last Sunday; so I shall preach at the Chapel next Sunday. I had a mind to have put off preaching at the Chapel at all, because some said there used to be strange Preaching there: but, on consulting Mr. Taylor about it, he said the Curate was a very good-natured honest man; that Strangers often preach there; that the Chapel was in disrepute, whilst Mr. Chapman served it, who now lives in the Country; but that now all the Methodists have forsaken it for Lady-Huntingdon's Chapel: and he desired me to officiate there. Your Mamma and Fanny, I suppose, will go the Abbey, where I am much importuned to preach in the Afternoon: Fanny may be afraid of the Spiders: for sure there is Reason; but I would have her go to the Abbey, where the Service is so decently performed, and the large Congregation so decently behaved, and every Seat quite full, that it is quite heavenly. – If Mrs. Hearle's Desire for me to stay in Bath had come, before Places were taken in the Coach, we should have paid so much Deference to her Judgment, as to have done as she desired. I have put her to little expence in Chair-Hire; and shall put her to [no] more Expence, unless I want to go out in the Rain, and then I must take a Chair, for I am afraid of catching Cold. It was very kind in her, to form a Scheme for Fanny's Pleasure, if we had gone to London: but it is best as it is. It would have been very chargeable; and where would you have found money for us, Peg? Fanny is very well satisfied with having seen Bath, and would rather never see London, than we should be at the Expence purposely on her Account. Our Compliments wait on Mrs. Hearle and the Ladies. – If you chuse, Peg, you may print my Letters; but then we have fair Play; yours must be printed too, because mine will be unintelligible without them, yes and Dolly's and Jacky's, and Charles's and Mrs. Coode's too, as my Letters contain Answers to all of them. – I hope, Jacky was very complaisant to Mr. Billy Paynter. – I am obliged to Mr. Hocker for giving you so much of his Company. – We are highly thankful that Mary's Lowness of Spirits went so well off, and hope in God we shall find you all again in good Health, as we left you. – Mr. Coode's family are extremely kind to you all, and we hope we shall never forget it: but who can be kinder to Peggy, than Peggy deserves? – So poor Mrs. Rawling is dead: she did not long survive her Husband. What will the Youngsters do? we are very sorry for her. – If Mr. Hocker is of so spiteful a Disposition as to rejoice in the Misfortunes of others, and be glad that you were deprived of the Fat of the Land (for so Oil may be deemed) he did not deserve so good a Cake as he had; and, if he comes again under your care, pinch him in Butter and such Things as he best likes, till the Loss of the Oil be made up by his Loss of good Things, or you have good Cause to think him penitent. I observe the witty Gentleman's Proverb on the Occasion; but cannot possibly apply it:

> Now to apply, hath plagued me more,
> Than all he said or did before.

I hope, he makes more suitable Applications, when he makes his Sermons. Yet you were so forgiving, that you gave him Punch forsooth, and bribed him to mind all friends in Bath. We mind him at our own Expence, without a Bribe: but there he is a Vote in a Borough, so the Times will excuse him. – I am glad you have the

Licenses, and that the St. Agnes Man was not disappointed. If Mr. Hocker had not done me that Piece of Service in granting the License, I would have desired you to take the Price of the Oil out of the cash he put into your hands; but now, only do as I mentioned before, and keep it out of his Gut. Did you ever know me more provoked? I must resent every Indignity offered to you.

*Te nemo impune lacesset*, Construe, Jacky.

Mrs. Bath (more Latin for Jacky) *antiquum morem obtinet*, is just the Woman she was: We are glad to hear of any Thing, respecting the Welfare of all the family. – I hope, the Horses will be in good order for the Journey: then the cheaper they are kept, the better; but I am afraid Gratis Grass is not very plentiful, nor very nourishing: I have had the Grey almost starved upon it before now. – We are glad to have a Confirmation of Mr. Sam Enys's having a Place: I hope, his Brother will let him keep it.

The Paragraph in Mary's Letter, wherein she endeavours to raise Jealousy of you, need give you no concern. It is written with so much Humour, that I concluded it was not a fact, but an Attempt to display her Parts. The Wit is enough, if she has any malice, to make Atonement for it, and has excited such Laughter, that if she means seriously, we take all for a Jest. However, as she seems to have given uneasiness to my trusty Housekeeper, who has so many other Cares in her Pate, I must shew some Degree of Resentment. So far will I be from giving her the least Commendation or Applause, that when I come to that Part of her Letter, I intend, my dear Peg, to pass by in solemn State, and not so much as turn my Eyes towards it. Such Contempt shown to her Ingenuity may make her humble and modest. What think you of my Scheme?

Now for Mary's Letter. It is as hard to find the Beginning of Mary's Letter, as it was to find the Exit of Daedalus's Labyrinth; one must turn round and round, as a Dog does when he's going to Bed. Pooh! I will not trouble my self any more about it. Sour Grapes! No, no, I'll e'en go to Bed, and To-morrow send you Mr. Derrick's[43] Rules for the Ball Rooms at Bath, which will please Mary more than any Remarks I could make on her Letter.

Thursday, May 22nd.

The Master of the Ceremonies, the first of October last, was under a

---

43 Samuel Derrick (1724–1769), soon after the death of Beau Nash was appointed master of ceremonies at Bath, which place he kept along with a like position at Tunbridge Wells, until his death. His rules are clearly based on the ones published by his famous predecessor.

Necessity of reviving and republishing the following Rules, to be observed in both the Assembly Rooms here. As they are not in the *Bath-Guide*, nor in any Book that I know of, they may give some Entertainment.

No Chair or Bench can be called on Ball Nights for any person, who does not rank as a Peer or Peeress of Great Britain or Ireland.

No Lady can be permitted to dance Minuets, without a Lappet head,[44] and full-dress long Hoop, such as are permitted to dance Minuets at Court.

No Lady can be permitted to dance Country Dances with an Hoop of any kind; and those that chuse to pull their Hoops off, will always find a servant maid ready to assist them, and a proper Place to retire to for that purpose.

The Master of the Ceremonies is under a Necessity of causing all Ladies infringing on this Rule, to sit down.

No Lady, be her Rank or Quality ever so high, has a Right to take place in Country Dances after they have been begun.

Every Gentleman chusing to dance Minuets, must present himself in a full Dress, or a French Frock Suit compleat, and a Bag wig.

Officers Regimentals are an Exception to this Rule, being every where proper; but every other kind of Lapel is improper for a minuet, at Bath.

It is recommended to the Gentlemen frequenting the Rooms to remember that leather Breeches are by no means suitable to the Decorum of the Place.

Before the French Dances begin, such Ladies as chuse to dance minuets, are desired to acquaint the Master of the Ceremonies with their Names and Intention.

Gentlemen are requested not to stand between the Ladies sitting down and the Country Dancers, the Benches being brought forward solely for the use of the Ladies, and sufficient Space left for the Gentlemen to pass thro' behind.

The Music is always to be dismissed as soon as the Clock strikes Eleven.

No Ladies with Hats can be admitted into the Rooms at Bath, be their Rank or Quality ever so high, during the Season.

No large Screens can be brought to any Card-Party in the Rooms on any account, as they not only divide the company into secluded Setts, which is against the fundamental Institution of these Places, but occasion such a Draught of Air, as is not only disagreeable to the rest

44   Part of a lady's head-dress hanging loose.

of the Company, but often detrimental. There are small Screens provided for such Individuals as complain of Cold.

So much for Rule and Order. Now for ourselves. Your Mamma and Fanny, to my Joy, surprized me this Morning by coming unexpectedly to the Pump-Room. Oh, had you seen, how the Gentlemen flock about Fanny, fine gold-laced Gentlemen! I would fain have persuaded them, that Fanny was my Sister, and Your Mamma my Aunt: but, 'tis prodigious, not one but takes things as they really are. I thought I had so brisk a Countenance, I could deceive any one; but Age hath, I fear, stamped some indelible marks there; so for the future, let them take me for one of 53 or upwards. Before morning Prayers your Mamma and Fanny, waited with a How-d'ye on Lady Simpson and Mrs. Forster, then on Mrs. Backhouse: short visits! After Prayers with me at the P.R. where were Col. and Mrs. Sewell. From the P.R. we went to see Gainsborough's Portraits,[45] among which was one of Lady Wald-grave; no such flaming Beauty in my Eyes. In the Church, I saw an old Acquaintance, whom I have not seen since I left College, Mr. Atherton, Master of Tiverton-School. I asked him for George Scoble. He told me, he was now at Penzance. I enquired of his Character. The Words of his answer were these: "He is a very good Lad, sober, diligent, and capable: he will do very well." This Mr Atherton is to preach next Sunday afternoon at the Abbey, where I have been teized much to be: in the morning either Dr. Beridge, a Clergyman in Lincolnshire, of 2000 pounds per ann. or one Mr. Parsons; not yet determined. I shall be at the Cross-Bath Chapel in the Morning, to do the whole Duty, and read Prayers in the Afternoon when there is to be no Sermon. I had the Honour to preach last Sunday before Dr. Hume, Bp of Oxford and Dean of St. Paul's. Before Evening Prayer Mamma and Fanny walked out to bespeak a Trifle for each of you, to bring you for a Bath Present; and I went to wish Sr. Booth Williams and his Lady a good Journey to Ham near Richmond in Surrey, one of his Seats, for which they set out to-morrow. Col. Sewell, Mrs. Sewell and Master drank Tea and Coffee with us. The two latter went to the Play with Fanny: the first staid a great while after them. Major Tucker came in an hour before the Col. went, and staid long after him. Ah! poor Major! I shall lose him too to-morrow, and must bid Adieu to his innumerable Drolleries, excellent Stories in themselves, and excellent-ly well told by him. "May Joy go with him, whereso'ere he goes!"

When all were gone, away went Mama and I, took two Turns on the

---

45   Thomas Gainsborough (1727–1788) settled in Bath in 1760 and took lodgings
     at the newly built Circus. He remained there until 1774.

Parade and home to Supper. I have often mentioned the Pavement for Walkers, all flat Stones, and highly commended it. Let me now tell you, the common Pavements, which the Carriages go over, are of Stones not very roughly hewen and cemented with a mortar made of Earth and Lime-ashes. So that they are almost as level, as the flat Pavement.

If Jacky can come at my Silver Watch, let him wear it in his Pocket, but let him have a Ribbon instead of the Chain; and let him have a Key that will fit it, if the Key to it will not do; and let Mr. Coode set it right for him, and observe it's motions, that if it moves too fast or too slow, it may be regulated. I desire, he will not play Tricks with it, by opening it, or setting the Hand, or shaking it: and I desire, he will be careful not to over-wind it, and to wind it up always at the same Time of the Day, suppose the Evening. Let him take care of it, and it shall be his own.

Friday, May 23rd.
"Where nothing is, there nothing can come out."
So said Dr. Pinch of Ephesus, and so say all his Successors in Conjuring Art. This will excuse me, if I write but little to-day, because very little has occurred.

Fanny desires Mary to excuse her not writing this Post: she has had not Time, but hopes nothing will hinder her writing next Post. You see how her Time is taken. I may call her RAKE in capitals. At Play last Night, at the Ball this night. Well, but this is the last Ball for the Season, and a great deal of company expected, the more for that Reason.

"So, Peggy, I may call her Rake:<br>
Yet she'll nor Ball, nor Play forsake<br>
Call me a Rake, Papa, you may:<br>
I own, I love to see a Play.<br>
A Rake, Papa, you may me call:<br>
I own, I would see the last Ball."

This is a sad corrupting Place, Peggy: even sober Fanny is tainted. I hope, a little Country Air will sweeten her again. Don't you think, it would be a cruel Thing to bring another of your Sisters here? And yet Mrs. Sewell proposes it, proposes for us to put Dolly to a Boarding-School here. We have not yet considered the Matter, as it is fitting; but we suppose, Dolly will have no Objection, but will rather be here than at Glant, perhaps than at Exeter; surely rather than at George & Ury's.

Your Mama hath this day paid a Millener for clear-starching an handkerchief 6d. – hemming it, 1d. – could not you get your Live-lihood, with your Hands full of work at this Price? Could not Mary, with all her literary avocations?

Mr. Newcombe prevented my going to Church this Evening. – Mr. Morshead is gone West. I have got a good many Bath Acquaintance among the English and Irish Clergy: but no Devon or Cornish one remains, save Mr. Gregor, and Mr. Thomas of Truro. Mr. Newcombe lives in Bristol, so I don't reckon him; and Ld. Edgcumbe is still here.

So far I was come in Writing, when the Col. & Master Sewell came in to usher Fanny to the Ball, where Mrs. Sewell had appointed to meet them. The Col. having introduced her to where Mrs. Sewell was, went with me to Morgan's Coffee-house, the Corner-House between the Grove and Wade's Passage. Here we had Tea and Bread and Butter, tho' I was passed Tea before: but I can eat and drink at any Time. From the Coffee-Room the Col. went to the Ball, I to your Mama. We then took a Walk together, down Horse Street to the River, up King's-Mead to the farther End of King's-Mead Street, and so Home; a long Walk, and a tedious; for, near a Quarter mile of the Way towards King's Mead Street, they are building new Houses, and the Ground is tore up, just as if one Enemy had done it to retard the Progress of another. In this Street lives Mr. Taylor, who hailed us as we went by, made us rest ourselves a little, gave us some Cake and Wine by way of Refreshment, accompanied us to our Door, then went to the Ball. Thank God, I am very well after my Walk: and well we all are. Remember us to all friends, the Doctor, etc., Friends at Falmouth, etc. Our Blessing upon all you children at Vicarage, children and grand-child, blooming Molly, at Penryn: Fanny to all as due. Remember us to George and the Maids; me to the Clark, etc. A good Journey to dear Jacky and George. I must here conclude myself,

Your most affectionate Father,
JOHN PENROSE.

Bath, Saturday, May 24th. 1766.

My dear, dear Peggy, and all the rest of my dear Children, whom I long to see, and whose Welfare is the Thing ever nearest my Heart; If it please God, that all succeed according to our Wish, this is the last Letter you will receive from me dated Bath. For this will not go till Wednesday Night, and the next Day in our course of writing to you is not till Monday night, the which Night we hope to lodge at Taunton; and if we write from Exeter the Thursday, you will receive our Letter the Saturday, and till then you would not receive it, tho' we wrote you from Bath. The Exeter Coach sets out hence Monday morning at six o'clock: we breakfast at Wells, dine at Bridgewater, lodge at Taunton; breakfast the Tuesday at Tiverton (not at Cullumpton, as in the way up, the coach now takes another Route,) and dine at Exon at Mr. Paul's where we hope to meet, all in good Health, and with grateful Hearts to God for his Mercies, our dear Jacky.

From casting my Eyes forward, let me now look a little backward, and say a Word of Intelligence from yesternight's Ball. Sewell danced a minuet, and was much admired. Fanny made the Tea for the Company she was with; and, I dare say, she was much admired. The Ladies have a Dress coming into fashion, called a Minute Dress, because it can be put on in one Minute; and another, called a two minute Dress, because it requires but two minutes to put it on. One of these Dresses Fanny saw at the Ball, too distant for her to note it particularly; and were she ever so well acquainted with it, I must have left it to her Pen to describe. Madam came Home in a Chair, in very good Season. The good Hours observed here at all Diversions, render them much less exceptionable, than at Penryn and other Country Towns.

Rain this morning, and a considerable Perspiration, as I always have after Fatigue, (you know I had a long and troublesome Walk last Evening) made me Chair it to the P.R. and back directly. Notwithstanding the little Rain, it was very warm; even Fanny thinks it warm, and the Sweating Room would be too hot for her. – Mr. Grigg sent this morning, to know if I could conveniently serve St. John's (Cross-Bath) Chapel the 1st of June instead of To-morrow; but I cannot, because I am engaged, for the Rector of Bath, to read Prayers and administer the Sacrament in the Morning, and to read Prayers and preach in the Evening, of that Day, at Witcombe, a little Church in a Village the South-East side the Avon, not far from Lyncombe Spaw, exactly a measured mile from the P.R. So to-morrow I shall serve the fore-mentioned Chapel, according to Promise, and one Mr. Beavan, a young Gentleman, is to read the Morning Prayers.

While we are in Devon, do you continue to write us the same Posts, as you do now; and we will continue our Correspondence in like manner.

We dined to-day with Col. Sewell. Mr. Gregor dined there too. The Dinner was very sumptuous, such as became the Col. and Mr. Gregor, far above our Station. At the higher End three boiled Chickens, at the lower an Ham bought and dressed at Mr. Gill's', on one side Carrots, on the other Cabbage, in the Middle Butter. Second

Course, at the higher End Veal Cutlets richly done, at the lower End a prodigious fat Goose, on the sides Gooseberries, and Tarts. After, Cheese on a Plate, and Butter in a large Glass of Water for Coolness: Every Thing very elegant, Wines, Tea, Coffee, etc. excellent in their Kind. Vast Likeness between Doctor Coode and the Col.: in their Fondness for their respective Grand-children. Mrs. Sewell forbid to give the Servants: This, disagreeable.

At Mrs. Sewell's we saw a curious Advertisement, which not being able to get a duplicate of, I have extracted Part of it for your Entertainment. It is from one Mr. March, Surgeon Dentist, dated Oct. 2nd. 1765, who attended at his House in Pallmall London, every Day except Sunday, to be consulted upon the various Disorders incident to the Gums and Teeth, and to prevent any mistakes, fixed the following Fees.

For his Advice − £1.1.0.
For Every common Operation − £1.1.0.
For Filling a Tooth with Gold − £1.1.0.
For drawing a Tooth or a Stump − £1.1.0.
For putting in a common artificial Tooth − £6.6.0.
For putting in an artificial Tooth of his new Invention − £10.10.0.
For taking out a Tooth and replacing it, £6.6.0.
To transplant a Tooth with Success, a Folly.
For fortifying loose Teeth, the Fee according to the Nature of the Operation.
For an entire Set of Teeth of his new Invention, £105.
For any Number of Teeth of the same Kind, the Price in Proportion.
If any Operation be undertaken, the Money to be paid before.
For his Tincture £1.1.0.
For his Powder to clean the Teeth 5s.
For his Root for the Teeth, 2s.6d.

I beg you all, Children, take what care you can of your Teeth. If Artificial Teeth be of so great Price, how much more valuable those, that God and Nature has given you! Half Hour past Eight, when we came from the Colonel's.

### Sunday, May 25th.

This morning I preached at St. John's Chapel, Text John III. 3,5. and in the Afternoon I read Prayers there, after having been at the Abbey, where Mr. Atherton preached on 1 Cor. XIII.9. "We know in Part". Your Mama and Fanny were at the Abbey both Parts of the Day, where in the Morning Mr. Parsons, a Norfolk Clergyman, preached a flaming Sermon, of 50 minutes long, against the Methodists and other Oppugners of the established Church. His Text, 1 Thess, V.21. Between the Services was an Anthem sung by the same Person, who sung before the Wiltshire Society, out of Job XXII.21, etc. I came from the Chapel, and assisted at the Sacrament, with Mess. Taylor, Atherton, and Totton. Mrs. Sewell and Master were at St. John's Chapel in the morning; she generally goes there, because it is warm. The Roof and Walls have been swept since I spoke about it to the Curate, and the Place was very neat. Mr. Croxton, who died suddenly in the Pump-Room last Week, was buried in the Abbey this Evening. Mr. Newcombe drank tea here, and offered Fanny a Ticket to the Public Breakfast at Spring-Gardens To-morrow, but, as she has no particular Acquaintance going there, that she knows of, and he is going to Lyncombe-Spaw for his Health, she did not accept it. My Feet acked to-day so much with standing, that I am afraid walking to Witcombe next Sunday and back again, and doing all the Duty, will be too much for me; so I have desired Dr. Grant, at whose Request I was to go thither, to get one of the Bath Clergy to supply Witcombe, and me to supply one of the Bath Churches. Mr. Grant offers me a Chair, both thither, and home again; but if it can be done, I shall rather preach here.

### Monday, May 26th.

Lord Edgcumbe came to me in the P.R. this morning, and told me he should set out to-morrow for London, desired his Compliments to all Friends at Penryn, and told me he should be extremely glad to see me this Summer at Mount Edgecumbe. The Company are going away apace, the Music hath left off playing at the P.R. and yet the Bathonians, as well those of the Faculty as others, agree in one Voice, that from the middle of May to the End of June the Waters have most Virtue. Mrs. Sewell, whose Goodness to us is surprizing, has prepared a very pretty Present for Molly Coode. Our Thoughts now are all turned towards Home. This day se'nnight we are to set out. The Time will soon pass away. Pray God give us all an happy Meeting! What day that will be, must be fixed at Yendacot.

As I was returning from the P.R. I met Mama and Sister, reading Charles's Letter as they walked along: they turned back again, and away we went home to read over together your welcome Pacquets. It was exceedingly well done of you to get the two covers of Lord Falmouth; and I am surprized at your Courage.

It was exceeding kind of your Uncle and Aunt to invite you all to

Penwerris, and quite polite. Charles and Mary in particular ought to think themselves under great Obligation. We are glad, the Small-Pox are so favourable. We wish Jacky Joy of his Bird and Cage. Let the Clark speak to the Sherborne News-man for a couple of Quire more of ruled Paper, not gilt. – You do not any of you, say, whether there was a great Congregation, when the Friendly Society had their Sermon. I am glad they were so well pleased, and wish they may profit by the good Advice Mr. Harris gave them. I wish Mrs. Harris, if she goes to Bristol, may find Benefit by the Waters. I suppose, Mr. Harris would accompany her. I should be very glad, if able, to give him any Help in his Absence. – Mrs. Nevill is very good to you all. Mama intends to bring her a Trifle from Bath: we are too much reduced to deal in any thing but Trifles. – We think, George might safely enough have carried Mrs. Kempthorne's Candles. But it is too late to give him Orders about it. Were I to write by the Post, which goes out to-morrow morning, you would not receive my Letter till George is gone; or were the Post to come in early with you next Saturday, there would not be Time to let Mrs. Kempthorne know, that George would carry them. I am afraid Mr. Pierce will be vexed; but I cannot help it. – Mr. Trevanion is not yet dead, but there are no Hopes of his Recovery, – How came Mr. Hodge to ask Jacky to Tea? We suppose Mr. Neddy is home, and account for it that way. – Surely Peggy is an extraordinary Manager, if any thing will last longer under her care, than when Mama herself is at Home. I speak with Respect to the Ale. Tho' I suppose, by this Time, it is good for nothing; and, if so, it had better have been drank. Such Saving is Waste. But, why do I say a Word on this Subject? As if Peggy, my Butler in chief, did not understand the Things peculiarly in her Province. I must cry *Peccavi*, and ask Pardon. Dear Peg, you answer the Query, which I put you, with great Prudenc? and Tenderness of Heart: and I do assure you, I have received a good deal of Pleasure from that Part of your Letter. – Don't ever be alarmed again at any Spirity Story: for I doubt not, but the Apparition I mentioned is as real an Apparition, as ever appeared. All Accounts of Spirits, and such-like airy Beings, Spring from Fear; and if People had Courage, when any thing uncommon happens, to search the Affair to the Bottom, all Ghosts and Hobgoblins would vanish of themselves, without drawing Circles, or the Intervention of a Conjurer.

Thank daughter Coode for her kind Letter to her Mother. I have said Mama and Papa, in the former Letters and the Beginning of this, but the Mode is now quite altered. The old fashioned way of Father and Mother is come round again; and we old-fashioned folks like it best. – Most likely the Colonel's Cravats will come to-morrow: no doubt but they will please; and the Col. will be glad of the Pens; he can write with no other. – We are very sorry indeed, that the Doctor is still so indifferent, and at times so bad. He must come to Bath. Bath-Waters cure all Disorders, curable or incurable. The worst is, the Doctor hath mean Opinion of Infallibles. My feet are very weak, and ache pretty much at times, else I am very well. – Nothing can be more agreeable to us, than to hear of dear little Molly. Whether she laughs or cries, as we suppose she doth every Thing according to Solomon's Rule, There is a Time to cry, and a Time to laugh, all is quite agreeable: and we are glad to find her Cold is gone; Rudeness in her is an excellent Sign. We shall see her play a thousand pretty Tricks, which we cannot dream of, when we return. So long Absence will make her Improvements more sensible to us, than to you who are always with her. We wish Mrs. Rosewarne, Mr. Heame, and all the Ladies, Joy of the late Addition to the Family. May the Child enjoy every Blessing which can be, and give her Father, Mother, and other Relations all the Pleasure their Imaginations can form! Tell Dolly, that I think by Mrs. Coode's Letter, these are fine Times for Lying-in Women. – Tho' I don't know in what manner, yet am I glad the Parish of Budock have settled with Capt. Bown: Peace and Good-neighbourhood is a very glorious Thing, and almost at any Purchase is worthy the Price. – Sister hath taken care to bespeak for Mrs. Coode, what she spoke to her about. I was with her at Mrs. Brett's about it; so you may depend on it's being well done. – Our Blessing to Mr. and Mrs. Coode, and Molly, (pretty Creature! says the Col. 100 times a day, of Sewell,) our Love to the Doctor, and all Friends. Fanny's Love and Service every where, as due.

Tell Son Coode, that Mr. Heard is not now at Bath: as soon as he returns, which I expect in a Day or two, I'll not forget to speak to him about the Coode Pedigree: and I fancy, he will be very favourable.

Tell Dolly, that Mrs. Coode gives us the Pleasure to hear, that she is a good Girl. Your Mother hath got a printed Bill of the Terms of the Bath Boarding-School. But she intends going with Mrs. Sewell and talking with the Mistress. Mrs. Sewell says, if she comes to Bath-School, she will be as a Mother to her, and introduce her into polite Company, and she shall dine with them Sundays when they are in Town, and keep her Christmas with them. The Col. says, she is his Plumb-pudding Girl, and he will take care of her.

While it is in my mind, let me tell you, that if George does not take Mr. Pierce's Candles with him, (tho' I suppose he will, but he loves to raise difficulties,) you may desire Mr. Enys's Servant to take them to

Exeter in the Coach, when he goes to meet his Master, and leave them at Mr. Paul's.

Fanny will be so kind as to answer Charles's very kind Letter, He hath surprizing Parts, to write so much without being dictated to. Then, in one respect, he is equal to you all; I mean, in writing so much domestic News. We should not have heard, but for him, of the poor old Hen's Death, nor of the Fruitfulness of the others: we should not have heard of their furious Fightings, nor of the Bunches of Bees, which I thought were all dead; nor of the Order of his Gardens, nor the Frizzing of his Hair. These are very important Articles, and we take it kind in him to let us know them. Then, what is of still more Importance, we have it from his own Hand, that he is very good indeed: And I assure you, that is very good News. No wonder Mrs. Nevill gave him such a pretty little Book.

Before this comes to your Hand, Jacky will be (I hope) in Devon; so his Letter shall be answered by Word of Mouth. I must tell you, my trusty Housewife, he speaks well of your House-keeping; and was even with me for the Spirity Story, for with full as much Ceremony, and teazing Preamble, he introduced the pompous Article of News, "Mr. Evans has a new Wig." The Mountain was in Labour, and brought to Bed of a Mouse.

Not so Mary. Every Thing she says, is worthy her Ladiship. She is a very diverting Correspondent, and affords a good deal of merriment. And I find, by a Specimen she has given, she can spell well when she is careful. It is worth her while to be careful: and in a very little time, she will write fluently, and make very few mistakes. I observed Fanny's Countenance, when I read the hooked Paragraph concerning Mr. Bolitho; and, as she did not change Colour, I conclude her honest. But Fanny will answer her Letter.

I return to our own Affairs. Tea Visiters to-day Mrs. Marsh and Mrs. Graham. Before they came in, Lady Simpson was here, and Col. Sewell; but as soon as they came in, the Col. ran away, which he would not have done from the French Army; and immediately after him, away went My Lady. She is a very personable Lady, very dressy, between 40 and 50; has no Marks of Widowhood in her Words, Behaviour, Countenance, or Apparel: but is as buxom and gay, as one who sits as a Queen, and has never known Sorrow. Her Husband was Sr. Edward Simpson, Dean of the Arches, a Place of great Honour and Profit, in the Prerogative Court of Canterbury. The coast was hardly clear, when the Col. came again. I begged him to sit down; told him we were going to see Mrs. Sewell, and would come back to him presently; but he insisted on going with us. We found Mrs. Sewell just returned from a Rout at the Countess of Lauderdale's. We stayed a reasonable Time, and would have gone, but found an Embargo laid on us, till after Supper. We had cold Ham, (the Ham cost 11s. weighing 13 lb. and 1s.6d. dressing) minced Veal, and Tarts: preserved Orange, good Wine, etc. etc. etc. a hearty Welcome, better than all: and we were not home till near ten. This is the latest Hour we have kept, since we have been here.

Tuesday, May 27th.

I have spoke to Mr. Heard about making an Extract from the Herald-Office Books, relating to the Families of Coode of Morval – Methleigh – and Sethnoe; and desired the Arms of the Methleigh-Coodes may be emblazoned. He told me I should have it soon, probably before I go from Bath, and that the Expense should not be much. I did not let him know, Mr. Coode had desired the Extract might be made; but spoke of it, as if I thought such a Thing, through Mr. Heard's Acquaintance and Good-Nature, would be an agreeable thing for me to carry him from Bath.

After Morning-Prayers Mrs. Sewell was so kind as to go with us to Trim-Street to talk a little with Mrs. Pullaine, the Boarding-School-Mistress concerning her Terms: which are Sixteen Pounds a Year for Boarding, and learning to read and work, and a Guinea Entrance. Three Pounds a Year learning to dance, and Half a Guinea Entrance. Forty Shillings a Year learning Writing and Arithmetic, and Five shillings Entrance. Five shillings Entrance to each of the Teachers, which are Two. Two Guineas to be paid in Lieu of a Silver Spoon, a Pair of Sheets, Six Napkins, and four Towels. Two Guineas at Xtmas, or once in a Year, a Present, which the Mistress divides amongst the several Parties concerned as she pleases. Half a Guinea to be paid at Whitsuntide, and Half a Guinea at Xtmas, if the Ladies keep the Tides at the School: but this is not insisted upon, tho' every Body pays it. One Ball in the Year, at which is paid five shillings: and five shillings a year for a Seat in the Church. They now go to the Abbey; but the Mistress has taken a Gallery for the Ladies in the Octagon Chapel, now building at the foot of Milsom Street, when it is finished. The Mistress is a well-looking Person, and we like her very well. The House is a very handsome one, very near Barton Street. All Bills to be paid every Half-year. Great care will be taken to instruct Ladies in the English Grammar. If Dolly comes here, she will soon become acquainted with Apostrophes and all the Niceties of Spelling. From Mrs. Pullaine's we went to King's Mead Square with Mrs. Sewell. Just inside West-gate, as we walked along, your Mother dressed in green,

your sister in yellow, a fellow passed by, saying,
"The finest Ladies I have seen,
Are one in Yellow, one in Green."
In the Church-yard we met the Col. who came with us to Abbey-
Green, and staid till near Two o'clock, our Hour of Dining. The
Boarding-School Hour of Dining is a Quarter after One, of rising Six,
of going to Bed between Eight and Nine. The Col. and Mrs. Sewell
are very eager for Dolly's coming up; but We are to pay the Expence,
and we think it a great one; we shall consult our friends at Penryn and
Gluvias before we determine. The Colonel's Cravats and Pens are come
safe. How he likes them, I cannot tell, because we sent them to him by
Sally, and have not seen them since. He paid us the £1.17.6. for
them, as soon as he knew what they came to. The Coach-Charge for
bringing them was one shilling and six pence, and the Porter had three
pence for bringing them from the Inn, which is but in Staul Street at
the End of Abbey Lane. One Mr. Townsend, a Gentleman of Exeter,
who dined at Sr. Booth Williams's the first Time I dined there, is to
go to Exeter with us in the Machine. There will be but we four. I hope
for a pleasanter Journey down than up. Your Mother's Knee is still
very troublesome, and cannot be knelt upon. I am pretty well, thank
God, and read Prayers at the Abbey both Parts of this Day. – Erratum
in my former. The Name of the Anthem-Singer at the Abbey is Mr.
Hannaford. I was mistaken, or my Informer was. – I don't know, how
plenty Green-peas are with you. I have seen none till to-day, when
four shillings were asked, but two were taken, for so many Peas in the
Cod, as would (when dressed) have filled perhaps a good Sawcer. –
This Evening after Tea we all walked to the Iron House. It is in the
Bristol-Road, close by the River, near the Place where in the Map the
Word Bristol begins. As all that see the Inside of this House pay
sixpence apiece, Your Mother and I took a little Walk, while Fanny
saw it, and we rest satisfied with her Description of it. It is a little
House made entirely of Iron, and completely furnished with House-
hold Goods of all Kinds, of a minute Size, such as suits the
Dimensions of the House. So that it is a little House, and Goods in
Miniature. Fanny was within, and viewed it, and must be more
particular in her Account of it, when you meet. It would make an
excellent House for Charles's little little Crim of a Crim of a Giant.

## Wednesday, May 28th.

Mr. Williams of St. Ewe, who is returned from London, sets out for
Cornwall this Afternoon. Fanny was offered a Ticket to the Ball the
King's Birth-Day, half-a-guinea a Ticket, by a fine golden Gentleman:

but we set out the 2d. of June, and the Ball is not till the 4th. – Mrs. Grant's last Week's Bill, as follows:

| | | | | |
|---|---|---|---|---|
| May 22. | Roasting Veal | – 4d. | – Breast 1s. | |
| | Stewing Spinage | – 2. | – – 1d. | |
| 23. | Frying 3 Soals | – 6. | – – 1s. | |
| 25. | Roasting Lamb | – 4. | Bad – | ⎫ |
| | Boiling Potatos | – 1. | | ⎬ 2s.6d. |
| 26. | Roasting Lamb | – 4. | Shoulder | ⎭ |
| One Week's Lodging | | – £1.5s.0d. | | |
| 24. | We dined at the Colonel's. | | | |
| 27. | We had a Veal-Pie, price 1s. 6d. | | | |

A Quarter before Eleven we set out for Walcot Church,[46] which stands in that London Road, which joins to Walcot Street, a little beyond where the Map extends to. But there was no divine Service, so we trudged back again, in small Rain all the Way, through the middle London Road, by Bladud's Buildings, and through Broad Street, Hight Street, Cheap-Street, and West-gate Street, to the Colonel's: because Mrs. Sewell had sent us Word this morning, that it was too cold for her to stir out. While we were there, Col. Mansell, and his Nephew, a Gentleman who has acquired an immense Fortune in the East Indies, called also Mansell,[47] came in: by which means, we had an opportunity of seeing Sewell's Father, a well-made, well-looking man. He returns to Bristol this Evening. The Col. is very thankful to Mrs. Coode for getting the Cravats, which he likes exceedingly well; and to Mr. Coode for the Pens. If Mr. Coode will supply him, he may have all his custom; for he can write with no other. He has desired us, when we get home, to buy him some more Cravats, and he hopes Mr. Coode will with them transmit some more Pens. We had for Dinner a Brill, the same Kind of Fish we partly dined upon at Lyncombe. Your Mother bought it in the Market, where she saw a Butcher drinking Chocolate for Breakfast. To-day we lost another of our Acquaintance, Mr. Newcombe: and next Saturday Mr. Gregor goes. We shall leave no one behind of those we know but Mr. Sam. Thomas. Sister is not so well as we could wish: and I have lain two hours on the Bed this afternoon, affected (I fancy) by the Weather, which is very rainy. The

---

46  St. Swithin's was rebuilt in 1777.
47  It appears that this younger Mansell was Col. Sewell's son-in-law and young Sewell's father.

Rain kept all from Church this Evening. I went to the P.R. in a Chair. The Gentry are leaving Bath very fast. We have seen eight coaches, Chaises, or Chariots, set out to-day with Company, and Luggage. Coaches are common here, and almost as many Vehicles with Coach-Boxes as without, tho' Mr. Enys's Coach-Box was with us deemed so unfashionable. – Mr. Totton, whom I have several Times mentioned, is a Clergyman, beneficed in Northumberland, but lives within ten miles of London for the Benefit of his Lady's Health. – I hope in God, that nothing will prevent our setting out the Time appointed: Do you all pray to God, to give us a good Journey, preserving us in our going out and coming in.

> I am, my dear Children, with Prayers for you,
>> Your most loving Father,
>> JOHN PENROSE.

P.S. Mr. and Mrs. Hamilton, Mrs. Peter's Parents, live splendidly here in Bath, in King's Mead Street. I have seen him at Morgan's Coffee House. – Your Mother's Head aches very much, and has done so this day or two.


Bath, May 29th. 1766. Thursday.

My dear Peggy, and all my dear Children,

When first I wrote you from this Place, I only thought of giving you the Satisfaction (for such I knew it would be) of seeing my Hand-writing; because on the Road I had been so ill, and was so ill for some Days after my coming hither. Little did I think, that I should be able to hold out a single Page; whereas, by the Blessing of God, to my great Pleasure, as supposing I gave Pleasure to you, I have been enabled to carry on an Epistolary Correspondence with you for near eight weeks; for so long will it be from my first commencing my Scribble to the Time you receive this, this the last Pacquet, wherein (I hope) you will see me date from Bath.

The Pacquet, sent you by last Night's, or rather, this Morning's Post, being somewhat doubtful, whether it would pass uncharged, we sent to the Post-master, and desired him to examine the Weight of it, who said it would do very well. Else we must have gutted it, and should have been very sorry to have taken out either Mary's or Charles's Letters. – This morning, being the Day of the Restoration of

K. Charles II: the Day, in which the Ecclesiastical and Civil
Constitution was restored: a Day, which all true members of the
Church of England ought to celebrate with religious Joy; was ushered
in, with ringing of Bells from the three Towers of the Abbey, St.
Michael's and St. James's Churches; not only the Boys and Girls, but
the Chairmen, Collier's Horses, Coach-Horses, etc. are adorned with
Oaken Leaves; large Oaken Boughs stand up in the Front of most
Houses; the Union Flag was displayed, on Top of the Abbey-Tower;
Mr. Mayor in his Scarlet Gown, attended by the Magistrates, and
preceded by his Officers and the City Music went to Church in solemn
State, where an excellent Sermon, proper to the occasion, was preached
by Mr. Taylor, (his Text Psal. XCV.2 former part); Prayers were read
by Dr. Warner a Clergyman of Bath. You cannot think, how I was
pleased to see the Day so well observed; and I am sure, Mrs. Nevill
must have respected the Preacher to her dying Day, if she had heard
how he run down the Usurper Cromwell. Before we went out, to go to
Church; we had reason to think, some remarkable Good-Humour was
prevalent among the People; for the Baker let us have a farthing Roll
among the other Bread we had for Breakfast, which he said he did not
care to do, nor would to any one but your Mother; for they make
farthing Rolls, it is a singular favour to have less than two at a time.
The Weather is wet, and cold and very uncomfortable: it hindered us
yesterday from drinking Tea at Mrs. Corner's, as we had sent Word;
but it did not hinder us from Church this morning. It affects my
Bones; and tho' I have no symptom of an approaching Gout, yet I have
Aches in all my Joints, especially in my Feet. Notwithstanding this, I
read Prayers this Evening at The Abbey. Your Mother and Fanny
changed Clothes before Prayers; this was one Comfort from bad
weather: The former put on her Brown, the latter her Green.

I have sent a Letter by this Post to Mr. Feroulhet, desiring him to
send the *London Chronicle* to Penryn as usual. You will be so good as to
put the Papers away safely, after Mary and Charles have done with
them. I apprehend, when Mr. Enys went to London, he stopt his
*London Chronicle* from coming: if he did not, I desire you will speak to
one of Enys Servants for Number 1466 which the Carelessness of
Borrowers hath lost for me here.

As the Time of departure is drawing nigh, I have sent home to the
Owners all the literary Productions, which I had borrowed for my
Amusement. They are Hume's *History of England, vol. the 1st.* —
Wood's *Account of Bath, vol. the 2nd.* — *The New Bath Guide*, a poem, —
Colman's *Terence* — Rotherham's *Essay on Faith* — and the *1st Book of
Massillon's French Sermons*. I have dealt very little in reading. Writing

to you hath taken up almost every minute I have not been necessarily engaged.

Friday, May 30.

This Day hath not been fruitful of Occurrences, your Mother and Sister having spent all the Afternoon in packing, and preparing for our Journey, and we all drinking Tea this Evening at the Colonel's who came this morning to invite us, and to insist on our Dining with them next Sunday. They were vastly pleased with Charles's kind Letter and Drawing; and indeed they are both very pretty; the Drawing has several things in it well designed and executed, and it shall be carefully reserved for the ingenious young Artist. I took Leave of Mr. Gregor, this Evening, who sets out to-morrow morning at four, and intends being home on Monday. Miss Eliot called here this morn, and says her Aunt is so much out of order, that she does not come down-stairs. They were to have set out for Cornwall to-day, but are now obliged to stay here longer; so these are two more, we shall leave behind us. Tell your Brother Coode, that I have an Extract from the Herald's Office of the Coodes of Morvel, and of Breage. There is no Account of the Coodes of Sethnoe; nor any Arms to the Coodes of Breage. The Arms are blazoned in the corner of the Vellum-sheet, which contains the Genealogy of the Morval Family, very neat indeed. What the Charge is, I cannot yet tell.

Let me tell you another Instance of the Colonel's Kindness. He went t'other Day to Mrs. Brett, the Millener, whose Bill will not be inconsiderable, and took her out of the hearing of all others and told her, that he knew her very well, and her way of charging, and that she should repent of it, if she were not as favourable to us as she could be. He says She knows him very well too, and that she has taken hundreds of pounds thro' his Recommendation.

Your Mother thanks Dolly for her pretty Letter; and we both thank Mr. Coode for the trouble he has taken with her, especially in teaching her to write. I never saw such Improvement in so short a time. Surely she is a good Girl, as well as has a good Master: for I think her Writing, not only comparatively good, considering how she scrawled when we came away; but absolutely so. She is a lucky girl. We have a very genteel Present for her from Mrs. Sewell, and sure I hope she deserves Encouragement. Poor Dr. Turner! There is a good-natured man gone. I hope, without self-interested views, he was buried at Gluvias, because he told me, he desired to be buried in his own little Aile, and to have a plain monumental Stone inserted in the Wall with his Name and Time of his Death. – We are sorry Miss Goodall has the

Small-Pox bad; but hope, as they are in general favourable, by the Help of God she will get the better of them. She is a fine good-tempered Girl, and we wish her extremely well.

Tell Charles, we admire his both Performances; we congratulate him on the prosperous State of his Gardens, and the Health of his Hen and Chickens; and as he is so good a Boy, I will give him great Encouragement, by letting him enjoy his little Premises Tithe-free.

Jacky will be gone from you, a week before you receive this. God send him a safe and agreeable Journey! The Same to George! We are under concern about him; and what you will do, if he should be unable go the Journey. But why take we thought for the Morrow? Sufficient for the Day is the Evil thereof. We are obliged to Mr. Hodge for his civility to Jacky, and to Mrs. Williams for her Civility to your all. — Give our Compliments to her and say we heartily sympathize with her for the Accident befallen her little Boy.

Let the Clark get all the money he can. We shall come home very poor. We received the Bill safe. You are all very kind in writing all the News you know. One charming Piece of News, is, dear Molly's having a Tooth: the first Tooth is rarely long without a fellow. Lamb is cheaper at Penryn than here by 1d. or $1\frac{1}{2}$ per lb. Mackarel here $1d.\frac{1}{2}$ apiece. We are glad Mr. Bath is better. Mary did very well in writing Mr. Hocker. I hope to make Interest, to see the Letter. It pleases me, that the Mayor objected to the Bull-baiting in the Praze: it is a mobbing Diversion, always accompanied with horrible Oaths and Curses, as well as Fighting and Uproar. We wish Mrs. Tabois Joy of her new Scholar. I hope Charles and Miss Grace will be as loving as Sweethearts.

Our Blessing, Love, and Service, attend all you, Friends at Penryn, Falmouth, Burian, etc. as due. They will excuse my naming them particular.

### Saturday, May 31.

Oh, what a wet morning have we! Ah poor Jacky! poor George! We can hardly hope, in your rainy corner of the Island that the Weather is more favourable. I wish, my Oil-case had been left behind. But I am comforted with the Thought of my honest Peg's Carefulness and Thoughtfulness. She hath cloak'd up Jacky, I dare say, so as to fence him against being wet to Skin; and I flatter myself, the Inconveniences of the Journey will in great measure be made up to the Travellers, from the consideration of their coming to meet us. We shall be rejoiced to see them. As to our Health, Fanny is very well; Your Mother hath the old Weakness in her Knee, and complains much of

Deafness, and sometimes of Head-ach; I am a little on the Grunt, with a stiffness attended with a trifling Pain in the right side of my Neck, but it will wear off. We are preparing for our Journey and are in good forwardness. We shall let you see at Penryn our little Stock of Bath Household-goods, for we have packed up all, and use now borrowed Utensils: but the half dozen Dishes and Saucers, of new old china, you will see no more at Penryn, being made a Present of to Mrs. Sewell. If you can supply their Room, by buying others instead of them, before we come home, you are desired to embrace the Opportunity. Six pence more expended in Chair-hire, that I might have my Water at the Pump: Col. and Mrs. Sewell, and Master drank Tea here: Master and Fanny went to the Play. *The Provoked Husband or a Journey to London,* with the Farce of *The Citizen.* Fanny treated Master. The Col. and Mrs. S. went home in two Chairs. We have a Present from Sewell to Jacky, with strict charge not to see what it is, till Jacky himself opens it. We are ordering all as fast as we can for our Journey: have paid my Barber, 1s.6d. per week; paid Mrs. Brett the Millener, (What Pity 'tis milleners should be suffered in a Christian Country!) paid my Fees, a voluntary Payment, to the Gentleman attending the Pump, 10s.6d. and half a Crown apiece to two Pumpers; changed the Bill Peggy sent us, (who will come to Loss in the End, Mary knows as well as we;) taken our Leave of Mrs. and Miss Eliot, Mrs. Corner, etc.: and I of many Bath Acquaintance English and Irish, Clergy and Laity. Your Mother was at The Abbey in the morning; she and I in the Afternoon. We called at Mr. Haviland's yesterday, to pay him; but have not seen him: shall leave a Guinea for him with the Col. if he does not come in our way. The Col. and Mrs. Sewell well known at Bath, and well respected. She has given Pope Joan two Packs of Cards; and we have a trifling Present for Mrs. Walker from Mrs. Brett. I received yesterday compliments from Mr. Quick of Nanswhydden. He and I met the day before in the Pump-Room, but did not call one another to mind. As soon as we parted, he was told who I was. I would afterwards have waited on him, but he had left Bath.

### Sunday, June 1st.

Glorious Weather! Let it continue to dry the Roads; we shall have no Dust, but pleasant Travelling. We think every Hour of Jacky, and pitied him yesterday till we thought he might have reached his destined Goal. My dearest Children, what an Happiness is it, and how ought we to be thankful to Providence for it, that from the Time I began to drink the Waters, which was the third Day after my Coming, I have had no Interruption from Colds, or any Kind of Disorder! I hope in God, whatever Efficacy is in them, will shew itself in me. I have met with scores, who attest that they owe their Lives, the use of their Limbs, and all the Comfort they enjoy, to the use of these Waters. This is great Encouragement and tho' I set out an Infidel, I have now an Assurance of Faith in their virtue.

Your Mother and Sister this morning at The Abbey heard Mr. Yescombe preach on Heb. XII. 5,6. In the Afternoon Mr. Totton preached on Matt. V.6. but they did not hear him. As we dined and drank Tea at Col. Sewell's, they went to the Cross-Bath Chapel with Mrs. Sewell, where the Prayers this Evening were so much later than the proper Time, that they went and came away again, prayerless, supposing there would be no Service, as is sometimes the Case. I read Prayers in the Morning at St. James's where was a most splendid Congregation. I wrote you in a former Letter, that Service begins later at that Church, than at the Abbey, for the Convenience of Servants; which might be the original Design; but at present the rich and great assemble there, because Service begins later, and (there being no Sermon) is much shorter; and (the Church having but one Door to it) it is much warmer. In the Afternoon Mr. Morrison, son of Mr. Morrison Convocation Clark for Exeter Diocese, read Prayers, and I preached on Luke XVI. 19,20. Our Dinner at the Colonel's was like his other Entertainments, too costly for us. There were three large Mullet richly stewed, a Fillet of Veal stuffed and roasted, three fine Collyflowers and a fine Dish of Green Peas. These two last Articles came, I dare say, to a fine Penny. When we dined with the Col. the time before, the three chicken came to five shillings; and we reckon the whole Dinner came to little less than thirty shillings.

Mr. Heard was here this morning, and I paid him for Mr. Coode's Extract from the Herald's Register. The Blazoning the Arms cost ten and six pence to their Painter, the Carriage from London one and six pence; in all twelve shillings: the Vellum, Extracting, and Certificate, are a Compliment to me, which I transfer to Dr. Coode.

I have taken my Leave of the Waters; and we have been to take Leave of our fellow Lodgers, Mrs. Forster, Lady Simpson, Mrs. Marsh and Mrs. Graham, who came afterwards to desire, if any of us should visit London, we would visit Mrs. Marsh in Basinghall Street. Mr. Cooke was here, to wish us a good Journey: he is a well-disposed man, and we wish him Success in his Business. Mr. Haviland, my Apothecary's Bill is five shillings; so I sent him a Line and a Guinea by the Col.'s John, desiring him to accept the Overplus as a Token of my Respect for him. – Mrs. Mundy was here this Evening to pay her Compliment before we set out. We did not know, they were at Bath.

They came from London yesterday. Mr. Mundy much better, and set out for Cornwall to-morrow Evening. She saw at Vaux-hall Mr. Miss, Mast. Sam, three Misses Enys, and Coz: Fanny all very well. – Aurelia and John have helped us in packing up our Things; we have taken Leave of Mr. Backhouse, Dr. and Mrs. Grant, paid Mrs. Grant's Bill, and are all dressed in the same manner, as we shall go our Journey. As we set out of a Monday morning, Necessity obliged us to do several Things this Even. which we should chuse to have done rather on some week-day; and Necessity hath no Law, the Sabbath being made for Man, and not Man for the Sabbath, as we are taught in the Second Lesson this Morning. – I should have told you just now, that this is the Col's Birthday, he entring into the 68th Year of his Age. – I cannot send you a Copy of Mrs. Grant's Bill, because by Accident it is put up, so that we cannot come at it. – We have now nothing to do, but to pray to God to give us good Rest this Night, and to prosper the Journey we are to enter upon To-morrow morning. I trust, we have your Prayers, the Prayers of you all, and the good Wishes of all who know the Time appointed for our Setting forth. You here must bid Adieu to Letters from Bath. God be thanked, that I have been enabled, so contrary to all reasonable Expectation, to write to you from hence, as I have done.

Monday, June 2. Taunton.

Farewell Sally – Farewell Bath. The Servants at Mrs. Grant's we gave two Guineas and half to, which Mrs. Grant said she thought was very handsome, yet we were suffered this morning to go out of our Lodgings, without so much as one single Person of the Family arising to bid us Farewell. Sally and the Col's John saw us into the Coach, a little after Six. We had good weather before Dinner, constant Rain afterwards. Mr. Townsend, formerly mentioned, our Comrade. We breakfasted at Wells, hot Rolls and Tea; then went to see the Cathedral, the Chapter House, the Library, etc. all very pretty. The Cathedral indeed poorly paved, and inferior to Exeter Cathedral in point of Grandeur, but very elegant, and neatly kept. We dined at Bridgwater, in company with three ladies and one Gentleman, who came from Taunton in the Coach going from Exon to Bath: for Dinner, Salmon, fore-quarter of Lamb, sallad, spinage, and Tarts. But an Accident happened before Dinner, which was enough to take off the Edge of our Appetites. As soon as we came to Bridgewater, I sent away to Mr. Burroughs, desiring him to dine with us at the Inn. He soon came, and met me in the Back-Court of the inn, where our Luggage was weighing. He took off his Hat to compliment your Mother, and in the Instant dropp'd in a Paralytic Fit, or something of that Kind. The Physician and Apothecary were sent for, who ordered him into a Bath Chair, put him to his House, let him blood, put a Blyster to his Back, gave him a Vomit, and what will become of him, God Knows. He cannot use his left Arm, left leg, or any Part on his left side. Your Mother and Sister went to his House after Dinner, to enquire after him; and the Collector of Bridgwater, who was at his House, has promised to send us Word at Exeter, how it goes with him. We were obliged to set out at the stated hour, and got safe to Taunton. For Supper, two roasted Chicken, Asparagus, Mutton-Stakes, Tarts, etc. Our comrade is a very prating Gossip, with a large Fortune, and an infinite deal of saving Knowledge. Tho' Mary would not have us go to Monmouth Street, this Gentleman at Bath was at a Broker's Shop in Avon-Street, and bought many a Bargain, of which he exhibited a Specimen or two.

Poor Ben. Burroughs! When I was at Bridgwater in my Way to Bath, he complained that his Back aked, and that he had Pains all over him, to see me in that dreadful condition I was in: and now I had the pain to see him drop down in the Street in a condition much more deplorable, because much more dangerous,

We hope to set out to-morrow at six o'clock, being to dine at Exeter

## Yendacot, Tuesday, June 3d

About six this morning we set out from Taunton, and had no Breakfast till, after twenty two miles Journey, we came to Tiverton. It was Tiverton-Fair; by which means, we met such Numbers of Oxen, Sheep, Horses, etc. on the Road as retarded us greatly. The Coachman too stopped a great while, whetting his Whistle and prating, at Wellington and Maiden-Down: So we did not reach Exon till half past three. Near St. Ann's Chapel, commonly called Tan-Chapel, at the higher End of St. Sidwell's Street, we met Jacky and George: very well, thank God! They turned again, and Jacky ran along side of the Coach till we came to the London-Inn. God be praised for his Mercies, in conducting us safe, without the least evil Accident, so long a Journey. The Weather was sometimes fair, sometimes rainy, but upon the whole tolerable enough. – Jacky had a very pleasant Journey; slept at Uncle's the Saturday night; was at Broad-Oak Church the Sunday morn.; slept at Lanceston the Sunday night; (this was seven or eight miles out of way, but Mr. Baker had desired George to go that Road, to let him know how Billy was; ridiculous Errand!) got safe to Yendacot the Monday; and, as I said before, met us at Exon the Tuesday. Great Joy, Joy unfeigned, reigned on both sides at our

Meeting. Happy will it be, when we all meet together, as we hope in God we shall soon, tho' what Day we shall set out hence, or what day get home, we are yet in the Dark about. What we had for Dinner at Mr. Paul's, and what Entertainment we find here, must be trusted to memory, and hereafter we will tell you as well as we can: at present I can only say, that Friends at Exon and here are all well, and shew themselves friendly. It was nine o'clock, when we arrived here. Between Exon and this we met Mess. Geare and his Brother and Mr. Furlong, but were too late to hold a minute's conference.

Your Letters we received at Exon, and one from Mr. Hocker, which will be answered when Time will permit; but when will that be? Our Time is now less our own than ever.

We find by Daughter Coode's Letter, that she and her Husband were to go this Day to St. Enoder. Uncertain yet, whether we shall go home that Way or Broad-Oak Way. I am glad Dolly is so agreeable to the Doctor, as to stay with him in their absence. I hope she will keep all Spleen from him, and be very careful of her pretty Niece. That Molly Improves in Walking, is a most welcome piece of News. Her Grand-Mother was in no small Trouble about her Backwardness in that particular. – I think, in Gentility, Dr. Turner's friends, who directed the Funeral, should have sent Mourning to Vicarage: but that as they please. Mr. Harris could not have given him a Character, as he deserved, if he had not enlarged on his Charity and Hospitality. The Doctor was a humane benevolent Man, and hospitable to the highest Degree. I am glad he remembred Penryn Poor: and I presume, an hundred a year will be sufficient Maintenance for his widow, if she be a widow indeed. – Tell Mrs. Coode, Candles are six pence half-penny. – She approves of Dolly's going to Bath, and so (it seems) do you all: This we must consult about at our leisure.

Your Sister will not forget your Scissors. – Jacky gives you a very good Character, as Mistress of a Family; so I will not reproach you with gadding. A little Relaxation, in the midst of so many Cares, will make you go through them with double Spirit. – I hope, you gave our Compliments to Mrs. Clies: you know, we always remember to them that ask for us, or shew you civility. – We will make Enquiry about a Shovel for Charles; but believe, no Iron ones can be bought little enough for his pretty little hands. But Mama (I should have said Mother: Oh! how could I be so unpolite!) hath bought a pretty Thing for him at Bath; but they will not let me tell any of you, what you are to have.

Yendacot, Wednesday, June 4th.

This morning we had a little longer Time in Bed, than the two mornings past. Early Rising by no means agrees with me. Your Mother likes it better, than I do. Mr. Tom Pierce and his Wife dined here. They came in a Post-Chaise from Topsham this morning, and returned this Afternoon. We have promised to dine with them next Monday, Mr. Sam Pierce and this family are to go with us. We purpose to lodge there. On Sunday your Mother and I are to dine at Mr. Lake's, in Crediton Parish, about a mile from Shobrooke Church, where I am to do the Duty all that Day. To-morrow we go to Dawlish, where we purpose to continue till Saturday, when, God willing, we shall be here again. This Letter we must send to the Exeter Post-Office, in our way to Dawlish: so, if any thing memorable occur to-morrow, we must send you Word of it by Monday's Post. My Letters now will only be a dry Journal, where we are, and how we do: but we cannot, consistent with the Respect due to our friendly Entertainers, do otherwise, and you will all be so candid as to excuse it.

Yendacot, Thursday morn: June 5th.

We are now getting ready for Dawlish, where we hope to be about One, four Hours ride.

Our Blessing, love, and Service to all as due, concludes from

My dear Children,

Your ever loving father

JOHN PENROSE.

P.S.I have not been able revise what I have written; so you must yourselves correct the Errata.

Yendacot, June 9th. 1766.

My dear Peggy,

Remember us with the utmost Affection to your Brother, Sisters, Mr. Coode, the Doctor, Molly and all friends. It is impossible to keep up a Correspondence now, as we could (tho' with difficulty) at Bath: yet we must let you know in general, that we are pretty well, excepting your Mama's being a little troubled with Tooth-Ach. We went the Thursday to Dawlish; got there before Dinner, after a pleasant Jaunt of 18 miles; were kindly received and entertained, and invited to a longer Stay. Saturday we got to Exeter, about two: dined

My dear Peggy,                                    Gendarick, June 9th 1766.

Remember us with the utmost Affection to your Brother, Sisters,
Mr Coode, the Doctor, Molly, and all friends. It is impossible to keep up a correspondence now, as we could (tho' with difficulty) at Bath: yet we must let
you know in general, that we are pretty well, excepting your mama's being a
little troubled with Tooth-Ach. We went the Thursday to Dawlish; got there before
Dinner, after a pleasant Jaunt of 18 miles; were kindly received and entertained, and invited to a longer Stay. Saturday we got to Exeter, about two:
Dined on two-penny pies, drank Tea with Mrs Mason, supped at Gendarick. The Sunday
I preached at St Marks, morn & ev: Texts Luke XIV. 16. and Matt. XXV. 46. Your
Mother, Jacky, and I, dined at Mr Lake's; Tea at Farmer Reed's, where Mrs Taylor and
Fanny after their Tea, came to us: Saw at Church some few old acquaintance, but
most all the church was filled with new faces. We go this morning to Topsham, being to dine at Mr Tom Pince's. The Gendarick family go with us. Whether we shall
stay at Topsham one or two nights, we cannot tell; probably, two. as soon as we
certainly know, what Day in next week we are to set out, you shall know: we
think, on Tuesday.

This Letter we shall drop at Exeter in our way this morning.
Excuse this Shortness, and horrible Writing.

                    Your most affectionate Father
                              John Penrose

Mrs Weston has sent a
Letter to Lucky Dolly.

Facsimile of a letter from John Penrose.

on two-peny pies, drank Tea with Mrs Mason, supped at Yendacot. The Sunday I preached at Shobrooke, Morn. & Ev: Texts Luke XIV. 16. and Matt. XXV. 46. Your Mother, Jacky, and I, dined at Mr. Lake's; Tea at farmer Reed's, where Mrs. Taylor and Fanny, after their Tea, came to us: Saw at Church some few old Acquaintance; but almost all the Church was filled with new faces. We go this morning to Topsham, being to dine at Mr. Tom. Pierce's. The Yendacot family go with us. Whether we shall stay at Topsham one or two nights, we cannot tell; probably two. As soon as we certainly know, what day in next week we are to set out, you shall know: we think, on Tuesday.

This Letter we shall drop at Exeter in our way this morning.

Excuse the Shortness, and terrible Writing.

Your most affectionate Father

JOHN PENROSE.

Miss Weston has sent a Ribbon to lucky Dolly.

Exon, June 12th. 1766.

My dear dear Peg,

It is great Pleasure to hear, that you are all well: as, God be thanked, we all are, except that my feet ache to-day a little more than common. You seem displeased, that we are so long in coming Home. I don't see, how we can decently help it. We should be exceeding glad, if we could have gone directly to Penryn from Bath; but that would have been unkind to our friends here, whom we had not seen for ten or twelve years. Last Monday we dined at Topsham, at Mr. Pierce's, the Yendacot family went with us. At Topsham we lodged the Monday and Tuesday nights. The Tuesday morning Jacky had a Tooth drawn. It was very deep rooted, but he bore it very well. Fanny, and I, and Mr. Tom Pierce went out in the Morning to see my old Parish of Sowton, where every thing is very neat, and pretty, and much improved, by Mr. Granger the present Rector. Wednesday morning, We came to Exon. Dinner and Tea at Mr. Paul's: Supper at Coz: Mason's[48] tho' she is at Tiverton with a sick Uncle of her Husband. We lodged at the Swan Inn, where our Horses are kept. Breakfast this morning with Mr. Thorn the Bookseller: and we are to dine at Mr. Geare's. We sent for Melly Scoble; but she is at Totness. We were

---

48   Coz: Mason has not been identified. Perhaps she was a married sister of Mr. Robert Paul and thus cousin through John Penrose's mother.

yesterday to see Arch-deacon Baker etc. Mr. Phillips we met by accident in the Street on Monday. Where we shall go a visiting after Mr. Geare's, we are not determined. But we are to go to Yendacot to-morrow Evening, spend Saturday there; dine at Shobrooke Parsonage with Mr. Manning on Sunday; pack up our Awls on Monday, and Tuesday set out for Home. We think to take Uncle's in our way, to dine with him on Wednesday, lie at Lostwithiel that Night, and be at Vicarage Thursday Evening. But if any thing unforeseen should detain us a day longer than we at present intend, don't you be uneasy, nor expect us till you see us. We cannot go to Uncle's and Brother Bennet's too; so we must leave St. Enoder, till we go on purpose another Time, which we hope will not be long first. George is very uneasy about Grace, for fear she is worse than you write We expect no Answer to this, being (we hope) to meet so soon. All join me in due Remembrances. I am, my dear, Your ever loving father,

JOHN PENROSE.

Candles here are as dear as at Penryn, and bad Candles too. They send to Totness and Tavistock, and other Places for them. October is the Time for taking in a stock, so we must leave that matter till we come home. – We sent a large Box by the Caravan last Monday and we suppose, you will have it to-day or to-morrow.

# VISIT OF 1767

Exon. Apr: 9th, 1767.

Dear Fanny,

I sent Charles a Letter from Camelford by the caravan, acquainting you that I was better, than could be expected. One Mr. Murray, a Druggist of this place, saw me go into the Post Chaise yesterday morning, and promised to let you know it by Betty Downing to-morrow, he being to set up at Catty Jobe's. You will probably be surprized, when I tell you, that we reached Exeter last Evening about seven o'clock, having changed chaises at Launceston and Okehampton. If Mr. Coode be not yet set out, you may let him know, that the best chaise in Camelford is not at Smith's, but at the Lower Inn next the Market-house; and that there are the most excellent chaises at the White Hart in Okehampton. We sent for Mr. Evans at Launceston. He has been much out of order, had taken a Puke the evening before, thinks the Duty too hard for him, the cure very inconvenient, and has given Mr. Bedford notice of quitting the cure at Whitsuntide. He intends to set out for Penryn Good Friday, sleep at Camelford, and be at home Saturday even. He will do all he can for the Service and the Churches Easter Day and the Easter-week. You will let Mr. Evans sen. know this. I shall be glad to hear by you, that he is better as to Health. You want now, I presume, to know how I bore the fatigue of so long a Journey, 57 miles in one day. Why, extremely well. I was so much bettered by my travelling, that I can walk without a stick, and this morning dressed myself from Head to Foot. We lodge at Mrs. Thorn's. I purpose to be carried in a Sedan tomorrow morning to the Machine at the London Inn. Our company will be a Lady and her maid, the lady an old School-fellow, (I believe) both of your mamma and mine. Mr. Paul's family are all well. Dolly employs four or five of them in running about the City with her. She has been highly delighted from her first setting out, and wants to see her sisters, to entertain them with her observations. I desire you to let Mr. Harris of Falmouth know, that I have consulted Mr. Geare, as he proposed; who says, that Curates are greatly wanted, and that it will be impossible to get a Clergyman, at least from Devonshire, to serve Falmouth for nine months occasionally. He is of opinion that unless Mr. Buckingham resides upon his cure of St. Michael Penkivil, the Bishop will oblige him to residence at Stithians & Perran; that his Lordship does not care to encourage Clergymen's residence in Borough-Towns where they have no spiritual Business. Dolly has been to see Melly Scoble, who is very well. – We had our Post-chaises all the road at 9d. per mile, no one expected more: but in general, the owners don't chuse to go long Journeys. The Landlord at the White Hart in Okehampton will send a chaise to Falmouth or any where, and convey Gentlemen and Ladies where they please, at 9d. per mile or 12s.6d. per day. Our Blessing, Love and Service to all as due. I fear being more particular, for fear of being the worse for it: but don't let that hinder your writing one or other of you all you can. I am, my dear Fanny,

Your Affectionate Father, etc.
JOHN PENROSE.

To Miss Penrose,
at Gluvias Vicarage,
Near Penryn,
Cornwall.

My Dear Cousin. I am sorry to find you have not received my last to you, lest you should accuse me of neglect, but tis what I have been doubtful of, hearing nothing from you in return, I should have wrote by Mr. Paul to have enquired about it had I known the time of his setting out. With Mr. Penrose's leave I now insert this short paragraph just to convince you the fault is not on my side and to subscribe myself

Your affectionate Cousin,
M. MASON.

I hope to hear from you soon.
My Mother joins with me kind love to all our Cousins.

Bath, April 13th. 1767.

My Dear Peggy,

How we took a fresh chaise at St. Columbe, Camelford, Launceston, Okehampton, I wrote your sister from Exon, where we stayed a whole day. The Friday we set out at five in the morning without Breakfast, broke fast at Columpton, dined at Taunton, slept at Bridgwater; breakfasted the Saturday at Piper's Inn, dined at Old Down, and got to Bath about six o'clock. We drank tea at Bridgwater at Mr. Burrough's. He is able totle [toddle] about, and speaks intelligibly, tho a little wildly. He and his wife were very obliging, would fain have had us lodge at their House, and pressingly invited Dolly to come there on a visit, or to keep a tide. They live in a very pretty Place, in Castle Street, a Street quite regular and uniform on both sides, built with Brick, and having quite the air of London. At the Inn Door in Bath John and Aurelia waited our coming. The Colonel had provided Lodgings for us, very much to our Liking, tho' not so cheap as at Dr. Grant's, whose House was full. We have a Parlour and two Lodging-Rooms, the first forward, the others backward, all on a Ground-Floor. Our Landlord's name is Golding: he collects the tickets at the Public Rooms. The House is on the Grand Parade, the nearest House to the Parade – Coffee House. The Parlour window has a view of the whole street between Simpson's and Wiltshire's Room, and looks thro' the Passage leading into the Grove: the windows of the Lodging-Rooms front the South, between the Backside of Garroway's Buildings and Orchard Street. Fanny will be able tell exactly what House we are in, tho' since the Map of Bath was printed, such alterations have been made here as make the Map unlike the present places. It adds much to the Pleasantness of our Parlour-window, that it juts forth a little: so that from one side of it we can see every person in Lilliput Alley, and from the other side we see the whole length of the North-Parade. We are quite out of the way of Coaches; in other respects there is not a pleasanter Room in Bath: for whoever goes to either of the Public Rooms, and all who go to the Theatre, except those who dwell on the Parades and the other two Streets (Duke and Pierpoint) which connect them, come in view of our window. Dolly was highly pleased all her journey: but, if you had seen how amazed she was at the sight of the Buildings here, and the hundreds of fine Ladies and Gentlemen, you would have been amazed yourself. The Duke of Cumberland came to Bath the Day we did: the Sunday evening he gave public tea to all, townspeople as well as strangers. You may depend on it, he wanted not company. In the morning he was at the Abbey. When Service was over, such multitudes crowded into the Pump Room that poor Dolly was overcome, grew pale as a cloth, was forced to go out, and in the church-yard cast two or three times. Mrs. Sewell was with us. The Col. and she drank coffee with us yesterday. Tomorrow we are to dine with them. They like the cravats etc. exceedingly well, and wish for more. I would, willingly express to you, how kind they are to us. But it is not in the Power of my Pen. Imagine to yourself the utmost you can, and you will fall vastly short

The old Rooms, Abbey Walks and Parades. Watercolour by William Blackamore, 1785, showing Simpson's Rooms, the detached building on the right, and Wiltshire's Rooms with its three round windows opposite on the left. The Penrose family lodged in 1767 in the Parade on the extreme left.

of any idea suitable to their civilities. Sally[49] is in Place: but they provided for us a likely girl, about 16, of honest parents in their neighbourhood, who will do very well; her name Diana. She has liberty of the Kitchen: so we have more comfort of her than we had of Sally. I consulted Mr. Haviland about my Breath. He assigns it to the gout, and says the Bath-Waters will relieve me; but he has not yet permitted me to drink them. I have seen several of my old Bath-acquaintances but no Sr. Booth here, nor Major Tucker. Mrs. Sewell was here to-day and went with us to Mr. Pritchard's and Mrs. Brett's: the Col. is a little indisposed, and is threatened with the gout in his great toe. Thank God, we are all well, and begin to recover from the fatigue of our Journey. I have bought Fanny the 3rd vol. of *Clarissa,* a dirty dab price 1s. Dolly says, the other vol. she wants, is the 7th. If so, I cannot get it. I could have any odd vol. except that and the 1st. The house we lodge in, is small, has only two servants. The only Lodgers besides us, are Sr. Gilburn Lawson and Lady, who occupy the first chamber-floor. One Lodging-Room, and Servant's Room, un-occupied. Mrs. Sewell says, Mrs. Grant (who is gone to Portsmouth) was very assiduous in going with her, to provide our Lodgings; it being a difficult thing to get Lodgings, without a Servant's Garrat and Hall. We pay 10s. per week for each Room. Tomorrow we shall expect Dr. Coode: then Dolly is to be at Mrs. Sewell's. When you send the inclosed to Mrs. Hearle's, send it with our compliments. Compliments also to all friends. We have been to Mr. Pritchard's for Patterns of Silk, which he promised to let us have, so as to send them you by this Post: but now it is come late, and he cannot let you have them till we write again; unless we send a frank on purpose, which perhaps we may be able hereafter to afford; for I have written to Ld. Edgcumbe and Mr. Basset for a dozen covers each, and for leave to apply again on the same occasion. I hope the disappointment will not be great to Mary; nor to my even-tempered Peg.
At the Abbey yesterday.

Dr Warner read Prayers in the morn. – Mr. Web in the even. Morning preacher, Dr. Grant, Text, Luke XV. 18, 19, 20. Evening preacher, Mr. Smith, Text, Luke XVIII, 14. Your mamma and Dolly, with Mrs. Sewell, sat on the Forms in the morning, in the afternoon in a Pew. The Church hath lately been cleansed and beautified; all the monuments, the Roofs, the Windows, the whole Church throughout is as neat as possible and during the Lent, all the cushions; the Pulpit, Desk, Mayor's, Communion-Table, and other cushions and cloths are covered with Black; black curtains to

---

49   Their servant during the previous year's visit to Bath.

the Pulpit-sides, Organ gallery, etc. very decent. The Duke of Cumberland sat in the long Pew, which they call the Baronet's Pew; he was dressed in scarlet with gold buttons and button-holes, 3 or 4 officers accompanied him dressed exactly like him. To-day he appeared in Blue, as did his companions. In face he greatly resembles the Copper Plates of the King. But his appearance is mean, without any thing of the look of a gentleman. 'Tis said he looks wiser than some-body else: then some-body else does not look so wise, as I wish him.[50] – In the Gallery Book-case, you will find Abernethy's *Sermons* four vols and another vol. of *Tracts & Sermons* by the same author. I desire you to let me know the first Text in each of the vols., except that with the Tracts in it and the two on the Being and Attributes. I take it, that the 1st and 2nd vols. are on the Being & Attributes of God; if so, I want the first Text in the 3rd and in the 4th vols. – Our Blessing on You, Your Brothers and sisters, and the dear children at Methleigh. I long to hear how Jacky goes on. Mary will send us, I presume, a specimen of her Drawing.

I am, dear Peggy, your ever affectionate father,
JOHN PENROSE.

Bath, Apr. 17. 1767.

Dear Fanny,

I thought to have written to you all in the round; but Mary is at Methleigh, and Jacky will perhaps be returned to Truro before this comes to Penryn. However it is all one; for that I address particularly to one, the contents are communicable, and equally respect all. I wrote, that we should have a companion for Exeter; but the Lady, we expected, went in a Chaise: But from Bridgwater we had one, an old woman in her journey to London. Mr. Coode came on Tuesday even. We were at the Colonel's, where we dined that day; and Diana (Dinah we call her) waited at the Lamb-Inn with a ticket, desiring Mr. Coode's company immediately with us. We all drank tea too yesterday at the same Place. After tea Mrs. Sewell, your mamma, and Dolly, went to St. John's Court, saw the Boarding-house mistress, etc. and liked all exceeding well. Dolly promised to be very good, and we have reason to think, Mrs. Sewell will be very kind to her, and do what she can towards her Improvement. The Col. is confined by the toe; but his confinement does not seem as if it would last long. Your mamma, by

50  Presumably, the king!

Mrs. Sewell's advice, hath bought for Dolly blue sattin for a Robe, 18 yards at 7s.3d. per yard. Mrs. Sewell thinks it more lasting than lustring.[51] In present circumstances, it is fit she should have what Mrs. Sewell approves of. A Pattern of the Sattin we have sent inclosed. By the last Post Mr. Coode sent to Methleigh, in a Frank, a great many Patterns of Silk for Peggy and Mary to chuse out of. The Patterns they chuse, must be sent back: the rest Mr. Pritchard desires may be shewn to your friends. The Stay-maker and Mantua-maker have been here, and Dolly is to go to school next Friday. She now lodges at the Colonel's. They are extremely kind to us indeed. Mrs. Sewell desires, if you can, that you will get half a dozen dishes and saucers to match those your mamma gave her. But your mamma says, she will make Mrs. Sewell a Present of those she has at vicarage. Do you then buy half a dozen dishes and saucers of the same kind, but of the larger size, and let Pellew pack them up carefully together with ours, and send them by the Caravan, directed to Col. Sewell at Bath. When they are sent, you will let us know it, and also Mr. Pellew's charge for the Package. There is no limitation of Price. The weather is very cold, the wind being very piercing. It keeps me back from growing strong. I have drank the waters three days, with no sensible effect. I assisted to-day at the Sacrament, and bore it very well; but I walk tottering. Dr. Grant preached; his Text Zach. XII. 10. Every thing is excessive dear, so much dearer almost than when you were here. We received your letters with great Joy; tho' sorry to find by them, that dear Charles has been disordered. We doubt not of your care of him. I suppose yesterday was a joyful day to Jacky. I shall expect a particular account from him of every thing he can say relating to the School. I don't wonder that he likes it: he will like it better, when more used to it. If Mr. Osborn will take on him the trouble of consulting with an Attorney, and prosecuting the Fellow that preached in the Town Hall; I am willing, that it be done in my name, and I will be at the Expence whatever it be, and I shall be obliged to Mr. Osborne for doing the good and necessary work. For never was a Fellow guilty of a more impudent brazen-face action, than to go into the Mayor's seat to bid open defiance to the Laws, after warning given to his friends, and a Prosecution lately at Tregony on a similar occasion, and to ring the Town Bell to call a Congregation, – I am drinking Pine-Bud Tea; and so far I like it very well. Your mamma drinks Bath Water thrice a day. – We are obliged to you for all the Particulars in your Letters; tho' I am not able to answer them particularly, nor is it necessary. – I have

51  Lustrine. A glossy silk fabric.

sent to London for some Franks. Such of them as are directed to me at Bath, shall be sent to you as I have opportunity. Your mamma and I pray God to bless you all, our children and grand-children at Methleigh, and Jacky at Truro. Mr. Coode and Dolly, blessing love and service, repectively as due. Remember us to all Relations, friends, and servants, unnamed. I am. my dear Fanny,

Your ever affectionate Father,
JOHN PENROSE.

I have pd. Mr. Osborn's Tenths.
Send a copy of the *Receipt to make a Methodist*.[52]

Bath. Apr. 22. 1767.

My dear Fanny,

We received your's, Jacky's, and Charles' letters, with the copies of Ld. Edgcumbe's to Mr. Hearne, and the Bp.'s to his Lordship. I hope Mr. Hocker will succeed. The Bp.'s Letter seems to me to convey a Promise, as full as could decently be made before the Living became vacant. I don't see, what can hinder it, unless Mr. Barnes writes the Bp, that he should be glad to have St. Enoder, because it joins to Newlyn; in that case St. Merryn may fall to his share, but I should prefer St. Enoder to almost any of the Bp's Livings. I had a Letter from Ld. Edgcumbe this week with some Franks; but he did not write a line on any other subject. – Poor dear little Charles! We are truly concerned for him, but hope as we did not hear from you again to-day, that he is better. If it be an ague, Mr. Coode thinks he should take something to carry it off, as soon as it is certain to be an ague. We were glad to see his pretty Letter, and thank him for it. (This Instant, while I am writing, I received some covers, with a complaisant Letter from Mr. Basset, dated Imley in Northamptonshire.) We imagine you must be in a great fright, when Charles had the fit, and pity you: and we don't in the least doubt of your care of him. – I was glad to hear from Jacky; hope he will soon be in the Head class, the Books he learns now, he either had learnt before he went to Truro, or at least was so well acquainted with them, that they can throw no difficulty in his way. Whatever Books in my Study he thinks will be an help to him, he may take. There is a *Martial*, tho' not of the Edition used at Mr. Conon's; and there is a *Buchanan*. He may have them both: and any

---

52 A tract or lampoon.

other Book he wants. I beg he will be careful of his writing; and think it best he should write upon lines for some time longer. We are glad he is so well pleased; and he will find every thing agreeable, while he behaves himself well, as we hope he always will do. – When we came away, I through mistake brought with me the scheme for Sunday Service in my absence. I now send it inclosed. Our Texts here since my last at the Abbey, Easter day in the morning 2 Tim. II. 8. Mr. Daniel the preacher, in the afternoon Luke XXIV. 34. Dr. Warner: East. Monday, Heb. XIII. 14. Dr. Grant; Easter Tuesday, I Cor. XV. 53. Mr. Yescombe. I am sorry Mr. Evans looks ill, but hope Mr. Evans Jun. does the Duty this week, unless Mr. Hocker jogs home on this occasion. I am obliged to him for his late services. I find Peggy and you will take the advantage of our absence to gad about. – There needs nothing be said about mourning for your Unkle,[53] as you talked with your mamma about it before we came away. We take it very kind in Betty Trelease, that she shews such Love to Charles.

The Waters agree with me very well; but I am just as I used to be at home, weak-footed, and somewhat affected in my breath. Mr. Coode is better, than when at home; but does not readily attribute his being better to the Bath-Waters. – We are upon a quite different footing, than last year. Then we were never free from Company; we had hardly time to eat, or read a Letter: now we are all to ourselves, unless now and then we drink Tea at the Colonel's, who is confined with the gout, but with Mrs. Sewell is very obliging. We have had no Tea-visitant, but Miss Grant to Dolly. Mrs. Grant and her Mother were at Portsmouth, when we came here, to visit her Brother lately made Capt. of the *Romney*; they returned Good-Friday evening, and called at our Lodgings immediately in a very obliging manner. They and many others enquire for you. I thought so eminent a Lady would not soon be forgotten. – O sly Peggy! never to let us know of her Intimacy with Mr. Osborn. We must go to Bath to learn news, interesting news, concerning our own family. – I shall not trouble myself or you with a detail of our wandrings up and down the Town, nor what we have for dinner, etc.: only in general our weekly Bill for dressing victuals is much as at Mrs. Grant's only we have Potatoes, Spinach, etc. dressed by the Cook, and are charged for it, which we used to dress ourselves. – Since last year all the signs in Bath are taken down, and affixed to their respective Houses. – I think I am the weaker for the weather, which has been cold or wet, ever since we came. Sunday we had Snow; but it lay not long. I have been obliged to use a chair

53   Rev. Thomas Bennett; who had recently died.

three times. We remembered your Birthday, and wished you many years of Health & Happiness over a Glass of Wine. – Mamma has bought Dolly a Pair of Silver Buckles, and – don't be surprized – a Pair for herself. – I suppose you keep up a correspondence with your Sisters at Methleigh; so you will let them know what I write, and I suppose they communicate to you what the Doctor writes, who mentions many things, which I omit out of Kindness to my Fingers. –

As to compliments, I must express myself in general, that Mr. Coode, your Mamma and I, join in Blessing, Love and Compliments as due, to our children, grand-children, Friends and other relations. Dolly's Love and Service to all as due. Mrs. Aurelia is well, & sends her Duty to her Mother & to you with Thanks for mentioning her in your's

I am, dear Fanny,

Your affectionate Father,

JOHN PENROSE.

My *London Chronicle* for the Wednesday & Thursday, the 15th and 16th of April, did not come to me. If it was sent by Mr. Feroulhet to Penryn thro' inadvertence (as possibly it might,) then all is well: if not, desire Mrs. Hawkins to let me have hers, not sent hither, but preserved at home in order hereafter to bind with the rest: if Mrs. Hawkins', be not to be had, let me know, that I may write to London for another. If Mrs. Hawkins has received the Title Page and contents to the volume, ended at the end of last year, beg that also for me. Present our Compliments to her.

Bath. May 1st. 1767.

My dear Fanny,

Remember us all in the most affectionate manner to honest Peg, Mary at Methleigh, who we heard this morning is well, and to all that family, to Jacky when you have opportunity, and dear Charles. It rejoices our hearts to find this last is so well recovered. It was very good of you to humour his stomach, and we are obliged to Mr. Enys for his Pigeons. Dolly is now at our Lodgings, very well, and very well pleased with the School. We did not design to see her till Sunday next, the Col. and Mrs. Sewell so advising, that she might be a little weaned; but this morning Mr. Brinsden told me his niece, who is Mrs. Aldworth's scholar, let him know that Dolly yesterday asked lieve to go and see us; and on being refused, unless sent for, that the tears came into her eyes. This determined us to send Mrs. Aurelia to ask how she did, and she also reporting, that Dolly was unhappy, because she did not see us, we sent for her. Yesterday I was out airing with the Col. who insisted on my dining with him at our return. He is exceeding kind; so is Mrs. Sewell. When we dined with them our little Servant dined there too. They have put us in the way of saving expence in coals. We used to pay 2s.11d. an horse-load – so we pay'd at Mrs. Grant's: so here. They told us, we were imposed upon, and this morning sent us two horse-load for 3s, the two. They are so kind as to promise, Aurelia shall be Dolly's milliner; she hath made a very pretty cap for Dolly, and washed that which Coz: Fanny, (to whom and all friends at Falmouth our sincere Love) made for her. I wish you may have an opportunity of shewing Coz: Fanny the fine verses inclosed to Dr. Peters, written by Mrs. Trevanion of Caerhayes. You may copy them, if you please; then seal, and send by Post, for want of other opportunity. Mrs. Trevanion is a fine Lady. We saw her one day at the Col.'s. We every day see Mrs. Macaulay, the celebrated female Historian,[54] and Mr. Colman,[55] author of the *Jealous Wife,* and other Dramatic Pieces. And yesterday we saw Mr. Snow and Mrs. Snow, on whom we hope to wait very soon. Miss Howell with her sister are here for their health. They were two or three times at our Lodgings to enquire for you. We happened to be absent, and they would not leave their Names. But now your Mamma has seen them. They lodge in Chandois Court where Mr. Mundy did. Mr. Paul dined with us today. He came yesterday. Mr. Geare called on him as soon as he had Intelligence of Mr. Bennet's Death, and told him to send me account of it; which he neglected to do, on supposition I knew it before, and was reproved for it by Mr. Geare. Mr. Hocker is obliged to Mr. Geare for this, and when he sees him, must thank him. The Bp's letter to Ld. Edgcumbe is full and strong, and I wish Mr. Hocker Joy. I this morning received a line from Mr. Loscombe. I wrote to him, desiring to know what day in next week we should pay our personal Respects to him. He has fixed on Wednesday, when we hope to wait on him. I this morning have wrote to Miss Chudleigh,[56] praying her to back my application to Ld. Camden, and naming some particular Preferments in his Lordship's Disposal which I think my shoulders strong enough to bear. I have inclosed a Frank to her, if she chuses to send an answer.

54   Catherine Macaulay (1731–1791) published in 1763 the 1st volume of her *History of England from the Accession of James I to that of the Brunswick line.* The 2nd volume came out in 1766 and the 3rd in 1767.
55   George Colman 1732–1794). His comedy *The Jealous Wife* was the most popular piece of its epoch.
56   Elizabeth Chudleigh, later Duchess of Kingston. See Introduction.

Catherine Macaulay. Engraved portrait by Spilsbury after C. Read. The celebrated historian was at the height of her career, when the Penroses saw her in Bath.

If she do any thing for us, I hope we shall be thankful to God and her; if not, I shall think it all for the best. My duty obliges me to endeavour for my family, and to acquiesce if my endeavours fail. Tuesday last, we all went to the Square Chapel, the Circus, etc. I was an hour and three quarters on my legs. Oh my poor legs! they reproach me for it to this very minute. Mr. Coode was quite tired with such a creeping walk. But he finds great Benefit from the Waters, and makes no complaint. He dares not complain, for his Face would give his Tongue the Lie. When Mr. Coode wrote last to Methleigh, I took the advantage of his cover to send you a few advertisements. Your Mamma is pretty well; but has been busy the two last days in mending a rotten pair of black silk stockings for Mr. Coode. And were they mended at last? No: as well a blackamoor be washed white. Sir Guildford & Lady Lawson, who lodged over our head, are gone home to Cumberland, and are succeeded by others, who coming but to-day we know not their names. We have now very fine weather, a little cold in the mornings; but it has [not] been piercing cold. To let you know one Instance of our luxurious Living, from which judge of our general Proceedings, (tho' by the by, your Judgment may be wrong) we had Wednesday last a Fish Dinner, viz: 3 pair of Soals 2s, – Lard, 3d.$\frac{1}{2}$ – Butter, 4d. – Potatos, 2d. and after all was cooked, and double cooked, any one might have been welcome to my Home for the small Price of Thank you. The same Day Mr. Derrick had a Benefit Ball. It is supposed, he might clear £150 at least. Oh Shame! Shame! Shame! that such an insignificant Puppy should receive so rich a Subscription, and the Reader at the Abbey, who is a Gentleman of Sense, Virtue, and many approved Qualities, should have on his List of Subscriptions from March 1st to this Day not more than six guineas. One would imagine, the Gentry who resort hither, were Lovers of Pleasures more than Lovers of God. The Reader has been ill ever since we have been here, but at present has hopes of Recovery.

Your letter was extremely agreeable to us; but requires no particular Answer, only Thanks. I told you, when I came away, that you must excuse me, if we left abundance of things to be matter of conversation when we come home.

The news mentions several French Noblemen of high Distinction, as being in Bath last week; but I either saw them not, or did not know them. No Person of Quality arrived here, that I know of, since my last, but just now passed before our window Lord Newark. Mr. Coode and Dolly remember to you all.

I am your affectionate Father

JOHN PENROSE.

P.S. I read Prayers at the Abbey this even. Mr. Billy Robinson called here this Evening in his way to Oxford.

Bath. May 6th. 1767.

Dear Fanny,

I have the Pleasure of acquainting you, that I am very well, only weak in my feet; but able walk about tolerably. Yesterday I conducted your Mamma and Mr. C. to Avon-Street, and called in at both shops. The only thing we bought yesterday was Silks for Peggy and Mary. They are as near the colours of the Patterns, as if cut out of the same Piece, were never made up, and are as good as new. If they do not chuse to wear them, I shall attribute it to Pride, Rank Pride, and Haughtiness of Soul. Peggy's is not a blew, but cross-barred. Let them keep their own Counsel, and no one will think it second-hand. – We went from Avon-Street to the Col's: Mrs. Sewell saw our Bargains, and thinks them very pretty. There we drank Tea. In the Evening, Mr. Brinsden, Unkle to Mr. Gregor, sent his Servant, desiring us all and Dolly to dine with him to-day. The Col. and Mrs. Sewell dine there too. We were to have gone to Bristol this morning, and had a very obliging Letter from Mr. Loscombe; but were forced to postpone our Bristol Journey, if we shall be able to go at all. – George must carry the inclosed to Mr. Smith himself; and you are desired to send Word, whether Mr. Smith is sick, or has been sick, the Col. having not heard from him some time. The Col. is able walk about the Room, and go an airing in the chaise and is pretty well on the whole, tho' yesterday he began to grunt, and feared a Return of his Erisipelas. – In every Letter you write, write something, how Mrs. White is – I forgot to tell you, that your Mamma would have matched your white Duccape[57], where she bought the Silk for Peggy and Mary, but could not; so she will try some Shop in Bath. – I am obliged to Mr. Hocker for granting the License, and his other Services. You can hardly send me better news, than that of his being in Penryn. I presume, you have as yet no certainty, as to the Living; because I am pretty sure, as soon as it is determined, His Lordship will write word to the Col. – Mrs. Crowgey's tie was very handsome. – We are all very sorry for Miss Betty Hearle's Relapse, and dread the consequences. Burn some asafoetida to drive away the Rats: that has done it before now, and is

57 Ducape. A plain-wove stout silk fabric.

an innocent experiment. – We are heartily glad poor dear Charles is so
well recovered. – I have returned the Letter to Mrs. Boswarthack: I
cannot help her. There is no one of Chesham at Bath, so far as I can
learn. A litte more Patience, and I hope all will end well –

Dear Peggy. Thank you for your Letter. You will see by the above
to Fanny, what we have done for you; and we know from your Love of
economy, and regard to the good of the Family, that if we could save
40 shillings or three pounds in the price of two gowns, you would be
pleased with it. – Mr. C. has been a little out of order, with a
giddiness in his head; but he is pretty well again now. – You may send
for Jacky the time you propose – I have inclosed a Line to Jacky –
Mary's Drawing is very pretty – I have some Books from Mr. Thorn,
aboard Martins. Let George enquire whether he be come in – Mr.
Marshall has succeeded well, in the Point of Subscription –

Dear Children all, Charles among the rest – Dolly is very moody –
likes too much to be with us, but promises to do well, and thinks she
shall improve. Mrs. Aldworth gives her a very good character, and
commends her Diligence – Dolly's blew Sattin is died black, and with
a little addition will make a cardinal for her mamma, and another for
her – Last Saturday Mr. Billy Robinson breakfasted with us. The same
day, we sent home by his man, to be left at Mrs. Penrose's in Helston,
some few Books, an old cardinal, 4 Dolly's shifts, 2 petticoats, 2
shirts, 3 shifts – The same day the Music came to our new Lodgers;
but have no encouragement to come again. – We see a great many
Ladies in Riding-Habits; but Miss Michel's Fashion of Throat Ribbon
hath not yet reached Bath – Lord Edgcumbe's Son hath been
inocculated, and done well; he had eruptions enough to give entire
satisfaction to my Lord and Lady and no one sympton which gave them
any uneasiness. – Sunday last I read Prayers, in the morning at St.
James's, in the evening at St. Michael's. Dolly dined with us. Dr.
Dechair preached at St. James's. They call him the Garrick of the
Pulpit. But he is not fit to carry the Book after Dr. Stonehouse. His
Text James 1. 27 for the Charity School. At the Abbey Dr. Goodall,
Archdeacon of Suffolk on Acts XX.35 – and Dr. Warner on the
Parable of the unjust Steward in Luke XVI. – Miss Howell and her
sister now here; should have been quite happy, had you been with us.
Two of your schoolfellows married long since, Miss Yard to Mr.
Bullen, third son, and Miss Peggy Byrdal to Revd. Mr. Stukey of
Exon. –

8 o'clock returned from Mr. Brinsden. Our Entertainment there
shall be particularized in my next. After so much good Eating and
Drinking, who dare concern himself with Thinking and Writing. At

present only know in general, that we were entertained with Elegance, Plenty, and Friendship. I must mention one thing more, before I conclude; which is that I fear I have not expressed myself clearly concerning the Place where the Silks were bought, which was not in Avon Street, but at Mr. Pritchard's. Our Duty, Love, Service, to all as due, from Dolly, Mr. Coode, Mamma, and

Your ever affectionate Father,

JOHN PENROSE.

For Dinner at Mr. Brinsden's, May 6.

First Course – Pair of large Soals; one fried with Parsley, the other boiled, the Dish garnished with Horse Radish. At the lower end, roast rump of Beef. On one side crab-sauce and melted Butter, the other side cucumbers, a Sallet in the middle; the Sallet dressed, the cucumbers cut up and with them young onions not cut up. – The Soals cost 5 shillings.

Second Course – At higher end, 6 pigeons roasted; lower end a large dish of Asparagus; one side a goose-berry Tart, the other side an hundred large Prawns, the least as large as the largest at Penryn, almost all of them larger than you will readily conceive, price of them 3 shillings.

Afterwards – Cheese sound and rotten, the rotten like Stilton Cheese, Pats of Butter, Radishes. Then the napkin, which covered the Table-cloth, being removed, a Dish of Sweet-meats, viz. 2 preserved Pine-apples, in a high Glass, which stood in a salver of preserved Peaches, preserved in Brandy. Before the cloth was taken off, large glasses brought of warm water, without Sawcers. Our Wine was Port, Madeira, and Mountain; our other liquors Beer and cyder; all both eatables and Drinkables excellent in their Kind; and to crown the whole, an unaffected friendly Welcome.

We drank Tea in the Dining-Room. Coffee out of very large white china cups, Tea out of very large Dishes, next kin to Basons of a Rummer fashion. The Coffee Jug plain upon a square salver, about 8 inches square: the Tea urn plain except a Chinese Border round the Bottom, which stood on the Mahogony Table. The Tea and Coffee cups, etc. upon a silver Tea-table or Waiter, of an oblong square, which cost £44.19.0 at 7s.8d. per ounce. The Price of the Tea Urn about 30 guineas. The silver Tea – Table had Brackets, instead of Feet. The whole Service at Dinner was in china.

Bath, May 11th 1767.

Dear Fanny,

Writing to you, I write to all. The above Account of Mr. Brinsden's Entertainment was set down the Thursday, that nothing might be omitted. Occurrences here are so few, that, tho' I write but short, I set down all I know. Your Mamma's silk sattin is not yet come: but by a complimental Letter from Mrs. Barnett we have reason to hope it will be here soon. Mr. Heard could not write, having of late been greatly harried in attending the House of Lords, who are examining the Books, Records, etc, of the Heraldry Office, and taking care that their Pedigrees be well preserved, and that the antiquity of their families may be known to latest generations. – Canon Snow and Lady went for Exon last Thursday. It is reported at Bath, that a Gaol fever, or some mortal pestilential Disorder, reigns at Exon: we hope, it is not so bad as represented at this distance. In the afternoon Mr. Cook drank Tea with us: and at night I was very sick, perhaps from the variety of victuals at Mr. Brinsden's hospitable table the preceding day. The Friday morning I was well, as usual, perhaps the better for seeing the Col. here, being his first excursion on foot. He walked all the way: but returned in a Chair. Mrs. Sewell was here too. (He had received a Letter from Mr. Jones, who said he had seen you at Mr. Crowgey's, and that Mr. Hocker would have either St. Enoder, St. Merryn, or Newlyn, at least so he apprehended.) After Dinner we sent for Dolly, and walked a way to Walcot, to see the Church. But so Fate would have it, just as we came to the Church, it began to rain, as it did when you were there: away we hastened to Lady Huntingdon's Chapel, which was shut up; so we saw neither Church nor Chapel. Thence we posted in a running walk to the Latin School, drank Tea with Mr. Hele the schoolmaster and Mrs. Hele, and got home in the Evening. The Saturday Dolly was with us again, and had her blue Sattin Robe tried on, which is very handsome. Mem: the Mantua-maker, Mrs. Williams, has artificial fore-teeth, half a guinea apiece price, which are not distinguishable from pure Nature. Yesterday at the Abbey preached in the Morn. Dr. Dechair on Job. ii. 10. and in the Afternoon Mr. Barnstone, prebendary of Chester, on Matt. XXV. 21. Neither of them hath a voice loud enough for the Abbey; else the former is a very pretty Preacher. The Rector of Bath is prayed for in the Church, as lying at the Point of Death. It is generally supposed Mr. Taylor the Receiver will succeed him, tho' there will be several Candidates. I preached yesterday Even. at St. James's Church: One Mr. Barnet read

Prayers, a Gentleman, who has a Rectory in Berkshire, which pays him five shillings and three pence a pound for Great and Small Tithes. The Doctor is got acquainted with him, and a good-tempered Lawyer of Chester, and talks about farmering with them, with a high gout. The Doctor and I are two lazy fellows, but Mamma is a very Peggy for Industry. She is now about the second cardinal, one for herself, the other was for Dolly, and you would be surprized to see what a neat one it is. – Miss Grant drank Tea with us yesterday: Dolly dined with us. Mrs Grant has been out of order some time, and so continues. She apologizes from her Ilness for not waiting on us and desires our company one day this week in Abbey Green, if she recover well enough to receive company.

We all congratulate you on Mrs. Michell's arrival among you. You will give our compliments to her, and make her welcome. (I wish she were not of so troublesome a disposition: for Mr. Michell is very obliging and friendly, and for his sake one should be glad to shew all civility to his Wife and Children. Mrs. Coode has wrote your Mamma some brief account of your being at Methleigh. She should have kept our guest there till we came home as a Relief to you. Methinks you are driving about with her every day, to Gwenneys, Falmouth, etc, and methinks I see easy making a third in the Chaise. We pity you sincerely. Was not Coz. Fanny chagrined at Mrs. Michell's coming upon you just in the nick of time, when you promised yourselves mountains of Pleasure from your Methleigh Jaunt?) We are pleased to read your favourable account of Mr. Rodd's and Mr. Rosewarne's children, and that Miss Betty Hearle is better. Mr. Osborne knows our Determination about the Woods. Half a crown in the Pound, and an acre of wood after rinding, to be taken where I please, or two guineas in lieu of it. This my proposal, which I apprehended Mr. Ferris to have embraced. If Mr. Davis declined prosecuting the preaching Rascal, I suppose Mr. Thomas, Mr. Webber, or some body else would undertake the Prosecution. I don't care, who is the Attorney, so the fellow be punished for his Impudence. – We heard before of Mr. Grant's Death, and lament the Loss of so worthy a man to his family and mankind. We are glad Betty Williams and George behave so as to please you. Am sure, no one will be a Loser by doing their Duty, with whom your mamma is concerned. Give our Blessing, Love and Service to all as due. The Doctor remembers to all. When Charles favours us with a line again, let some one see he writes as well as he can. His last is scarce legible wrote worse than before he went to Medlyn's. I believe, Pope's Books were sent by Martyn. George had best inquire at Mr. Tresidder's. I will ask about them, when I go to Exeter. Mrs.

Aurelia's Duty to her Mother. I suppose Jacky will break up against Whitsuntide the 27th instant.

Your ever loving father

JOHN PENROSE.

Supplement.

Monday eve. May 11th. Mrs. Sewell drank Tea with us. – If Mary will have a Roll such as yours, or a set of curls to wear with her own Roll, let her send word what she will have, and some of her Hair that the Roll or Curls may suit her; or if she can send the Hair she cut off, when she was under Inocculation, the pretty thing shall be made of that: and if Peggy will have one too, let us know it, and she shall have it. If one Frank will not do for conveyance, take two. – Yesterday passed before our Window a Funeral Procession for a Deceased chairman. First came two men with long staves, in mourning; the Tops of the staves wrapt round with Black, as if Streamers were tied in. Then the Clergyman: Then the Corps, born on Shoulders, with a Velvet Pall trimmed with white silk, supported by six Men: Then two women mourners: Then fifty Chairmen, in pairs, all with long crape Hatbands. – The Rector of Bath died at three o'clock this afternoon – You see by the printed Bills we send you, what is to be had at Bath: if you want any thing here, write Word. – The Col. had a Letter from Lord Edgcumbe this Day, wherein he sends compliments to me, but says not a word about the Living for Mr. Hocker. – We now look homeward: thinking to set out either the 29th inst: and stay the Sunday at Exeter; or the 30th and stay the Sunday at Bridgwater, and perhaps the Tuesday at Exeter or the 2nd of June, and not stop at all by the Way – Chuse the Present yourself, which your Mamma shall bring you home. This is not said in order to stint you, but that you may have, what will be most agreeable and useful to you. Your Mamma is willing to lay out for you a guinea & half.

Bath, May 15th 1767.

Dear Children,

I am so excessively fatigued with a long walk, which I took this afternoon, that I have been forced to lie down for a little Refreshment from the Time we came home till now near eight o'clock. So you will be good enough to excuse my writing but a few lines. Indeed I should not have written at all, were it not for my engagement. I have been very ill ever since Tuesday, first in a violent Pain in my Belly which I suppose to be the gout, and then in Pain less violent from an uninterrupted Inclination to make Water and go to Stool, which is much abated now, but very troublesome still, and affects me to a great degree. Mr. Coode is my Doctor: without him I must have had Mr. Haviland. The Cause of my Disorder we attribute to washing my Feet with Bath Water two or three evenings according to the advice of Mr. Snow. Notwithstanding my being so greatly disordered, we drank Tea with the Col. yesterday, and they with us the day before. The Col. called here again to-day, and made us send to his House for a Bottle of Genuine Sherry. To-day also we went, (Mrs. Sewell with us) and saw Mrs. Aldworth's Scholars dance; After dinner we sent for Dolly, who is now at our Lodgings. Her Mistress gives her a very good character, says she is good-tempered and desirous of Improvement. It is time for her to improve, and play the Woman; for here is a young Gentleman deeply smitten with her, a young Gentleman about her age who comes to enquire about her very feelingly, and declares she is his Favourite, and that no Lady in Bath appears so lovely in his eyes. Indeed the Bath Ladies are not very lovely. The very Fashions, which fine Ladies must follow, or they had as good be out of the World, will not even suffer them to be wholesome. Such Ladies as have their own Hair, not artificial, and have it dressed by the Barber, do not comb their Heads for three months together. Whether they kill the Lice with Quicksilver, or Mr. Coode's hammer, or by what other contrivance, is a secret; but they endeavour to conceal the Stink of their filthy Heads with Perfumes, Essences, etc. This is worse, than Painting an inch thick: but Painting too is very necessary to a fine Lady.

We received Fanny's Paquet on Wednesday.

We are sorry to hear by Charles of Billy Baker's ague. Mind Charles, to write carefully and on Lines.

We thank Jacky for the *Receipt to make a Methodist*:[58] but hope, we shall never make use of it. For the Methodist, who is of the best composition, is a worthless, very worthless creature. Jacky's letter to Fanny, as well as that to me, are written very well. We are sorry for the misfortune which happened to his Eye, which might have been of sad consequence. May that Providence, which has shewn him by this accident, how liable we all are to unexpected evils, evermore protect him; and may he daily see more and more, how much we all are beholden to divine Protection. I like his account of Mrs. James going

---

58   This was the tract that John Penrose had asked should be sent to him.

with him to Mr. Jenny's, of Mr. Conon's accosting him in Latin, of
the Various entertainment he finds, not forgetting the Stuffed Veal
and Plumb-Pudding. That Mrs. Walker is better, gives us pleasure.
Mr. Michel was always kind to Jacky. As we dare say, every thing was
done, that could be done, to make Mrs. Michel welcome, it is strange
she should make so short a stay at Vicarage. We have no account yet
from Ld. Edgcumbe about Mr. Hocker; so we conclude you have not
yet heard any thing. Dolly had a very pretty Letter this morning from
Mary, inclosed in Mr. Coode's to his Father. The account she, and
you, and all give, about Molly's Improvement is very diverting, and
comfortable, and sets the Doctor in Raptures. Poor little Edward!
Would God, we could hear a better account of him!

Dear Fanny, No Letter from Miss Chudleigh – Mr. Taylor's
Subscription increased – Your Letters very pretty – Mrs. Michell must
come to Bath – When Miss Michel visits Miss Enys, she will take her
Front with her – Sorry Mr. Harris cannot get a Supply for Falm
[Falmouth] – Aurelia is well: her Duty to Mrs. White – Col. goes
away next week – The nest of Boxes was bought at Exon; the largest of
them is with us – You don't say, whether Pope's Books are come – Our
Blessing, Love, Compliments etc. to all as due. Mr. Coode, the Col.
Mrs Sewell, etc. all remember to you all.

I am your ever loving father
JOHN PENROSE.


Bath, May 20th, 1767.


Dear Fanny,

We this day received yours, dated Methleigh: and should have been
extremely glad, could we have heard, that dear little Edward was as
well as Molly, every account of whom is truly delightful. No news yet
from Ld. Edgcumbe: but last Monday Even. at my Desire, the Col.
acquainted His Lordship with what Mr. Rawling said, that He might
mention the affair again to the Bp: and also that St. Enoder would be
more acceptable to Mr. Hocker and his Friends than any other Living.
For, I feared the Bp. upon Mr. Barnes's making St. Merryn his option,
unless applied to again, might job an exchange with some other
Clergyman. Our Precaution may be useful, can do no Hurt. – Peggy's
Letter is quite characteristic. Her Honesty & Regard for the Family
good is conspicuous throughout. – The character Mrs. James gives of
Jacky gives us an heartfelt Joy. We pray God, he may always preserve

himself pure, fearing God and regarding Man, so as to find favour
from Both. So far as we can do, he shall want no proper Encouragement. – Make our compliments to Mr. Hocker, and thank him for his
Letter. He will be kind enough to excuse my not answering it: for I
have been very much out of Order, many days; and tho' better now
than for some time past, Mr. Coode thinks I have somewhat of the
Jaundice, and to-morrow I am to take a little Purgative. Mr. Coode
goes to Bristol to-morrow, whither I shall not be able go at all. Mr.
Loscombe is so obliging, and Mr. and Mrs. Richards too, that it is
with extreme Regret I am detained from paying him my personal
Respects. But my Disorder hath forbid me to think of going abroad
far, and doth forbid me. This being a fine morning, we sent for Dolly,
and shewed her Spring gardens, with which she is well pleased, and
from which (imitating you, and would she would do so in most
things!) she has presented the inclosed Briar Leaves to Miss Mary, who
might methinks have thanked us for her Avon-Street gown. Dolly is
now answering her very pretty genteel Letter. – Miss Howell and her
sister drank Tea with us on Monday. The Sunday we were at the
Abbey. Mr. Barnstone preached in the morning on Mic. vi. 8. and Mr.
Yescombe in the Even, on Rom. vi. 23. I assisted at the Sacrament. –
One would think by your last, and a foregoing Letter, that Sweethearts were plenty in your neighbourhood. But what do I mean? One
Swallow never makes a Summer, and it must be a Neighbourhood of
Fools and Blind, if my honest Peggy with all her endearing Qualities
want admirers. – Your many Articles of News merit our Thanks. I
wish Mr. Biddulph, tho' I look on him as somewhat insignificant in
point of real ability, may not prove a Fire-brand, in the Hand of Mr.
Rawling, whom I take to be a Man of much superior Talents, and
who, tho' probably well-meaning, does not appear to me to have that
Regard to Decency and good Order, which is absolutely necessary, or I
grossly err, in the Constitution of the Christian Church. – Our Hearts
ache for poor Charles on the Return of his Ague. He may learn the
New Singing, if he likes it; and we wish him to be a good Proficient. –
Probably we shall set out hence Friday in next week, and be with you,
God willing, the Tuesday or Wednesday in the week after that. The
Doctor, as brisk as a Bee, and fresh as a Rose in June, will go from
hence in a chaise, if he can get a Partner to Exeter; otherwise in the
Machine; and from Exeter in the Post-coach: I think, we shall have
Post-chaises all the Way; I am sure it will be our pleasantest method,
and the cheapest too if we can take all Luggage with us. An answer
from you to this Letter, if it please God to prosper our Designs, will
not reach Bath before we set out; but if you write us to-morrow

sennight, we shall meet your Letter at Exeter. —

Evening. — Just returned from Col. Sewell's where we all drank Tea. Dolly was dressed in all her finery, and made a very grand appearance. She is so pleased with her School, that were it left to her choice, she would prefer staying here the time appointed to going back with us. — An eminent Miniature Painter hath drawn the Portrait of my Gown, Cassock and Band. It is finished, and exhibits a most striking Likeness. — Mrs. Sewell being a little out of order, their Journey to Frenchay near Bristol, for which they did intend to set out Friday next, will probably be postponed to another week. I would not wish her the Loss of one Hair of her Head thro' any selfish motive; but surely, if they leave Bath before us, Bath will become very insipid indeed. — Give the inclosed Letter to Mr. Williams, to forward to Dr. Peters, when opportunity offers; there being no Hurry required in the case. —

Your Mamma, the Doctor, myself, send Blessing, Love, Compliments, etc. The Col. & Mrs. S. are yours. Aurelia's Letter will speak for her.

I am, my dear Fanny,

Your ever loving Father,

JOHN PENROSE.

Bath, May 22nd. 1767.

Dear honest Peggy,

As I wrote your Sister last Post, you probably are surprised at receiving a Letter now; and I fear you will not much like the Occasion of my Writing. You know, in my last I desired Fanny to direct her next to me at Exon, because we intended to set out from hence this day se'nnight, when Mr. Coode does, and should have accounted it a great happiness to be with our dear children June 6th, as you wish: but I have been very much out of Order, in a Kind of Jaundice and otherwise, and Mr. Haviland and Mr. Coode think it best that I should stay at Bath a Fortnight longer than we designed. I pray God, the Weather prove warmer: for this is a winter-day, and it has been cold almost ever since our coming hither, and the cold has hindred my receiving so much Benefit as I had reason to expect from these Waters. But what will become of my Churches? We must do, as well as we can, if not so well as we would. Get them supplied, if that may be: otherwise, let them go unsupplied. Mr. Hocker will be there next

Sunday: and if he can be there on Trinity Sunday too, it will be charming; if he cannot, let Mr. Michel be applied to directly. If the Friendly Society have a Sermon the Tuesday in Whitsun-week, desire Mr. Hocker or Mr. Osborn to preach it; and let them know privately, that in a Parcel of printed Sermons upon a Shelf in my Study, against the Store-Room, there is one by Adams preached upon the like occasion, which I think would do very well at Gluvias with a little curtailing. I would not mention Mr. Hocker so often, but you see how hard I am put to it, by Peter's leaving Falmouth, and Mr. Philipp's gout. If possible, I dare say you will provide for the Service some how or other. This is the Day, that you go to Methleigh in Exchange for your Sister: but what I write here, concerns her as well as you, and I warrant her most zealous endeavours will not be wanting; and probably she may have more Interest with Mr. Hocker, than you have. No news yet from Ld. Edgcumbe. – Mr. Coode went yesterday to Bristol, and returned this even. well. Your Mamma and I visited Mr. & Mrs. Brinsden after morning prayer, and then dined at the Colonel's where Dolly drank Tea with us. Mrs. Brinsden says, when Mrs. Sewell and we are gone, she shall take great notice of Dolly, and advise her freely: and Mrs. Sewell says, that next Season when she comes back from Frenchay, she will equip Dolly with Jewels and Gold Watch, to make a Figure at the Balls. Mr. Orchard has orders to make a Roll for you, and another for Mary, as near as he can match the colour of your respective Hair. Mary says, you are such a Belle, that we almost question whether a plain Roll will be smart enough for you. If you would have a Sett of Curls besides, tossed off A la mode de Paris, let us know in your next. – I am much afraid, as I shall not return so soon as I thought, the Impudence of the preaching Rascall will go unpunished. It was a great misfortune upon me, that I was forced to set out so immediately upon his Preaching. But Mr. Thomas's Reason for leaving him alone longer, because he has been left alone so long, does not seem very weighty. – We will mind the Pine-bud for Miss Kitty, and are sorry to hear she is in any danger of Consumption. – Thank God, Charles is well again, We hope, the Methleigh air will give him strength. – We are sorry for Miss Betty Hearle. – 'Twas very kind of you to go to Truro to see your Brother. – I desired Mr. Thorn to get for your brother the *Martial* (as he calls it) used in Eton-School, and a *Camdenus illustratus*. I will inquire about them. We are very glad to find he and you all so love one another. Let Brotherly Love continue. – The Col. desires to know, how Ensign Smith is? How long he has been ill? What is his Disorder? In what House is he confined? Send particular answers. – Aurelia is well, and sends her Duty to her Mother. – I took

Physic yesterday, and did not go out for the Day. Your Mamma's
Nerves are just as usual, but she is better as to the complaint she used
to have in her Back. – As Mary does not take amiss any Present made
her, I will not take amiss any Petition made me. I think, we are quits.
– Remember us to Mr. Hocker and all friends. I must coax Mr.
Hocker; you know why. Our Blessing, Love, Service, etc., from Mr.
Coode, your Mamma and

Your ever loving father,

JOHN PENROSE.

P.S. What Time in the morning does Iliff's Post-coach set out from
Exon? Where does it stop upon the Road? Where dine? Where lodge?
What Time the next day does it reach Penryn? – I shall write again
next Post, that your Letters and ours may continue in the old course. –
Seal and send Mr. Coode's Letter.

Bath, May 25th. 1767.

Dear Fanny,

Ere this you are again at Gluvias, where we hope all is well, as also
at Methleigh and Truro. Your Request concerning the Black Cloke
will be duly complied with. No News yet from Ld. Edgcumbe. If the
Bishop does not give Mr. Hocker St. Enoder, or one of Mr. Barnes's
Livings, but exchanges it for another inferior in value, he will pay His
Lordship a poor Compliment, and shew that he has not that Regard to
His Lordship's Recommendation which he professes to have. Col.
Sewell wrote about it last Monday, and told His Lordship that Mr.
Barnes had made his option, and that this Delay in the Bishop made us
fear some Jockeying in the case, and that St. Enoder was the very thing
by which Mr. Hocker and his friends could be most obliged, and that
a less Living would not answer the End of one who wanted to settle
himself: but he has received no answer. When an answer does come,
you probably will know the Result before I shall, because the Col.,
Mrs. Sewell, etc., etc., etc., set out this morning for Frenchay; the
Col. very gouty, Mrs. Sewell not well, the Servants all in health. It is
well they were not gone on Saturday; for we were forced to take Refuge
at the Colonel's to save ourselves harmless, after a most bloody Battle,
which happened near Westgate, wherein you would hardly guess such
a feeble poor cripple, as I am, to be engaged as a Principal. You shall
have a true Narrative of the affair from me. Mr. Scoble, his son, young
Gurney, Mr. Coode, your Mamma, Dolly, and myself, were walking

very peaceable-minded, and without the least murderous Intentions (at least I can answer for myself) to see the Square, Circus, and whatever we thought most curious in this fine City. As we went through the Postern at West-Gate, which you know is a narrow Pass not capable of two abreast, without some inconvenience, I was at the head of our little company, when I heard some noisy Fellows behind cry out "Stand away," and one of them rushing along pushed the Ladies in upon me. I put back my hand to screen them from violence, when a fellow with too much Liquor in his Pate pushed me with his Backside against the Wall. I then took him by the Shoulder, and pushed him in my turn, and with my stick gave him a little Rap on the head. The fellow turned about, lifted up his Club, and attempted to strike me. I warded the Blow with my Stick, and hit him again on the head, no mortal Blow; neither my Hand, nor Weapon, were Instruments of Death. Indeed I was most easily disarmed; the fellow got my stick into his Possession. My stick however was soon restored by the undaunted Courage of Mr. Scoble, who was in furious Passion with the fellow for attempting to strike a Clergyman, and laid on manfully. The Doctor from behind stretched out a Herculean Club, very knotty and broke the fellow's Head, which streamed with Blood. The Enemy being wounded, and his Spirits failing, (doubtless thro' loss of so much Blood), the affair seemed at an End. But Fate had still more Difficulties in Reserve for us. But before I mention those, I must observe that all the preceding action was in the Postern Way, the narrow Pass before mentioned, and may justly enough be compared to that most famous one mentioned in ancient History, where Leonidas, the Spartan Hero, with only 300 men, all men of valour, defeated the whole Power of Persia in the Straits of Thermopylae. With respect to the two Places, where the Engagements were fought, they correspond exactly; so with respect to the Courage of the Combatants: In some points there is a difference: the Fate of Nations did not depend on our Success, whether good or ill; I, the Captain, may not so justly be compared with Leonidas, as Mr. Coode might; the Spartans were all slain to a Man; the Persians being routed, never made head against Greece again, whereas our Adversaries, as soon as we got out in the open Street in Kingsmead Square, rallied, and begun a fresh attack. If you ask, how many the Enemy consisted of; I believe, of as many as attacked Sir John Falstaff, dressed in Kendal Green; and Mr. Scoble acted the Part of the Fat Knight and would have made many a mournful widow wish that day blotted out of the Kalandar, had not Mr. Coode with great Providence (the Poets would have said Minerva did it) conducted him to Col. Sewell's: where we all took proper

Refreshment after the manifold Fatigues and Dangers of this memorable exploit. You must know, that as, when the Servant eats the Roast meat, Button bears the Blame; so Mr. Scoble bore the Blame of Mr. Coode's breaking the fellow's head; all the vengeance of the mob was levelled at him: but all ended well, and all's well that ends well. No Blood was drawn on our side, but a little from Mr. Scoble's Hand; and that drawn, not by an Enemy, but by striking it against the wall. You may judge, what a noise this affair made all over Bath and how much it was in every Body's Mouth from this, that the next day at St. James's Church, where we went, Mr. Barnstone thought it worth while to give us a Word of exhortation from these Words in Gen. XLV. 24. See that ye fall not out by the way. In the morning we were at the X Bath, and heard an excellent Discourse from Mr. Grigg, who living in the country did not seem to have heard the important news: his Text was Matt. VI. 33. By the Bye, he is the best Preacher I have heard here, except Dr. Stonehouse: and as the Bishop of Derry constantly attends his Chappel twice a day, it may probably gain some credit. After St. James's Service was over in the Evening, I read Prayers at the X Bath. At the Abbey, in the morning Mr. Yescombe harangued on Prov. IV.7. advising the congregation to get Wisdom and Understanding. I don't hear, that he expressly mentioned our foolish conduct in fighting with a Hydra Mob, but to be sure he gave many hints, which we should have taken, had we heard him. Dr. Warner's Text in the Abbey, in the afternoon, I have not heard; but I dare say, the Sermon, had we been there, would have been found to concern us. While I write this, several fiddlers are at our door, consoling us with their celestial Strains: but we shall give them nothing; it would be derogatory to our honour to suppose such noble Spirits could ever be cast down. How the News should reach Bristol in so short a time, is marvellous; but Mr. Loscombe came yesterday to see us, and was kind enough to dine with us; and if it be fair weather next Monday we have promised to dine with him. Mr. & Mrs. Hele are coming to drink Tea with us this evening; it is very kind in them, but we want no comforters. Mr. Brinsden too was here this morning.

### Monday evening.

Mr. Coode sets out next Friday. You will probably see him the Wednesday after. I am prohibited from going so soon. Yet I hope, I am better. Mr. Coode has put a Ticket in the Pump-Room inviting some one to take part with him in a Post-chaise. If he gets a Partner, he may possibly set out sooner. – Mr. Taylor is elected by the Corporation Rector of Bath, to the universal satisfaction both of

Inhabitants and Sojourners. It is to be feared however, he will have little enjoyment of the Rectory, as he has an abscess in his side attended with many dangerous symptoms, and complicated with other Disorders. – Mr. and Mrs. Brinsden sent here this Evening to desire our Company at Dinner next Wednesday; which invitation we are obliged in civility readily to comply with, tho' neither of us seems fond of Feasting. – The Balls are over, the Music ceased in the Pump-Room, the Plays end next Saturday. Aha! sly Mr. Coode. Now we see the Reason you stay at Bath only till Friday. – Mr. Scoble & Company came hither last Saturday about two o'clock, dined at the Lamb Inn, drank Tea with us, and about eight that evening set out in one Post-chaise all three of them, hoping to reach Oxford, 71 miles, by the Sunday morning. – We all remember as due to all friends, with our Blessing upon you, your Brothers, Sisters, Nephew and Niece. I am, dear Fanny, your ever affectionate Father,

JOHN PENROSE.

Bath, May 29th, 1767.

Dear Fanny,

The Bells are ringing merrily on this Church of England Holiday, the Towers of the several Churches are adorned with Colours, and the Houses decked with Branches of Oak in memory of K. Charles the second's Preservation in the Royal Oak. We were at the Abbey in the morning and heard a Sermon suitable to the Occasion from Mr. Humphreys, Curate of St. Michael's on Psal. CXLV.4. After Dinner I walked to Mr. Brinsden's, to return him Thanks for the Two Tickets to the Play to-morrow, *The English Merchant* and *Polly Honycombe* which he kindly sent last Night to your Mamma for herself and Dolly. They are for the Stage-Box, 4 shillings a ticket. Now you know, your Mamma could not use it, and we could not handsomely dispose of it to any other Person, as on the Back of the Ticket was written "Mrs. Light's Stage Box." So Dolly is to be at Mr. Brinsden's to-morrow at five, and go to the Play from thence with some Ladies of Distinction; afoot, if they walk; in a chair, if they are carried. She is to be dressed in her Robe. If the Weather be fair, we shall see her parade before our window. I suppose, Madam will be too proud to call in. If foul, we'll keep a Look-out and get a glimpse of her, if we can. She is now with us, and I can with Pleasure assure you, her Governess and Masters speak much in her Praise. Can any one be more obliging, than Mr. Brinsden? Wednesday last we all dined with him: There were a Dish of

The Old Theatre in Orchard Street. Aquatint by T. Woodfall, 1804. Fanny Penrose attended the theatre there.

very large Soals, Scotch-collops, two Ducks, sweet-meat Tart, with Sauces, Garniture, etc., all in Perfection. Let Mr. Coode recount the Particulars, and when he hath said all he can, in favour of Mr. Brinsden's unaffected Hospitality, it will be, like Solomon's Wisdom, related but by Halves. "Three Goddesses, no more, could Paris boast." Mr. Coode will tell you of an equal number, all in one Day, not contending with one another, but separately looking with wistful eye after him. Paris had a Golden Apple, to compliment one of the Contenders with: but Mr. Coode must have a Goddess and a Golden Apple too. Upon the whole, what might have proved a Temptation to some others, had not charms for him; nothing could engage his attention, but the Idea of Molly, dear Molly, sweet Molly, Appn's Idol. Her attraction was more potent, than that of the Bath-Magnets; and this morning at five, he set out in the Exeter Machine, with his Face homewards. Our Hearts are all turned the same way, but it is thought absolutely necessary for me to stay here longer. We hope, my yellowness or Paleness gradually lessens; and I am not internally disordered, so far as I know. I have not the least imaginable gouty Pain, nor do I feel any other Pain or Sickness. But where there are bad appearances externally, they must proceed from some inward cause, tho' hidden. Whatever that cause be in me, we hope it is going off. Mr. Coode will give you a full account of my Illness, and you will learn from him, that I do not continue here through a frolicksome Disposition. As Mr. Coode has a Hat-box with him, your Mamma has taken the [opportunity] of sending a Hat to you, which he will give you Leave to take out at Vicarage, where he will be a few hours after you receive these Lines. He will hardly let you see the Silk he has bought for Mrs. Coode: but it is very pretty, and far exceeds the Price to which she limited him. If any Blame is incurred by going beyond her commission, let Mr. Coode bear it; for it is all owing to his own Inclination. It is a Pompadour[59] Tissue with white Flowers, of 11s.6d. per yard, and of a very rich Look, warranted by Mr. Pritchard as of good quality in every respect. We were informed, since buying Peggy's and Mary's Silks, that it is customary for the Mercer to give Sattin for a pair of shoes over every gown, the Buyer being half-a-crown towards it. Mr. Pritchard denies any such custom; but was prevailed on after much Importunity, and your Mamma's pleading most eloquently, (never did Demosthenes, Cicero, or Mr. Pitt plead like her,) to give Sattin, on the foresaid condition, both for Dolly, Peggy, and Mary's Shoes. This will be a Present for them, beyond

59 Pompadour. A shade of crimson or pink.

their Expectation. Your Mamma hath bought at Pantir's a dozen
Wires, eight Bows of a side, very good ones indeed, for tenpence the
dozen: If you think them cheap, and would have more bought, write
so in your next. Here is plain gauze for eighteen pence per yard, and
striped in Proportion: if this is cheaper, than at Penryn, and you think
it worth while, Mamma will buy some. – Yesterday, being Ascension-
day, we were at the Abbey, where Mr. Yescombe preached on Mark
XVI. 19. In the afternoon The Minister and Parishioners of St. James's
Parish went in Procession, from the Church thro' Abbey-Green before
our Window to Simpson's Rooms, then thro' Simpson's Walk to the
River Avon, preceded by two Tip-staves, about twenty Boys with
Rods in their hands in pairs, then two French-Horns, two Fiddles, two
Haut-boys, and followed by a Rabble Rout. At the River the Music
and the principal Persons went into a Barge, as many as it would hold;
the Ropes all enriched with Colours; to the lower end of the Quay.
There they disembarked again, and went on to Simpson's Door, where
ended the Procession. A drunken Bout in the Evening: but that was a
Deed of Darkness, and so we could not see it. – We have not heard
from the Colonel, since he went to Frenchay. Mrs. White's Letter to
Aurelia did not come till they were gone: but it shall be sent to her.
Sewell is expected every day from Greenwich: it shall be sent by him if
no opportunity presents itself sooner. Mrs. Evil, where the Colonel's
Lodgings are, is very obliging on his going away, has lent us a Coffee
Pot, and says we should be welcome to any thing in her House. – I had
almost forgot (to use an Expression familiar to you) to tell you, that
Mr. Brinsden put us to see Mr. Hoare's[60] Paintings in Edgar-Row, and
genteely gratified the Servant's Expectations, not suffering me to give.

Dolly's Spark is called Middleton; his father an Apothecary, who
has left off Business, and lives on his private fortune. Her sister
Coode's father-law is another such. – The Doctor will give you a full
account of the Ladies in the fashion of this year. I fear, he will
aggravate [Exaggerate]. It is a pity he should; for the simple Truth
will be as entertaining, as any thing he can say; and be as much more
instructive, as History exceeds Romance in real Goodness. – I have
wrote Mr. Thorn about Jacky's Books. He is now at Vicarage: and I
intreat him to improve his Time. Besides his Task, and proper
Play-hours, he will have Time on his Hands, which will find it more
comfortable to spend in useful Study, than in Idleness; as well as that
it will be pleasing in the Reflection forever. We are heartily rejoiced at

---

60  William Hoare (1707?–1792), a portrait painter, settled in Bath where many
    of the distinguished visitors sat to him.

the good Report we hear of him. So we are at Edward's being better and your pleasing Intimation about Molly. I observe all you say concerning Mr. & Miss Michell, etc., Mess. Hocker, Corker, etc. But you will be good enough to excuse my stopping short here: only giving our Blessing to you and the children at Home: to our children and grand-children at Methleigh, our Love to our other Relations, Compliments to all friends, especially enquiring ones. Dolly's Love etc. to you and all.

> I am my dear Fanny, (longing to be home)
> Your ever loving father
> JOHN PENROSE.

Bath, June 3rd. 1767. 4 o'clock.

Dear Fanny,

Dr. Coode, before I write this, hath told you the State of my Health at His leaving Bath, which I think continues exactly the same, tho' your Mamma thinks I am not so much yellow, as pale. We came from Bristol this morning in the Stage Coach, the Weather very wet and remarkably cold. The Coach set out from the White Lion in Broad Street, and we were forced by the Rain to have a chaise to put us from Mr. Loscombe's thither. When I say We, you must know Dolly is included in the number: for she, little Hussey, accompanied us, and partook of a Pleasure, which we repent the not taking when you were here last year, because it certainly would have been most agreeable to you. To give you a concise account. The Monday morning we went in the Machine from the Angel Inn for Bristol. We had a poor Prospect before us, because of the Rain; but having taken Places the Sunday Evening, we were bound down to take our chance. We had three ordinary women, our Coach-fellows, who being before-hand with us had seated themselves in the Back-part of the Coach, and gave an Intimation very shortly that they could not ride with their Backs to Horses without being sick. We put up at Bristol in Thomas Street, this side the Bridge. We had a long walk to take, but is was better weather, and we footed it stoutly. At the Head of High Street, a Voice hailed me, "Mr. Penrose, Mr. Penrose"; which proved to be that of my old friend Major Tucker: he invited us cordially to his House, and we promised not to leave Bristol without waiting on him. His Lady has been very ill, and is scarce recovered. While I was exchanging a Word or two with him in the Street, a Man came to me and asked if my

Name was Penrose. I told him, "Yes". He said, His Master had sent him to conduct us to his House, and that his Master's Name was Loscombe. Here begun a Series of such Civilities, as no one ever experienced greater. Mr. Loscombe received us with every Mark of Respect; treated us very handsomely with a plentiful and elegant Table; invited company to dine with us, tho' none was more agreeable was himself; walked out with Dolly on the High Grounds near King's Square to shew her the best view of Bristol and the adjacent Country; while your Mamma, and I, who could not walk so far or so uphill, went to call on Mr. Newcombe; but he, and Mrs. Newcombe, were gone to Gloucester. Our Guide was one Mrs. Ramsey, mother to the Revd. Mr. Berjew and Mrs. Parsons, which three were the Persons who dined with us. The next Morning by Eight o'clock Mr. Loscombe had provided a very genteel carriage to take us three to the Hot-Wells, he himself on Horse-back. That we might see every thing curious, as far as the Time would permit, we went first to Queen's Square, then to College Green, called en passant on the Major, excused our alighting by reason of Mrs. Tucker's Ilness; proceeded the lower Road to the Wells; drank the Water which is very soft and agreeable; met there Miss Nelson, a Lady who is Guest to Mr. Loscombe; ascended the Hill, and on to King's Weston, where we went into the House, made a second Breakfast on hot cake buttered and coffee; drove on to Pen-poll near the fine Seat of Mr. Southwell, Knight for Gloucester-shire, where we had Sight of the Severn, the Bristol Channel, King-Road just under us, Wales on the opposite Shore, in short, the most delightful View my eyes ever beheld; and we had most glorious weather to enjoy it in. Our Return was thro' Clifton, the best built and most pleasantly situated of any village in England. When at the Wells, we enquired after Capt. Bown and Mrs. Harris, to no purpose; we examined the Books at the Room; no such names appeared; so we concluded, poor Mrs. Harris had not Strength to bear her Journey: but as we came back from Pen-poll towards Clifton, we met her and Mrs. Bolitho in the Chaise an airing. Our conversation was but short. She is prodigious hoarse. We reciprocally told one another where we lodged and parted. We were under Mr. Loscombe's command, and we had but just Time to get to Stokes Croft by Dinner-Time; for our Expedition took up near six hours. And never was a cheaper six hours Pleasure; for Mr. Loscombe with Generosity, we had no cause to expect, paid for the Chaise we went in, and satisfied the Driver, as well as defrayed the Expence at King's Weston: and I don't believe we passed by any thing, whether near or distant, worth seeing, but he stopt our Chaise and pointed it out to us. In our return, Mr. Loscombe conducted us through Horse Street, that we might see Mr. Allison, and invited him to spend the Evening at his House. After Dinner, Mr. Loscombe Jun. who is sensible gentleman-like Person, went with the Miss Nelson before-mentioned, Miss Bartle another guest of Mr. Loscombe's, Miss Champion and Miss Lloyd, and Dolly, to Baptist Mills to see Brass cast; they carried good Prog with them. Mr. Loscombe went out on Business. Mamma and I drank Tea at Mr. Allison's, about three quarters of a mile off. I walked forth and back very well, tho' coming back a smart Rain fell and made it disagreeable: Mr. Allison accompanied us, and spent the Evening according to Invitation. While we were at Mr. Allison's, Mamma took the Opportunity of going to Orchard Street near College Green, to wait on Mrs. Gwatkin. She was not at home, but this morning sent by her Servant the inclosed Ticket. In the interim Capt. Bown and his Lady came in their Chaise to Mr. Loscombe's; but the Servant could not tell where we were gone. We should have been sincerely glad to have spent an hour with them. They left a message, desiring our Company to-day; but it was not right to go so far, and at such Expence, for Bath Water at the Fountain, and their neglect taking it. Be pleased to let Mr. & Mrs. Richards know, presenting our best compliments, that we have been at their Father's and he desires us to acquaint them, that he & his Son are well. Our companions in the Coach to-day were a Gentleman of Worcester related to Mrs. Hooper, a master Builder of I know not what Place, and a Bath woman whom we take to a slatter-pouch mantua-maker. Don't you think Dolly hath her share of pleasure? I dare say, Mary envies her. It was but last Saturday she was at the Play, and sat in a Box, dressed out as fine as a Lady of Quality in her Robe etc. But she did not go to Mrs. Brinsden's, to have company from thence, as I wrote in my last was the projected Scheme; for Mr. Brinsden in the morning gave me another Ticket for Mrs. Aldworth to go with her. This was obliging to a degree. By the way they drank Tea with us; and the Mistress and Scholar give each other a very laudable character. To be sure, Dolly was not a little proud on this occasion; and it is fit, Pride should have a Fall. So it happened with her; for just outside West-gate, that memorable Spot where the late bloody Battle was fought, one of her chair-men, whether drunk or sober, tumbled down, received some Hurt, and there she sat in the Chair, all mortified, till another fellow took his Place as Chairman, & put her home, not at all hurted, but somewhat hurried. She dined with us the Sunday, and went to St. James's Church in the afternoon, where I preached. In the morning we heard Mr. Grigg at the Cross-Bath on Luke XXIV. 50,51. The Sermons at the Abbey were, by Mr. Clark in the morning, and Mr. Anonymous in the evening, the Texts unknown. Miss Howell told us the Saturday, that Ralph Baron has Simon-ward, Dolby St. Pinnock, one Vivian Duloe, and Mr. Hocker St. Enoder. Concerning Mr. Hocker & St. Enoder I wrote Ld. Edgcumbe Saturday-night, and pressed the matter in pretty strong Terms. I told him, that I feared the Bishop's Delay boded no good, and that a less Living would not do; that if the Patron exchanged it with any Incumbent for a Parish of less value, his Lordship's obligation to him would be very small, and he would be as liable as ever to Solicitation from your Friends. I think notwithstanding, Mr. Hocker will be Vicar of St. Enoder, tho' I cannot account for our good Bishop's conduct. I find I must take another Piece of Paper, before I note any thing in your last kind Letter.

You will receive this on Monday. Mr. Hocker will be at Penryn that Evening, to preach the next morning. Let me communicate the above to him through you. And, lest Ld. Edgcumbe may not have wrote to Mr. Heame, let Mr. Heame know immediately the contents of the above. Your Mamma & Dolly join me in congratulating Mr. Hocker and you. Mr. Hocker will immediately thank Ld. Edgcumbe for his kind Offices; and if he writes a Line or two, under a cover to me, to Col. Sewell, thanking him for his most friendly Zeal & Importunity on his Behalf, he will do no more than ought to be done: for the Col. has been a true and sincere advocate for him., as ever man had. I wish Jacky may not jump out of his skin for joy.

#### Wednesday Even.

What Effect the Waters have on me, I am no Judge of. This I know, that I walk exceeding well, provided it is not too much against the Hill; then my Breath a little fails me. But the weather is very cold and very damp, and keeps me back. There have not been above 3 or 4 fine temperate days since I have been here. Your Mamma grows thin. I intended the Miniature Painting as something mysterious. Mr. Coode, I suppose, has revealed it to you. Lest he should not, I will tell you, that Mr. Harrington, Rector of Powderham, had his Picture drawn, and borrowed my Gown & Cassock to be drawn in. – I am glad Mr. Hocker will preach the Friendly Society Sermon. I would not have him be too short; such Gentry like somewhat for the Money. – I am glad Mr. Philipps is better and that Peter stays at Falmouth: question not Mr. Harris's Readiness to do any good Office, and Mr. Michel's serving on Trinity Sunday. We have got two Rolls for Peggy and Mary, and curls to each, to be worn or not at Pleasure. – You did not answer my Queries about Ensign Smith: your general account will not satisfie the Colonel. – The Society's Books had best be kept, till I come home. – The Things were right by Mr. Robinson's man: but Mr. Robinson gave us liberty to send them by him, and "Thank ye" was Reward enough without a shilling. The fellow had as much in that, as the carrier (if he has any conscience) would have expected. – It will be too late to punish the anabaptist when I come home; because the Process will require some Time. – We think to come home in a Chaise, and not trouble the Exeter or Falmouth Machines. The Expence will not a great deal more, and the Journey much more comfortable. The Redruth Singers had better have staid at Home: but it does not signifie. – Why you have Loads, Oceans of Company, and a multitude of Frolicks: such Flaunting, Galanting, and Jaunting, such Frolicking you do see. Well, poor Souls: do enjoy yourselves, but be careful not to spoil sober Peggy. – We are glad, you speak so well of Jacky. Thank him in my name for his Letter, the News in it, and what he says, about the School: and I beg of him to revise his Task Exercise again and again, and then transcribe it on good Paper as fair as he can, the Lines not too close; and deliver it to Mr. Conon with correctness and neatness. If he has time to go to Writing-School, we are very willing of it, and desire him to be careful. Writing is a useful accomplishment, and I am sorry when I see any thing written by him with any Marks of Negligence. His news about Mr. Mundy, we learnt also by Miss Howell. – I am sorry Mr. H. should have so much Disturbance from Mr. P's Tempers. – Sorry too for Miss Betty Hearle. Thought Miss Harriet was to be a Boscowan. Wish her very happy – Glad Edward is so recovered, and dear little Charles's ague is gone. Hope Mrs. Coode's cold is gone. Wish Dr. Coode may not kiss away Molly's cheeks. The Colonel's John called here yesterday: we were at Bristol; he had no Line, nor left any message. – Mrs. Michel's Silk shall be matched if possible. – Our Blessing, Love, and Service to all as due. Dolly joins us in suitable compliments. I am, my dear,

> Your, & your Brothers and Sisters loving father
> JOHN PENROSE.

P.S. The little Book was bought at the Hot Wells, and is Dolly's Present to Charles. –

June 5th, 1767.

Dear Fanny,

To give you all the Satisfaction I can, I write out of course and send you a Letter which I received yesterday morning from Lord Edgcumbe.

Where you will see the good News confirmed, had it needed
Confirmation. Keep the letter, till our Return.

You may tell Dr. Coode, I continue in statu quo, only my
Yellowness or Paleness is rather abated: I took yesterday 40 grains of
Rhubarb; but cannot perceive any Alteration in the Symptoms of my
Disorder, except what I have said respecting my colour.

Yesterday being the King's Birthday, one Mr. Gulstone gave a
publick Breakfast. The Company were very numerous, tho' the Season
is over; and the entertainment was very elegant. In the Evening was a
Subscription-Ball, very brilliant.

This morning I read Prayers at the Cross Bath Chapel: in the
Afternoon we were at the Abbey. Before Evening Prayers we went to
every Mercer in Bath to match Mrs. Michel's Silk, but in vain. The
Pattern is too old for Bath, but it may probably be matcht in London.
The Mercers here are mostly such as come for the Season, and are
supplied only with Silks of one, two, or three years old Patterns. After
Evening Prayers we waited on Misses Howell, and drank Tea with
them. There we met Dolly.

While we were at Church in the Morning, one Mrs. Swinney
enquired for us at our Lodgings, and left a card: We recollect no
Person of that name. Pray, do you? Nor know we her Lodgings.

I shall write again next Post, that this Letter may not interrupt the
Series of our Correspondence. May God Almight bless you all with his
choicest Blessings, is the constant Prayer of your affectionate Mamma,
& your affectionate Father

JOHN PENROSE.


Bath, June 8th. 1767.

Dear Fanny,

This Day, if not before, the Colonel's and my Letters have given a
Quietus to yours and Mr. Hocker's mind concerning St. Enoder. The
Colonel's being at Frenchay occasioned the Loss of one Post; but one
Post was a thing of Importance, where the mind was in so great
Suspense. To be sure, Mr. Hocker will not refuse St. Enoder, which you
say Mr. Bennet did Simon-Ward, which is scarce credible. When we
received your's to-day, as it was not the Day we expected to hear from
you; we concluded, before opening the Letter, that Lord Edgcumbe
had let Mr. Heame know the good News, and you were communicat-
ing it to us: but I have Reason to think, it was his Lorship's Design,
that you should have the good News through me. I received a Letter
from the Col. this morning, which I send you, to save the Trouble of

copying. But why do I mention Trouble, who yesterday did not save myself, as I might, from hard Duty? We walked in the morning (having crossed Spring-Gardens Ferry) to Bathwick Church, about half a mile from hence, where I read Prayers, preached and administered the Sacraments; and then walked home again. I had a convenience in the Desk, to sit during the Second Service, and during the Lessons and Athanasian creed: and there were but six communicants, viz. 5 men and your Mamma. In the afternoon I preached at St. Michael's; one Mr. Brereton of Derbyshire read Prayers. Your Mamma went with me and Dolly, and Misses Howell. (The Sermons at the Abbey were by Mr. Barnstone on Rom. VIII. 16. and by Mr. Chapman, the new Reader, on John XIV. 16.) I was not a little wearied; but am very well again this day, so that Misses Howell and we walked to Walcot Church, which is small, but pretty; many monuments about it, but none for Capt. and Mrs. Prowle, as we were told. In our Return, we met Mr. Haviland, who says I must not yet leave Bath. He advises me to chew Rhubarb twice a week, enough to give me two or three Motions. I think I am bettering; my Stools are most substantial, and not white as they were. You may depend on our coming home as soon as ever we can. We hope, next week, if I continue bettering a few days. But don't you leave writing to me at Bath, till I give you Notice. I write this soon after Dinner, because we expect Mrs. Grant, Mrs. Corner, and the two children, at Tea Time. Remember my Love to Mr. Michell. I am glad you have had an answer from him. If I should not be home, as I long to be, the 1st Sund. after Trinity, can you get a Supply? The two Franks from the Col. are for Ensign Smith. You need not be a niggard of Franks, when you have anything to communicate: I have a fresh supply both for ourselves and you. We wish Dr. Street's children all Success. We will buy a Nest of Boxes for Mrs. Michell. We are sorry, Miss Betty Hearle is in such danger. We are glad the family at Methleigh are well. Mr. Coode promised, we should hear from him this Post: but Molly hath put us out of his Memory. We are sorry for Polack; because we presume, his Poverty not owning to Extravagance or Idleness, but an unavoidable Want of Business. Though we do not answer Jacky's Letters to him, we thank him for them, and are very glad to read them. Dolly must answer Mary's, who writes very well to her. Mrs. Brett shall be spoke to, about Mrs. Richards and Mrs. Crowgey's Request: and Mamma will buy 3 yards of plain gawze. Mamma has less Trouble now, than when Dinah was here: she was more a Plague, than of Use, by reason of her surprizing giddiness. Thank Charles for his Letter. We wish him Joy of his beautiful Buckle; hope he is well, as well as good; and desire, when he goes to School after the Holidays, he will mind his writing. Let Dr. Coode know, we were much disappointed at not hearing from him this morning, according to Promise: We expected to hear from him, how he got home (but that we hear from you, by accident;) how all at Methleigh were; how Molly looked on him; how Mrs. Coode liked her silk; and to have had a Line from Belle Peggy under his cover.

Tea is over. Dr. Grant was in the Company, but not Miss. I have now only to give our Blessing, Love, and Service, to all as due, and to conclude myself

Your ever loving father

JOHN PENROSE.

P.S. Make Mr. Hocker do as much duty as you can.

Bath, June 12th, 1767.

Dear Fanny,

We have been most egregiously disappointed at not hearing, how you relished the News which you received last Monday. We concluded, that neither your Methleigh Jaunt, nor want of a Frank, nor it's being not your regular Day of Writing, would have hindered you from acknowledging the Receipt of my Letter. This week has seemed a fortnight through the tediousness of Expectation, and now we must expect three tedious whole Days longer, You should at least have been as ready with your communication of your Joys, as with that of your Complaints. I have heard from the Colonel again to-day, but nothing particular. I shall send him a Letter by this Post, and in it include Coz: Fanny's to Aurelia. It is not yet determined, when we shall set out homewards. Mr. Haviland is against my going as yet, and says he would not advise me to continue here an Hour longer than he thinks necessary. I have still a very yellow Tincture in my skin; tho' Abundance of Gentlemen and Ladies congratulate me daily on my looking better and better. I take Rhubarb twice a week, no other Medicine except the Bath-Waters, which are thought sovereign in such cases as mine. You must let us know, when Mr. Hocker is called to Exeter, what the Bishop or Mr. Geare writes; when Mr. Hocker sets out; when he shall be at Exon. I would have him be inducted in his Journey homeward. And he may take his fittest Opportunity of reading Prayers and The Articles by Way of Qualification, any time within two months. But Mr. Geare will give him, if he asks particular Instructions. I presume, he must have his Induction at Lostwithiel: if he goes thither, let him give my Compliments to all Friends there, and in that Neighbourhood. Last Tuesday Mr. Allison came from Bristol to see us. We walked about with him a great deal. I walked with him, and without him, that Day, as to make up, by a moderate computation, more than four miles. The Wednesday we walked in the Meadows with Misses Howell, and elsewhere, at least two miles. Yesterday the Wind was too cold and too rough, to permit us to make any Excursions; and the Wind is pretty much now, as it was yesterday. I had a very complaisant Letter on Wednesday from Mr. Basset, with some Franks. I hope, you will not be out of them again. Should that be the Case, we should not grudge Postage. – We heard from Dr. Coode last Wednesday. He gave us a very entertaining account of his Journey; but never let us know, how Mrs. Coode liked her Silk, or how the other Persons, to whom he carried Presents, were pleased. I told the Doctor, Molly would look strange on him at first, as children always do. We wish Mr. Dell Joy; hope Mr. Street's children are recovered; are glad victuals fall with you; sorry for Miss Betty Hearle. You should have sent a copy of Dr. Turner's monumental Inscription. You did well in sending for more Licenses. If I should not be home at the Visitation, which is to be (or I mistake,) on next Monday sennight. I depute Mr. Hocker to eat my Dinner for me, and desire the Chancellor or Mr. Surrogate to excuse my non-attendance. If Mr. Hocker does not attend, desire Mr. Osborn or Mr. Evans to make my Obeisance and Excuse, as aforesaid. We often see Dolly. She often drinks Tea, sometimes dinner, with us. We had yesterday a fine young Duck for Dinner, which cost in the market eighteen pence; and to–day we have a pair of Soals, price eight pence. Sawce and Dressing add greatly to the Expence: tho' our Dressing Bills are very reasonable. There is a deal of Company now in Bath, tho' the Season is out. This Instance will prove it; viz: The London Players are now at Bristol, and the last Play Night so many Ladies and Gentlemen went from Bath to the Play, that there was not one Post-Chaise, or genteel conveyance of any kind, left in Bath, notwithstanding such Numbers of Carriages are kept here. Mr. Taylor, the late Reader at the Abbey, now Rector elect, still continues very ill, and is prayed for; and it is feared, he will never enjoy his new Preferment. Capt. Hayes, a due Church-man, frequently enquires for Mrs. Hearle and Family. – Mrs. Middleton has made an offer to do any thing for Dolly: but we can securely trust her with Mrs. Sewell and Mrs. Brinsden. – Seal and send Dr. Coode's – Mr. Brinsden gave five shillings for a Green Goose this morning –

Saturday, June 13. This morning we waited on Mr. Haviland, desiring to know his Opinion, whether we might prudently go hence the middle of next week: This he does not consent to, but he consents that we set out the middle of the week after. So we hope to be Home before to-morrow fortnight: as for supplies for to-morrow se'nnight, do your best, not forgetting to consult Mr. Hocker.

Our Blessing, Love, Service, etc.

Your affectionate Father

JOHN PENROSE.

P.S. If you answer this per Thursday's Post, we shall receive it the Monday following. Probably before the Wednesday's Post arrives, we shall be set out. So your answer to this, will be the last Letter we expect to receive while at Bath, barring casualties. We shall remember Charles's Birthday.

Bath, June 17th, 1767.

Dear Fanny,

I doubt not, but all was Joy in every Heart and every Face, when the News came of the Bishop's Intention to confer on Mr. Hocker the Vicarage of S. Enoder. You should have wrote the Colonel a Letter of Thanks by the first Post. As Mr. Hocker was not at Penryn when the News came, his Thanks passed well enough, by means of my cover. By a Line from the Colonel, dated Sunday last, I find he expected to have heard from one or other sooner than he did. You know his eager impatient temper. He says about Dolly, "Love to Miss Dolly. She must write to us often, about her own Health and every thing else: for Mrs. Sewell says, she must be her girl and mine. So you must tell the sweet girl." The Col. and Mrs. Sewell are now at Bristol. They have taken Lodgings for a week in College Green, the better to return the many Visits they have received at Frenchay from the People of that City. I sent your and Mr. Hocker's Letters, which I like exceeding well, by the first Post. I fear Mr. Hocker has been too hasty in writing Dr. Boscawen. But this depends upon the way in which his Letter is worded. Lord Edgcumbe's Interest ought ever to be in his Eye: and he will not be able vote for him, in case of a contest, if he become an House-keeper at St. Enoder before the General Election. This Hint shall be explained, when I have the Pleasure of meeting you. I remain just as I was, my colour indeed slowly growing better. My appetite not extraordinary. But I walk very well, on this flat Pavement, and not too far. The Weather has been warm for two or three days, till yesterday brought cold again. Warm again to-day, with a little Shower of Rain.

It is amazing, that with all this cold weather, and in this Place of piercing Winds, I have not caught the least cold: I, who used at home to be so much confined, and was so liable to ill-affected by every Blast. Nor have I had one Stitch or Ach of Gout all the while I have been here. Yet am I glad the Time draws nigh when I hope we shall have an Happy Meeting at Vicarage. Next Thursday, perhaps Wednesday, is fixed (God willing) for our Setting out. We do not purpose to stay at Exon, but to get Home in three Days. We think an Interruption of our Journey, and Feasting at Friends Houses, not so adviseable as to proceed directly from Bath to Penryn. Let George brew against our coming, the Day after you receive this. – We are sincerely affected at poor dear Charles's Ague returning. He is a very good Boy. I hope, his Mamma will soon have the care of him, tho' we doubt not of your care. The inclosed Books are all for him. We are glad Mrs. Coode's Silk was liked, and the other Things. – We hope, the Doctor's Indisposition did not last long enough to discredit the Bath Waters, and that he will experience a lasting Benefit from them, notwithstanding a Memento now and then from his old complaints. He was in general very well here, improved to a Miracle. The principal News here is, that Mutton is fallen one penny per pound, the price now $3d.\frac{1}{2}$ – It is now past nine o'clock. We are just returned from a Tea Visit at Mrs. Brinsden's. She made a morning Visit here yesterday. Two of her sons, the Counsellor and Merchant (the latter having been at Oporto the last six years) are now on a Visit to her. Friendly People indeed! God Bless them. I must pass by some Particulars in your Letter for Want of Time, and having wrote the Col. a long Letter by this Post. Yet I must let you know, because it relates to myself, that I preached and administered the Sacrament (with two Assistants) at the Abbey last Sunday morning, and preached at St. James's in the afternoon, with no Inconvenience but a little weariness from long Standing. Write us again by return of the Post, directed to me at Mr. Paul's in Exon. – Misses Howell went away last Monday. – Last Saturday we and Dolly drank Tea at Mr. Grigg's in Bathwick. – Give our blessing, Love and Service to all as due, not forgetting Friends at Methleigh, and Jacky who we suppose is at Truro.

I am, dear Fanny,<br>
Your ever loving father,<br>
JOHN PENROSE.

P.S. Mamma is obliged to Mrs. Coode for her Letter, and wonders honest Peggy did not write. Did the Doctor buy Jumps for Mrs.

Coode? A young Lady, daughter to Mrs. Light, is going to the East Indies a Husband-hunting. She goes in company with a Lady, wife of Col. Draper. Her Mother has expended £800, the young Lady's whole fortune, in cloaths, to equipp her for her long voyage, and matrimonial state, if she be so lucky as to succeed.

# Index

(numbers in italic indicate illustrations)